THIERRY MAERTENS – JEAN FRISQUE

GUIDE FOR THE

CHRISTIAN ASSEMBLY

REVISED EDITION

LENT — EASTER

FIDES PUBLISHERS, INC.
NOTRE DAME, INDIANA

TRANSLATED FROM THE FRENCH BY MOLAISE MEEHAN, O.S.B.

Nihil Obstat: V. Descamps
can. libr. cens.

Imprimatur: J. Thomas, *vic. gen.*
Tournai, March 12, 1969

© Copyright, 1971, Fides Publishers, Inc.
Notre Dame, Indiana

LCCCN: 72-114245

ISBN: 0-8190-0003-5

GUIDE FOR
THE CHRISTIAN ASSEMBLY

PREFACE TO THE NEW EDITION

With the introduction of the new lectionary we have undertaken a complete revision of the *Guide for the Christian Assembly*. The purpose is twofold. We want to provide a manual which studies the new formularies in depth, and to indicate in our commentary how the Word of God proclaimed in scripture is complemented by his word elsewhere – the word, that is, which mysteriously informs actual happenings in the world and in the history of the Church.

We have entirely reworked our material and hope that our readers will find it a useful source for personal meditation and prayerful lives as Christians. In order to take account of everything the new lectionary provides we decided to revise the structure of the commentary. We concentrate almost exclusively on the readings, and do not provide extensive treatment of other material such as prayers or hymns. Greater liberty of choice, and some improvisation, is to be expected in that area.

Consequently the old headings of *Liturgical Analysis* and *Biblical Theme* have been eliminated, and commentaries are divided simply in two parts: exegesis and doctrine. We have however incorporated all the former material in one or other of our present divisions.

A. EXEGESIS

The reader will first find a brief exegesis of the readings for each Mass of the liturgical year. This is a minimal requirement if the thought of the inspired author is to be respected. Pastors who wish to comment on the text or lay people who seek to penetrate its content do not always have a ready means at hand of finding the exact meaning, and may resort to dubious expedients. In recent years there has been considerable development in the field of exegesis, but pastors and laity encounter isolated items only. Our function is to make the work of the specialists available for them.

It should be clear however that the function of exegesis is preliminary; it does not cover everything. It keeps us from following false trails or seeking verification in the text for *a priori* views. But it does not exhaust the possibilities of the text in deepening our understanding of the liturgical celebration. Another sort of study is necessary.

Specifically, the exegetical part comprises three paragraphs. The first places the reading in its context and provides the critical material necessary for interpretation. The second gives the exegetical commentary proper, the various themes, the really central message, out of which a homily can be built. Some doctrinal, moral or liturgical comments will be found in the third, which relate the biblical text to the whole context of life in the Church and in the world today.

B. DOCTRINE

The doctrinal discussions are centered on the Sunday formularies. Usually there are two for each Sunday, which consider the principal themes of the exegetical commentary. For the weekdays there is, strictly speaking, no doctrinal commentary, but in the course of the exegetical commentary we have suggested avenues of doctrinal reflection.

A word of explanation about the method followed in doctrinal exposition. We do not really study an isolated theme in purely analytic fashion. Theological reflection should be centered on the eucharistic celebration because this is the essential act of the Church's life, involving the whole mystery of both Christ and the Church. Because various approaches are necessary to gain insight into the totality of the mystery, eucharistic formularies, in an attempt to indicate the totality, will utilize various themes. The different themes however do converge, and in this convergence lies the key to deeper understanding. The living relation which unites a man with Jesus Christ crucified and arisen, the one mediator of salvation for everyone, is shaped more than anywhere else in the eucharistic celebration. It begins at that extraordinarily complex historical moment of baptism, which brings a man from unbelief into faith. It is developed as the liturgy of the Word initiates him into salvation history, the thread of growth, at once continuous and discontinuous, which links Adam with Jesus by way of Abraham. The thread always lies in the background of every formulary, reminding us where we stand and whither we must go. It is important for each one to know throughout life where he stands on the road that leads to Christ, what is still pagan in him, what still remains at the stage of Jewish man.

Whoever is admitted to the Eucharist is a member of the Church. In the mystical body he has his essential role, the implications of which he should constantly weigh. It requires him to cooperate in the building of the Kingdom, in the always actual shaping of salvation history. It ought to dominate his life, because it is in the warp and woof of actual living that the Church has the mission to bear witness for men to the salvation acquired once for all in Jesus.

Considerations such as these determine our style of reflection. Our treatment of each theme has two broad angles. First there is question of clarifying the continuous-discontinuous line from pagan man, ancient and modern, *via* Jewish man to Jesus Christ. The progressive consciousness that we find traced in scripture is somehow normative for all time and we must discern its tenor. It is essential that the Christian have a full appreciation of what coming to the faith means, and the steps he must take to achieve recognition of the man-God. Secondly, the light derived from consideration of the mystery of Christ is cast upon the mystery of the Church and the new state that Christian life in the Church means. So we go on to show how the liturgical theme being treated clarifies the missionary dynamism of the Church and of all authentic Christian life. All that remains is to point out how the day's eucharistic celebration, by the appeal made in the Word proclaimed, brings the assembled faithful to realization of their active role.

As we reflect on each formulary we shall attempt to follow these broad lines. It is a method, we think, that furnishes pastor and people with a tool that is fairly easy to handle, and that contributes to a continuous deepening of their faith under the sign of Christ and the Church.

A METHOD OF TEAM PREPARATION

The materials made available in the new volumes of the Guide for the Christian Assembly do not lend themselves to immediate use in the conduct of the celebration, or the homily. What we have sought to provide, for layman and pastor, is a cultural instrument, and it should be clear that this kind of study can be further developed on the pastoral level. The pastor will derive items of information and ideas, we believe, that give him a suitable perspective for preparing his homily and commentary according to liturgical tradition.

Furthermore the materials are suitable for teamwork. We should like to describe the kind of treatment we have ourselves frequently attempted. To begin with, all listen to the readings of the liturgy about to be celebrated. In that God himself is speaking, and people are properly disposed for hearing his will, the subsequent work will be inspired by the Spirit. Then a member of the team presents the exegesis and liturgical analysis. We might call this the "objective part." The commentary is discussed, and care is taken to isolate the central point that emerges from all contributions. Once this is agreed, another team member reads some relevant biblical passages.

Now comes the "reflective part." The section we entitle

Doctrine is presented by the person who best combines the qualities of pastor and theologian, always with an eye to the concrete situation of the particular assembly. This is a delicate task. The priest's habitual style of meditation is not readily developed into articulate reflection on the lived life of the Church.

It is possible at this point for the joint work to proceed. All that has taken place enables each one to say how he sees the Mass of the coming Sunday as a new stage in salvation history. The stage can only be reached by having recourse to the mystery of Christ. Again, with regard to the principal theme of the celebration, he might state the questions with which, in his opinion, the Church could be confronted by the world. It is important to linger over this discussion, even though it is time-consuming in the beginning.

Finally the team comes to grips with the actual pastoral procedure for the Sunday. Here, obviously, there is no need to be concerned with each detail of the matter considered. During the course of the celebration the homily and commentary will be developed with full consideration for their functional laws. Once again, the homily is not an exegetical or doctrinal discourse; but exegesis and doctrine are a good preparation for the sort of homily and commentary that will meet actual needs.

At the end the meeting should determine suitable chants. These, entrance hymn, communion chant and recessional, should be chosen to illustrate the theme selected. All these are merely suggestions. Trial and error will enable us, whether individually or in teams, to develop our own method.

CONTENTS

WEEK OF ASH WEDNESDAY

I. Joel 2:12-18   The book of Joel was written during a catas-
1st reading   trophe which struck Judaea about 400 B.C.
Wednesday   The land was so ravaged by a plague of
locusts (1:4; 2:3-5) that it did not even yield
sufficient produce for the daily oblations and libations in the
temple (1:9). The prophet reacts to the disaster in two ways.
First he demands an official fast (our passage), because it is
within God's power to end the calamity. Next he transfers this
"day of Yahweh" to the eschatological plane (3-4). He describes
what the judgment of God will be like and the paradisal age
that will suceed it, if God spares his people, as he will surely
spare them finally in the present crisis.

God has the power, once the plague is over, to bless his people
and leave them sufficient produce to maintain the daily oblation
and libation (2:14), if only their *fast* demonstrates that the
people are unanimously converted (elders, children, nurslings,
spouses, priests), and becomes also the sign of a genuine interior
conversion (2:13). He describes God's response to such a fast
as a return to the age of paradise (2:19-26). So both calamity
and official fast are made the symbol of the purification and
suffering the people must endure on the day of judgment, when
the definitive age of happiness comes (4:18-21). When Joel
prescribes the conditions for a fast that will be pleasing to God
(one that is general, and that is interior), its dimensions become
eschatological. Such a fast is the pledge of prosperity and of life
with God.

II. Matthew   This brief discourse of Jesus about accom-
6:1-6, 16-18   plishing our justice in secret is in fact a
Gospel   portion of the sermon on the mount. An
Wednesday   exact parallelism of vocabulary and structure
establishes the unity of the verses:

1

> when . . . not . . . like the hypocrites
> to appear before men . . . in truth I
> tell you, they have received their reward . . .
> But you, when you . . . (your Father)
> in secret . . . And your Father who sees
> in secret will recompense you.

We need only fill the spaces with terms from the vocabulary of almsgiving, prayer, or fasting to reconstruct, with slight variants only, the three strophes of the discourse in their entirety.

The central point of the discourse is that traditional works of justice should be inspired by a new mentality: the desire to please God, and him alone. Almsgiving, prayer and fasting should not be matter for ostentation; all should be within the secret of God.

Almsgiving was looked upon as the work *par excellence* of justice (vv. 2-4; cf. Si 3:14; 3:30 - 4:10; 7:10; 12:1-7; Tb 4:11; 12:8-9). It was given some publicity with the idea of kindling a sort of rivalry and forcing benefactors to keep their promises (Mk 12:41; Lk 19:8; Si 31:11). Prayer too was fairly generally public. As for fasting, even though in Jesus' time it was not very widespread in official Jewish circles, there were sects who liked to practice it frequently, and who, for propagandist reasons, made it matter for ostentation (Lk 18:12; Mk 2:19-20). Jesus is not suggesting other things in place of such observances; references to being anointed when fasting, or not knowing what the right hand does, are a sort of literary hyperbole. His real intention is to produce the proper dispositions for such works, and to denounce the hypocrisy of people who think they are serving God in vaunting themselves. Prophets previously had tried to bring about a similar spiritualization (Is 58:1-12; Os 8:11-13; Mi 6:6-8; Am 5:21-25): Jesus continues the tradition, and shows that filial life with the Father depends on this sort of interiorization.

In our secularized age there could be no more imperative

change in moral attitudes than this: the readiness to be unaware of contributions by right hand or left hand, to be blind to public awareness or recognition in our turnings to God, who sees only in secret. When we are unconscious of the good we do (as in Mt 25:31-40), we are asserting that the scales for judgment of good are God's, not ours. He alone can appreciate, the imperceptible God who dwells in secret and gives account to none. We are renouncing that knowledge of good and evil, which man in his egoism coveted in paradise.

III. Deuteronomy The author of Deuteronomy is always insist-
    30:15-20 ing on the necessity of choice between the
    1st reading "two ways." The topic becomes a pervasive
    Thursday refrain.

It is imperative for Israel now to choose the first of the *ways:* the one of blessing and happiness. Happiness is a blessing because it is produced by God's own life communicated to his people, and misfortune is a curse for the opposite reason. God communicates his life because he loves his people, and gives them prosperity and success. This may seem a very material view of the life of God. But there is little reason for surprise. It is important to realize that God wills the happiness of his children and wants to define what that is, because by themselves they cannot achieve it. Hence it is imperative for them to choose between disobedience and obedience.

IV. Luke 9:22-25 This passage is closely linked with the an-
    Gospel nouncement of the Passion. It proclaims the
    Thursday conditions necessary for following Jesus in the
    new path he is about to follow.

Jesus is not content with demonstrating the eschatological necessity of his own suffering. He has prepared his followers too to accept, in the same spirit, a life of trial. In order to emphasize this teaching, Luke makes a somewhat artificial collection of Jesus' sayings.

The verbs *renounce, take up the cross, follow Christ* are really synonymous. Each in its own way indicates what is the essential element of *Christian life*. In that he himself anticipates the punishment of the cross for his revolutionary ideas, Jesus is warning his followers that, if they remain loyal to his teaching, they must expect the same fate. Consequently one must reject all personal security and accept the master's counsels (the rabbinic meaning of "following someone") not only in theory but in practical life ("carrying the cross").

In this context saving one's life means abandoning Christ's group of followers, deciding that it is dangerously revolutionary and looking for safety. Losing one's life means risking life by remaining part of the group. The risk can only be undertaken in complete solidarity with the person of Jesus ("for my sake").

If this solidarity is maintained throughout one's earthly life, it will be rewarded by an active share in Christ's resurrection and his eschatological kingdom. It is thus that the paschal mystery is fulfilled for every Christian. This experience in death and resurrection becomes the lot of all his disciples. They in turn carry their cross so that they may live in glory with him.

V. Isaiah 58:1-9a *1st reading* *Wednesday*

VII. Isaiah 58:9b-14 *1st reading* *Saturday*

These two readings reflect the prophetic movement which arose to challenge formalism in Jewish worship after the exile. The voice of the prophet takes the place of the trumpet which hitherto used to summon the people to the ceremonies of fast (v. 1). They are now being summoned to a new form of asceticism. Not the ostentatious fast of the man who dons sackcloth, bows his head (v. 4) and marvels that he is not heard by God (v. 3a); but a fast from egoism so to speak, whereby a man renounces selfish conduct of his affairs (v. 3b), or conflict with other people (v. 4). The fast which is pleasing to God is that which is concerned with "sharing" (vv. 6-7). And such a fast constitutes a stage in the preparation of the eschatological era (vv. 10-13). The two verses which conclude the passage give a similar interpretation to sabbath observance (vv. 13-14).

Like most contemporary religions, Israel regarded *fast* as an essential act of religion, above all at the feast of Expiation (Lv 23:26-32), or to commemorate the grim period of the Jerusalem siege (Za 8:19, 7:3-5; 2 K 25:1, 4, 8, 25). There were however prophets who queried such observances to the extent that traces of Manichaeism were displayed in fasting because of the impurity of matter, or when the climate of the ceremonies was over formalist (Is 58; Za 7:1-14). Some prophets favored fasting (Jb 1:13-14; 2:12-17), on certain occasions at least because they regarded this as a sign of greater sincerity in conversion than, for instance, a simple sacrifice. Fast signifies the desire to be converted; it is only valid when undertaken in the love of God (prayer and cult: Za 7), or the love of men (almsgiving and social justice: Is 58), or to signalize one's expectation of the last days (Jb 2).*

The Church remains faithful to this understanding of fast, as her latest legislation demonstrates. Fasting devoid of charity is not countenanced; and practice has recently taken a high direction in the organization of "Lents of sharing," which will doubtless one day succeed in giving their specifically Christian stamp, according to Matthew 6:3, of "losing ourselves," to the various secular enterprises of charity. Christian fast is an opportunity for encounter with God (vv. 8-9); and it is on that basis, particularly because of the repentance it signifies, that it is observed at certain times of the year when the Church is in a particular state of watching and prayer.

So it is that the essence of fast is not privation of nourish-

*See doctrinal theme: *asceticism,* p. 84.

ment, but the quality of faith manifested in our daily lives, so that they become vivid examples of service to God and our fellow men.

VI. Matthew
9:14-15
Gospel
Friday

The passage from which these two verses are drawn describes the meal offered to Jesus and his disciples by Matthew the publican after he had been invited to follow the Messiah. Verses 9-13 raise the question about Jesus eating with sinners, while verses 14-15 are concerned with the question of fast. In the interval the audience has changed, the Pharisees being succeeded by the "disciples of John."

John's disciples are astonished that Jesus and his disciples do not, like themselves, fast to a degree that exceeds normal Jewish observance about fast. Jesus' answer reveals that the Baptist's disciples have not yet discerned in him the messianic "spouse." If they had, they would realize that henceforth fast does not have the same meaning.

Fast is connected with the time of waiting. Jesus himself had fasted indeed, in the desert, living through in person humanity's long preparation for the inauguration of the Kingdom. However, once the public ministry had commenced he could with good reason say that the Kingdom was already here. The spouse had come: it was not proper for the "friends of the spouse" to fast as long as the spouse was with them; in this time of accomplishment fast no longer had meaning. Only after the resurrection will it again have meaning (cf. allusion to the passion in verse 15), to the extent that the time of the Church must be considered preparatory to the construction of the Kingdom.

The ecclesial symbolism of fast is very important. Here on earth the Church must be seen as something which awaits its hope, and yet already possesses the object of hope. Day after day it marches towards the Kingdom, of which it is already the manifestation. Such is its rhythm; what it possesses gives true meaning to what it is still building and what it is still building is in terms of what it now possesses. In this cycle fast gets significance. Certain days of waiting and preparation are appointed for it by the Church. On such days in the early liturgy the Eucharist was not celebrated at all, or celebrated only in the evening, because the Eucharist is the moment *par excellence* of the Church's life, where "possession" is the keynote, where expectation is fulfilled. Fast was never permitted on Easter Sunday.

VIII. **Luke**   Commentary on this gospel is included with
      5:27-32   that of Matthew 9:9-13, the gospel for the
      Gospel   tenth Sunday.
      Saturday   This passage describes the meal at which,
                       immediately after the call of Matthew (v. 9),
Jesus, his disciples and some sinners were gathered. Luke 5:29 and Mark 2:15 tell us that Matthew himself was the organizer of the banquet, and Luke adds that it was a sumptuous one.

The Pharisees expressed astonishment to the disciples that their master ate with sinners. Christ then asserts that he has come for the sake of the sick and the sinners, not the healthy or the just (vv. 12-13).

Doubtless the "just" he has in mind are those incapable of transcending the conventional notion of distributive justice and recognizing God's mercy. Their attitude is that of the workers in the vineyard (Mt 20:1-16), or of the elder son who resents his father's generosity to the prodigal son (Lk 15:11-32), or again of the Pharisees who fulfills all justice to the smallest mite but resents the sinner seeking divine mercy (Lk 18:9-14). He is actually opposing to a religion constructed on human justice one that depends on divine *mercy.* When he cites Hosea 6:6 (v. 13) he is pointing out that the prophets had already questioned the value of ritual, even perfectly executed ritual, as against a religion of love and mercy.

The numerous meals taken by Jesus with sinners, the father's pardon for the prodigal which takes the form of a sumptuous banquet (Lk 15:22-24), Jesus' attitude to Judas at the Supper (Mt 26:20-25), his anxiety to offer the bread and wine for the remission of sins (Mt 26:28), are a clear demonstration of the early Christian concept of the Eucharist as a sacrament of pardon (Mt 18:15-18). An overly specialist theology of the Eucharist and of penance has tended to render obscure the link between the two sacraments. Penance actually derives its efficacy from the Eucharist. Any theology of penance which makes it a purifying rite preparatory to the Eucharist, on the basis that the Eucharist itself is not in essence a rite of pardon, lessens the value of both sacraments. When the father assembles his family at a meal and communicates his own life to them, does not that simple gesture include pardon? Our great theological and pastoral need is eucharistic celebration which will be once more "for the remission of sins."

FIRST SUNDAY OF LENT

A. THE WORD

I. Genesis
2:7-9; 3:1-7
1st reading
1st cycle

The most plausible explanation of Adam's sin, which is described in this reading, makes it a sexual sin. In fact, in the near East the serpent represented the deity who controls male and female fecundity. Many women, in Israel and neighboring nations, turned to serpent-cult in order to ensure a fruitful marriage.

From the 8th century onwards, Hebrew prophecy objected to such sexual practices (Gn 31; Tr 44:15-18; Ds 4:12-14; Ba 6:42-44; 6:27-29) claiming that Yahweh alone was the true source of fruitfulness.

By having recourse to idolatry, to a serpent cult, in order to secure fruitfulness, Adam and Eve were proposing to achieve by their own efforts something that was reserved to God, thus setting themselves up in opposition to him. Hitherto innocent and adolescent (Gn 2:25) they now discover the laws of sexual attraction and feel shame (v. 7). There is nothing abnormal here. Man and woman reach an adult state of knowledge; but they acquire this through transgression. Have we not illustrated here the basic ambiguity of the human predicament?

The purpose of the account as we have it, in the rehandling of the primitive myth by the author, is not so much to make precise the nature of Adam's *sin*. He probably concentrates on the theme of sexual fruitfulness, as distinct from other possible areas, because he wants to condemn the idolatrous practices of his time.

Thus the point of the passage is to be sought in the author's way of emphasizing the real nature of sin. This consists not of any material element: it is pride, the pride of the man who sets himself up against God, failing to acknowledge dependence.

We do not have here (as in Gn 6:1-4, 6 for example) transgression traced to sources outside man. It is found in the very heart of man* (Si 15:11-20). That is the key to interpretation of the dialogue between God and Adam about Adam's transgression (vv. 10-13). Man is entrusted with a function in the universe that is determinative; consequently a share of responsibility for disorder in the world is laid at his door.

II. Genesis An extract from the discourse, of priestly
9:8-15 origin, that God is represented as having held
1st reading with Noah after the flood.
2nd cycle

a) The essential theme is that of the *covenant*. Noah, just like Adam, becomes the father of humanity. God makes a covenant with him, as he did with the first man (Gn 1) and he blesses him in the same way.

As in the case of other covenants in the priestly tradition sealed by God, the initiative comes from Yahweh. He alone binds himself. The covenant is evidence of his goodness. It has a cosmic and universal application like the covenants with Adam (Gn 1), with Abraham (Gn 17) and with Moses. They are all distinguished by a sign, the blessing of Adam, the circumcision of Abraham, the sabbath arrangement of Moses, the rainbow for Noah. The rainbow is the instrument by which Yahweh launches his lightnings (Ps 7:13; Ha 3:9-11) upon the earth; but for the moment it is lodged in the clouds and God does not use it.

b) In fact the admission of a deluge narrative to their scriptures by the Hebrews is not so much to be explained by interest in this catastrophe. The real point is God's promise that there would never again be a deluge. Here, in any case, in the allusion to this promise, the biblical tradition is sharply distinguished from pagan traditions about the flood. No pagan god had made such a promise, because none of them had, like

*See the doctrinal theme *Satan*, p. 33.

Yahweh, power over creation. It was only a *creator* who could assure the stability of his work, and the security of human beings on earth. Pagan gods had willed the flood as a means of destroying surplus mankind, who were threatening the gods. For scripture, on the contrary, Yahweh is someone who wants to bless mankind, who wishes fruitfulness and increase. In these priestly views about God and the world, already set forth in the first chapters of Genesis, what we have is optimism.

III. Deuteronomy This passage has to do with legislation about
26:4-10 first fruits and tithing. All that is contained
1st reading here is the prayer which the Jew had to offer
3rd cycle at the offering of gifts in the temple.

a) The offering of first fruits is a rite essentially religious, but at the same time altogether pagan. The religious man is aware that nature, which governs his life, is subject to mysterious laws of fruitfulness and barrenness, renewal and sterility, which he cannot fathom. He sees nature, too, as something greater than himself, and usually he imagines God, the greatest of all, standing side by side with nature and the laws which govern it.

Offering first fruits then is an act by which man recognizes the fact that nature comes to his aid, because the laws of God are directed towards the blessing of men.

This is a religious attitude, but a primitive one. Modern man does not see his relationship with nature as a relationship with something greater than himself. On the contrary, for him it is a relationship where he is the important element. Furthermore, he does not see God in nature (such a God would not inspire trust because he underlies a force that man controls). He no longer offers first fruits, and if he believes in God, that can only be because he discerns here a force capable of controlling and dominating nature.

b) This passage then from Deuteronomy, above all the prayer

contained in it, already points to a transformation of nature-
religion into salvation history. The God to whom the Jew offers
first fruits is not a nature-god, but the *God of history*, who is
manifested to man not by laws of nature, but by a covenant
between two free agents (v. 7). It is true of course that man
here in Deuteronomy is not yet the secular man of the 20th
century, to whom God is manifested in freedom; but neither is
he a man completely at the mercy of the laws of nature.

IV. Romans We recall that, in the letter to the Romans,
5:12-19 Paul veers between proclamations of a keryg-
2nd reading matic nature (as in Rm 3:21-31) and scrip-
1st cycle tural or dialectical analyses (as in Rm 4).
Here, in chapter 5, he embarks upon a new
kerygmatic demonstration. The justification about which he has
been talking since chapter 3 is seen in the early verses of
chapter 5 (vv. 10-11) as a reconciliation: the point being to
prove that not alone does man have no right to justice, but no
work of his has any value because he is fundamentally sinful
("feeble," "sinners," "enemies": vv. 6, 8 and 10).

This justification-reconciliation is brought about by Jesus
Christ (vv. 2, 6b, 8, 10). In this context Paul points out how
the divine initiative of justification and man's response to it are
summed up in Jesus, even anterior to any impulse of Christian
faith.

a) The first question that arises concerns the meaning of
verse 12 in particular, about *original sin,* to which Paul seems to
allude. Paul's style (he usually dictated) is not quite precise.
Verse 12 begins with a conjunction (*dia touto:* because of this),
and a comparison (*ôs ei:* as if), which remain incomplete.
Subsequently, one cannot determine whether death, which he
personifies almost in a mystic manner, is physical or spiritual
(likewise in vv. 13-14). Neither can we tell whether the relative

eph' ô should be translated *"in whom* all have sinned" (the Augustinian understanding of original sin); or *"because* all have sinned" (an allusion to personal sin only); or again *"from the moment where* all sinned" (personal sin being somehow a ratification and augmentation of all mankind's sin; because from one generation to another it repeats and proclaims the basic revolt of humanity against God, throwing into direct relief the spectacle of an enfeebled and quasi-impotent mankind).

In all one cannot be sure whether Paul, when he says all have sinned *(anastein),* uses this verb in the classical sense (the *act* of sin) or in the passive, as sometimes found in the Septaugint (the *state* of guilt: Is 24:5-6). There is too much exegetical uncertainty about such delicate problems for us to be able to elicit from this single verse a doctrine of original sin. We should not forget that, as in the preceding chapter about Abraham (Rm 4:18-25), Paul's reflections about Adam are those of a theologian not a historian (cf. further Rm 7). As he considers the basic factors of human existence, what looms in the foreground is collective responsibility and the dominion of "death" over all humanity.

b) The position described by verses 13-14 is that, after the conscious sin of Adam, God's will is not manifested again to mankind until Sinai (a situation which is continued outside Jewish environments, among nations who have not yet knowledge of the law). Among such communities without the law, without knowledge of God (v. 13b), personal sins doubtless are not imputed to individuals; but nevertheless death falls upon all men, even those ignorant of their sin (v. 14).

To understand how Paul came to write these verses, we must remember the biblical distinction between conscious and unconscious faults. Numbers 15:22-16:35 is very revealing on this point. The deliberate sinner (Nb 15:30) should be wiped out, without any opportunity for forgiveness, whereas the multitude who unconsciously or inadvertently participate in his crime can escape death by offering a sacrifice for the sin (cf. Lv 4). The legislation is well illustrated in the case of Core. He with his family is exterminated (Nb 16:31-34); but the "community" which followed him into crime, is spared (Nb 16:22).

Now consider the position of the people who have no knowledge of the law and sin unconsciously because they are involved in the human situation. Certainly they die (either by natural or spiritual death) . . . so long as "sacrifice for sin" Christ's immolation on the cross (Rm 5, 6, 8, 11) is not being offered. The whole idea of the Jewish feast of *expiation* was precisely the remission of personal fault due to error, to limit the extension among the community of an individual's crime (Lv 4:1-3). The suffering servant then took upon himself the continuance of this ritual (Is 53:10). Finally, Christ on the cross brought to completion the effective "sacrifice for sin" of those who more or less unconsciously participate in the crime of an individual.

This expiation ritual, so often cited in the New Testament concerning the sacrifice of the cross, is then the backcloth of the Pauline passage. It enables us to distinguish two types of sin: formal, personal sin (in this case Adam's) which leads inevitably to death; and unconscious sin or sin by association which can be remitted by the sacrifices of expiation and by the suffering Servant.

There is no point in expecting the apostle to explain the why of solidarity between Adam and the people: for him, against a background of expiation ritual, this goes without saying. The originality of his thinking lies in the thesis that the guilt of collective sin is remitted by the sacrifice of the cross.

c) The passage is structured around a series of antitheses between *Adam* and *the Christ*.

Verse 15

— how much more —

by the fault	by the grace
of one man	of one man, Jesus
so many	over so many
encounter death	spread abundantly

Verse 16

the judgment	the grace
of one single fall	—
brings condemnation	works towards justification
(that is; the multiplicity	for a multitude of faults
of personal faults on the part	
of a humanity given over more	
and more to its passions)	
(cf. Rm 1:18-32)	

Verse 17

by the fault	by the gift . . . of justice
of one	—
death	in life
reigned	those who receive it reign
through this one man	through Jesus Christ only

It is notable that in this verse Paul leaves aside the nuance of expiation on the part of Christ, and turns to consideration of eschatological life with him. Such a gift has yet to be realized, but it is a consequence of the gift of justification already bestowed.

Verse 19 (conclusion)

by the disobedience	by the obedience
of one man	of one only
the many	the many
become sinners	will be made just

The parallelism between Adam and Christ does not, however, attribute equal importance to them. One should be careful not to regard Christ simply as the person capable of redressing the debacle for humanity that began with Adam. His obedience and his sacrifice not only cancel the disobedience of Adam and the guilt of the many; the Christ has become Lord of eschatological life (cf. the "how much more" of v. 17); there is more here than simple restoration or expiation, this means the beginning of a new providential economy.

d) Our last point is essential for Christian anthropology. If it were true that Christ simply redresses the debacle begun by Adam, Adam would be the primary figure because we would not comprehend Christ except in terms of Adam. But if what Christ brings ("life") is radically different from anything that Adam left to his own resources was capable of bringing, then we see Adam in terms of Christ. "Adam is no more than the figure of him who was to come" (v. 14b). It is not a matter of balancing Adam against the Christ as two persons of equal dignity, as if sin on the one hand, and justice on the other, counterbalanced one another. Thus we see that Christian anthropolgy is essentially rooted in the notion of man in Jesus Christ, who enjoys the promise of "life," Adam enters in only as the object of a backward glance, some figure from an ancient order. In the Christian view humanity cannot be defined in terms of Adam. Only the Christ, not just Christ of the cross but Christ become Lord, is the key to the mystery of man.

This, the most difficult passage in the letter to the Romans, is also one of its most important theological sections. True, there is a parallel between Adam and the Christ: each is connected with the many by an extraordinary bond. But there is no question of old and new, of first and second. There is only Jesus Christ and those who prefigured him, figures who find their meaning only when the one they herald has come. The two persons of the Adam-Christ parallel are so unequal, for all their brotherhood, that it makes little difference ultimately for Christian faith whether science one day demonstrates the truth of polygenism, and tears away the veil from the allegedly mythical thinking of Saint Paul in his commentary on Adam. For us the only important point is that there is no way for humanity to find the meaning of existence except in the light of Christ's lordship. Where we came from is not important; whither we are bound is.

V. 1 Peter
3:18-22
2nd reading
1st cycle

This reading is probably inspired by a primitive baptismal hymn, sung by the early Christians during the paschal vigil. It can be reconstructed as follows:

(The Christ)	
(known since before creation)	
manifested at the end of days	1 P 3:18
brought to death by the flesh	1 P 3:18
to life by the spirit	1 P 3:18
evangelizing the departed	1 P 3:19
entering heaven	1 P 3:22
subduing powers and dominations	1 P 3:22

Other New Testament passages (Ep 3:7, 11; 2 Tm 1:9-11) have been inspired by this same hymn.

We should note that these verses are in groups of two. The first two celebrate the lordship of Christ over time, of which he is the alpha and omega. The following two describe his life on earth, his passage from death to life, and his mystery as man vivified by the spirit. The last two describe his lordship over the cosmos, from his sojourn with the dead to his ascent to heaven.

Into this acclamation the author of the letter has engrafted a brief profession of faith:

(I believe in the Christ)	
who died	1 P 3:18a
arose again	1 P 3:21b
is at the right hand of God	1 P 3:22

Subsequently he adds a marginal note about the meaning of the descent into hell, and of the deluge as seen from the baptismal and paschal angle (1 P 3:20-21).

We do not know the real meaning of this *descent into hell*. One tradition sees it as a manner of describing the expansion of lordship over the nether world (Ep 1:20-21; Col 2:5; P 3:22 and especially Ph 2:10). In fact Jewish cosmology distinguished three levels in the universe: heaven, earth, hell. The Christ, enthroned by his Pasch as Lord, extends his empire simultaneously over the three domains.

In other traditions the descent into hell indicates total human participation in God's salvation. Even the ancients who died before Christ (Mt 27:52-53; He 11:39-40) are included. From an angle such as this the author of the letter would be emphasizing the shortcomings of the old economy. Only eight persons escaped the deluge (v. 20) and Christ had to descend into hell to liberate the others, sinners though they were. Baptism as a result of the universal salvific power of the risen Christ is capable of ransoming the multitude.

The theme of descent into hell raises the question also of primitive credal formulas and the modern interpretations of them. If the descent finds place in the Christian *credo* it can only be because it has meaning, and indicates the status of man before God after the Christ event. To say that Christ has been in hell means in the first place that he has been really dead, hell being the abode of the dead. Consequently he has undergone the total human experience. However, he is the Living One, and "arises" from this abode of the dead.

But Christian faith pushed the search for meaning further. When the Lord of life descends to hell, he does so actively. His sojourn there takes on the aspect of a victory over spirits. He announces their decisive defeat, and makes this effective by setting the men who are their captives free.

There is not however any question of localizing hell; a state rather than a place is envisaged. Furthermore the same New Testament which speaks of descent to hell mentions ascent to paradise in that context too (Lk 23:43). Such phrases express in cosmological language what people try to state in anthropological terms today. The Christ, living in a deep intimacy with the Father brings all capable of following him to that state. By "descending into hell" he demonstrates that the state of dereliction which is that of *sheol* is now replaced by the state of intimacy with God.

VI. Romans   In 57, the success of Paul's mission to the
10:8-13   Gentiles had already reached such remarkable
2nd reading   proportions that he was contemplating an
3rd cycle   early journey to Spain (Rm 15:17-24), and
                   thinking in terms of the time the gospel
would have reached the limits of the world.

The problem of Israel itself however was far from being so encouraging. In each community there were Jewish converts; but they were a small minority, like the stump of a tree that has been shorn of practically all its out-growth (cf. Rm 11:17).

a) Revolving in his mind this paradoxical image of a tree (the new Israel) which is made up almost exclusively of grafted branches (the Gentiles), and shorn of its own growth (the Jews); he contemplates with some elation a growth where there is neither Jew nor Greek (v. 12), and decides that it is all a matter of *belief or unbelief.* Belief grafts us on to the tree; unbelief cuts us off (Rm 10:4). The latter takes the position that man by himself is capable of achieving justice (Rm 10:2-3). The former springs from the conviction that man can only achieve salvation and fulfillment by placing his trust in the name of Christ (vv. 11, 13).

b) Turning to analysis of what belief in such terms means, Paul depends on a combination of Deuteronomy texts: 9:4 and 30:12-13. There we have a distinction between the *mouth* and the *heart,* to demonstrate that belief is made up of a word that is heard (the word of the gospel, v. 8b); adhesion by the heart to this word (v. 9b); and finally public confession of one's adhesion (v. 9a). The heart then and the lips must cooperate: the heart whereby we submit ourselves to the initiative of God, who raises up the dead; the lips which distinguish us from Jew and Gentile by the profession "Jesus is Lord" (I Co 12:3), which set us forth as a challenge before the world until the day of recognition by God at the final judgment.

VII. Matthew
4:1-11
Gospel
1st cycle

The narrative of the temptation is structured with a view to demonstrating that Christ relived in his own person the "temptations" (Dt 8:2)* of the Jewish people in the desert. By preserving his obedience towards God unsullied he will again set in motion the plan of salvation, which was interrupted by the people's disobedience in the desert.

a) The temptation of food (Ex 16:4; Dt 8:2-5; Mt 4:1-4). In Deuteronomy 8, God himself is "tempter" of the people: in Matthew 4, Satan has the role. The difference is altogether due to the development of Jewish theology (compare 2 S 24:1 and I Ch 21:1). But the moral remains the same: man must turn towards a new nourishment, the will of God.

The temptation of signs (Ex 17:1-7; Dt 6:16; Mt 4:5-7). The people had sinned by demanding a miracle of God; Christ shows such a complete confidence in his Father that there will be no need of marvelous signs (Mt 12:38-42; Mk 8:11-13; Jn 6:30-33).

The temptation of earthly gods (Dt 6:12-15; Ex 23:20-33; 34:11-14; Mt 4:8-11). The reference here is not so much to worship of the golden calf, as to the injunction not to worship the Canaanite gods. When they entered Canaan, the Jews had made some gesture towards the local gods. Would Christ, destined for universal reign (and after him the Church), also temporize with the Prince of this world?*

b) Christ undergoes these temptations as a *second Moses*. The mention of "forty days and forty nights" recalls the similar fast of the patriarch (Dt 9:9, 18; Ex 34:28). The mountain from which Christ sees the kingdoms corresponds to that from which Moses saw the land of promise (Dt 34:1-4). The portion of the narrative about a mountain from which all the kingdoms of the world were visible is not intended literally. In Deuter-

---

*See doctrinal theme: *temptation*, p. 27.
*See the doctrinal theme: *Satan*, p. 33.

onomy 34 the exaggeration was already there. It is not possible to have a view of all Palestine from Mount Nebo.

c) He also relives the temptations as *Messiah*. It is thus that we must understand the service of angels and the insertion in the narrative of Ps 90/91. True the psalm sings of how every just man has God's protection, and previously Elias had an angel at his disposition "for service" in his temptation (1 K 19:5-8). It is beyond doubt, however, that, both in Jewish circles and in the primitive church, a messianic interpretation of the psalm was customary.

The various echoes of the old Testament in the narrative are designed then to demonstrate that Christ represents in his person the remnant of the chosen people. In this capacity he is confronted by a choice: between human means and the means of being at God's disposal, which is that of the Kingdom. His personal sense of vocation though is also somehow deepened. He becomes aware of his capacity to be legislator (a new Moses) and leader of the people (Messiah); and he opts for a new manner of understanding those functions, one which depends altogether on faith and openness to the Father.

VIII. Mark
1:12-15
Gospel
2nd cycle

Mark has only a very summary account of the sojourn in the desert (vv. 12-13); but it is worth noting that he makes this pivotal as between the baptism (vv. 9-11) and the inauguration of Jesus' ministry (vv. 14-15).

In fact Mark is the only evangelist to feature the baptism of Jesus as the inaugural event of the gospel. Here he follows primitive apostolic preaching (Ac 10:37). The rite is described in a series of incidents which must be analyzed individually: the opening of the heavens (v. 10), the descent of the Spirit (v. 10) and the voice from heaven (v. 11).

a) The prophets often tell of visions where, to begin with, the *heavens part* to enable the visionary to see (Ez 1:1; Rv 4:1).

Here we have a poetic image characteristic of the genre of apocalypse. Nor is the opening of heaven solely to give access to divine secrets: it is also intended, as in Isaiah 63:19 and John 1:51, to clear a passage for God. Henceforward there will be no barrier between heaven and earth (a similar nuance in the rending of the temple veil: Mk 15:38): the proclaimer of the Kingdom (vv. 14-15) will be veritably equipped, like the ancient prophet, to speak of God to men.

b) Israel's prayer (63-64) which is the origin of the motif of heavens opening (Is 63:19) suggests something else also. It recalls the action whereby Yahweh, pastor of his people (Is 63:11), parted the waters of the sea and spread the spirit over his flock (Is 63:14). Surely we have here the whole source of inspiration for a *descent of the spirit* on the new Moses, the just one, at the moment of his emergence from the water (v. 10). The new Exodus foretold by Second-Isaiah is about to begin, and Jesus is seen as the inaugurator, the pastor of a new people. Seen thus, he is more than a prophet, more than a preacher: he has authority over the people.

c) Since the baptism is presented above all as an answer to Isaiah's prayer (63-64), where the Father is implored to draw forth from the water a new pastor who will lead his people in a new Exodus, the sojourn of Jesus in the *desert* takes on a particular significance. The Exodus is really entered upon. Jesus spends forty days in the desert as the people spent forty years. He is led there by the spirit as the people were led by the cloud. He is tempted as they were (Dt 8:1-4; Ps 94/95). But because he is also Messiah, he is, as Messiah, served by angels (Ps 90/91: 10-12), and subdues savage beasts (Dt 8: 15; Ps 90/91: 13) according to the messianic interpretation of Psalm 90/91.

Being baptized basically means being immersed in the water, above all in the human condition (including death) represented by the water. When Christ underwent it, he accepted his human condition with its ambiguities and sufferings, with death as the term. His election as preacher of the Kingdom has its roots in just this acceptance. At once temptation comes to assail him so that he will be reassured about the quality and actuality of his choice. Was he to be totally man, or would he evade that condition by banishing hunger, escaping death, or resorting to the weapons of power? The temptation proves that he is engulfed in existence. So is he fitted to preach the Kingdom of God, the coming of which hangs upon man's fidelity to his own human state, right to the very end in death.

IX. Luke 4:1-13 Luke's account of the temptation resembles
Gospel   pretty closely that of Matthew. Consequently
3rd cycle   we need only refer the reader to the com-
                mentary on the Gospel of the first cycle. One
important difference has to do with the use of Psalm 90/91. Luke refers us to it in the context of the last temptation (vv. 9-12): Matthew uses it for the second. Moreover, Luke's citation of the psalm is a little more elaborate than Matthew's (compare v. 10 and Mt 4:6), even though both of them tend generally to coincide in citations, and both have probably omitted the allusion to Ps 90/91:13 which is preserved in Mark 1:13. Then Luke does not mention the "service of angels" which for Matthew and Mark is so important.

There is another difference between the two in the order of temptations. Matthew, no doubt the more primitive account, has a geographic bias: the desert, Jerusalem, the entire world, in that order. He is concerned to present his narrative as a parallel of the temptations in the desert, following the order of Exodus 16:17 and 32. Luke has no such anxiety. He is addressing Gentile Christians for whom parallels with the ancient people of the desert were of little moment. He prefers, too, to present the three temptations* in a new order, recalling the temptations of the first man, Adam, whose descendant, as he has just men-

---

*See the doctrinal theme: *temptation*, p. 27.

tioned (Lk 3:38), Jesus was; recalling also not only those of Adam, but the habitual temptations of all human beings.

a) Thus the second temptation (Matthew's third) is somewhat retouched. Satan's role as sovereign of humanity is probably a reminiscence of man's dominion over the earthly paradise. Thus his proposal to Jesus is not a messianic royalty that is universal as in Matthew, but a possibility of which all men dream, that of dominion one day over all the world at whatever price. Adam had the power of "dominating the earth" (Gn 1:18), but he chose to exercise this function under Satan rather than God. Christ by his victory over temptation undid the degradation that had been wrought by the *first man*. He is not so much then a new Moses, as in Matthew, but the leader and the model for a new humanity.

b) Likewise, we must pause to consider the significance of the reference to Psalm 90/91 in the temptation narratives.

Clearly Satan*, in suggesting that Christ cast himself from the pinnacle of the temple, is not just suggesting an ostentatious gesture before an assembled crowd, because there is no mention of spectators. There seems rather to be reference to certain Jewish traditions which alleged that the people had been "borne" throughout the wandering by the *shekina* (the divine glory). A temptation for Jesus to be similarly borne by the *shekina* or by the angels and thus preserved, would amount to asking God that he escape death (cf. Mt 26:53). He refuses to make such a request, recalling Adam (Gn 3:3), and undertakes the burden of life with complete acceptance of the human condition. Consequently he will be a *suffering servant*.

c) Luke then, in the matter of collaboration by *angels*, differs in his emphasis from Matthew 4:11 and Mark 3:13. For him the point is that Jesus refuses to have recourse to supernatural means or celestial powers to avoid his destiny. Matthew and Mark on the other hand put forward the service of Christ by

*See the doctrinal theme: *Satan*, p. 33.

angels as a means of demonstrating to Jewish readers that he really was the prophesied Messiah.

There is significance in the fact that Luke, in concluding his narrative (v. 13), points out that the temptations of Jesus are such as any man may encounter, and they will recur at the "appointed time," at the moment when Jesus encounters death. In fact his whole temptation-narrative raises very profound anthropological considerations.

Man is seen as naturally subject to temptation. He wants to eat from the tree of knowledge of good and evil, to have God's own knowledge. That is to say: he would make absolute his own ethical insights, judge everything, and reject what he wants to reject. This life, essentially precarious, is made an absolute too, when he strives to overcome death. No longer can he have angels to bear him up; but he finds other assurances and certainties to give him the illusion that he is master of his fate. So in the anonymous masses of the streets he reassures himself, among the paraphernalia of publicity and propaganda, worshiping the dull divinities of the masses, lest he be forced to find personal, free solutions.

There is a basic need in man, one that must be respected, for security. What Jesus shows is that this need cannot be satisfied by making human solutions absolute, by divinizing ideas and techniques. There is only one way. We must accept the fact that all earthly existence bears the stamp of death, and live life on such terms, seeing its ambiguity, its absurdity. We must grasp with both hands this double-edged challenge, and encounter it side by side with the one person who successfully made the human pilgrimage all the way.

What is under consideration in the temptation narrative is the human predicament. Jesus does not content himself with saying that human life has no meaning except in communion with God. He is demonstrating that such communion can only be achieved when we reject the various human absolutes, and accept death, Christ's death and that of all men, as something that will always make nonsense of the divinized Adam.

The eucharistic assembly brings together those men who freely accept the human predicament, and also, in turn, that area of themselves that is of God. In the Word and in the breaking of the Bread we find a way of being faithful to what is in us of God. After Jesus it is called the Spirit of God, and it is this Spirit who "groans in us in mysterious language" that only the Father hears, groans ceaselessly until we, too, comprehend, and live our lives accordingly, though surrounded by the temptations of this world.

B. DOCTRINE

1. The Theme of Temptation

At the beginning of Lent the Church summons Christians in assembly to a closer look at the fundamental sources of their inspiration. Following the path of salvation acquired by Jesus Christ requires constant readjustment from everyone. Sin is always operative here below, and the danger of our faith being undermined or distorted is always present.

The desert temptations never lose the dimension of actuality. They concern the good Christians, those who are aware of their responsibilities in the people of God, just as much as those who fall victim to the various brands of modern materialism. The Tempter is quite subtle, and no area of life escapes his attention. Even in these days of Church reform, sometimes painful reform indeed, if Christians are to respond more vigorously and with open eyes to the challenge of modern paganism, it is imperative for them to reexamine their understanding of God's plan, and to have a fuller insight about the depths of degradation, where the Tempter is capable of leading.

Temptation for pagan man

In his search for happiness man naturally tends to the ways of security. He looks for the solid, the stable, the immoveable, the forseeable. He rejects time, the fluidity of history, because this brings him suffering, frustration, meaninglessness. Everything in nature, both within and without himself, that is permanent or cyclic seems to hold out hope of grasping the happiness for which he yearns.

Insofar as it is anterior to man the natural "order" could theoretically be regarded as a sign of the benevolence of a transcendent God, and be accordingly the basis for authentic thanksgiving. But as a sign it is ambiguous because there is no clear distinction between Creator and creation. It is when God is apprehended as the principle of natural order that he can be wrested into the scope and compass of human aspirations.

Here lies the temptation . . . why should not man be like a god? It is more reassuring to accord oneself salvation than to await God's initiative for it. So it is that man, constantly liable to confuse creation with Creator, has so often been plunged into every form of idolatry and magic.

For modern man this temptation to manipulate God takes a new form. The ever increasing mastery he exercises over nature tends to make him more and more oblivious to the fact that nature is anterior to man. He is only interested in nature to the extent of subduing it for transformation and humanization by himself. He doesn't have to reject time or the fluidity of history; he can dominate this area too and bend it to the service of his projects. His temptation is precisely atheism. It's not necessary to manipulate God: God is dead . . . For humanity to fulfill itself there is no need of his existence.

Temptation for Jewish man

A decisive turning point came with Abraham and the people who made up his progeny. Israel does not wish to cancel time or renounce history. For Jewish man the event — human history in its unforseeable, unique and irreversible texture — constitutes the very core of the salvation towards which his innermost being yearns.

So it came about that temptation for pagan man was annulled in a radical fashion by the advent of faith. It was no longer possible to confuse creation with Creator for people who discerned in concrete history, and in the events which punctuate it, the antecedent initiative of God. The God of Israel is the master of a history which transcends human powers. He is the transcendent being, eminently personal, who intervenes with full freedom in the daily life of his people. Between Creator and creation now stretches a gulf, henceforth unbridgeable.

Under the regime of faith man no longer attempts to divinize himself, or to manipulate God. His temptation now takes two forms. It is more subtle, and manifests itself precisely in the context of the covenant and the choice of Israel. The first form of temptation: if Yahweh chooses for himself one people from among all others, would he not naturally reserve for them certain securities and abundant blessings? And if today, because of infidelity, he does not shower these upon his people, at least in the final times of salvation he will do so. Of course, in the search for security here and now, many Jews continued to have recourse to the favors bestowed by pagan divinities. The second form of temptation for Israel arises from the specific nature of Jewish theorizing. When he makes the covenant, Yahweh expects from the Jewish people the fidelity of a partner. How is that fidelity achieved? By strictly human effort, or by waiting for God to bestow it, a gift in the future? Too often wrong turnings occurred in the first direction: Israel would seek a fidelity in purely human, and thus inadequate, terms, something that set apart and bestowed certain nights.

Had Israel lived at proper depth this religion of awaiting, it could have overcome its particular temptation. Any merely human contrivances would have been engulfed and overwhelmed. The virgin Mary, because she was without sin, was certainly the only believer of the old covenant to demonstrate complete allegiance to the religion of awaiting. Open as she was to the definitive covenant, she could give birth to the awaited Savior.

Jesus' victory over the temptations in the desert

For the New Testament authors the temptations of Jesus in the desert are closely related to those undergone by the people in the desert, and remembered always throughout Jewish history as archetypal. But on this occasion, for the first time, the Evil One fails to prevail. The regime of faith reaches perfect fulfillment in Jesus; the danger of corruption is finally removed.

After the fast of forty days Jesus is hungry; but he will not exercise his messianic powers in his own favor, even though such exercise is legitimate. He will not inaugurate the proclamation of the Good News by a miracle; he will not cast himself from the pinnacle of the Temple. It is not by such sensational means that the Kingdom comes! Jesus could indeed have given the chosen people domination of the universe, but it is from God that the Kingdom issues, and that needs no mobilization of human power.

In short Jesus is conquering the most radical temptation that the regime of faith could encounter, that of depending on human resources to build the fidelity required by the covenant, having human destiny hang upon the realization of any human project, of whatever kind. But his victory was paradoxical because humanly speaking it had all the semblance of defeat.

Here, at the beginning of his public ministry, Jesus is called upon to affirm once again his decisive choice in incarnation. "Father, thy will be done" is the governing principle in all his individual actions. The radical poverty indicated here gives us the time image of the regime of faith which Abraham began. He saved mankind because he was able through his human nature to bind man in a real sense to God. Jesus did not derive this capacity from any reliance on human resources, but from his Divine Sonship. The relation of Son to Father is a timeless one and invested him in his humanity as well.

The Church's victory over the temptations in the desert

The desert temptations were resisted by Jesus. Does this mean they have vanished for ever, or is the Church still assailed by them? Is not the victory of Christ automatically that of his Body, the Church, because of the closeness of the link?

The truth, of course, we know: the same temptations do continue to assail the Church. For Jesus they were part of a human experience the true nature of which was revealed by the death on the cross. For him, of course, there could subjectively be no compromise with evil, but his experience was not devoid of failure and frustration.

In the latter domain, for the Church, nothing has changed.

Trusting in Christ's victory, she pursues her mission in continuation of his, and in its pattern. Her human experience always exhibits the appearance of failure. Satan, the great antagonist, who was laid low by the resurrection, still has the capacity to tempt her. It is easy for him, here below, to manipulate the gap that lies between this goal of universal salvation and actual experience, as the Church continues her human struggle. He is always proposing that she change her concept of mission and turn to human means. Like her Lord, she can always emerge from the temptation victorious.

Her victory will always be assured by the swelling of the Word within her. And the individual Christian too, in proportion to his surrender to the Word, can for his part share in the victory. But insofar as he continues in sin he yields to the desert temptations. He can never, of course, bear a witness to Jesus Christ that is perfectly in alignment with the gospel that is the essential core of the Church. For each one the victory over the temptations remains constantly to be won. But the Christian has confidence; this "eschatological" victory which lies before him will be his if he clings to the Word and models himself more and more in accordance with it. The power of Satan has been definitively crushed.

The tension is characteristic not alone of Christian lives but of the ecclesial institution too because the institution bears the marks, in appearance and development, of the sinful men who make it up. The Church may be more than the sum of baptized persons at a given time, but there is also a sense in which it *is* that sum. Christians collectively are capable of making mistakes, grave mistakes, as we know from history. Divided Christianity is one of them.

No collective sin, however, perpetrated within the Church, can ever destroy her triumphant holiness, which is that of her Master. This will always be the living source in her of constant "reform," at once institutional and individual. By refreshment at the source the Church and her members will succeed in conforming their will to that of Jesus Christ.

The temptations of the apostolate

The apostolate is the collective work *par excellence* of Christians. What are the temptations that beset it? Today's gospel tells us in unmistakable terms.

Because nothing could possibly sway Jesus towards self-interest, every authentic apostolate must necessarily be carried on under the standard of absolute detachment. The Kingdom can never be confused with secular pursuits, however noble. There is sometimes a subtle temptation here. If the ecclesial institution tends to feature itself as philanthropic, an instrument for social revolution, a wholesome leisure occupation, there is a very real danger of confusion.

Jesus refused the facile prestige that propaganda would bring, the power over the masses. Liberation was his object, not persuasion or dominion. The witness of salvific faith cannot be allowed to mask violence done to liberty. Every apostle consequently must beware of seeking success in such terms.

Satan tried to kindle the ambition of Jesus. This is the temptation *par excellence*. Yielding to it really means corruption of the message, because religion is swallowed in the will to power. In his stern rejection of this final assault, Jesus indicated condemnation of what we mean by ecclesiasticism, or clericism, in all its manifestations. It is not mindless paternalism that keeps the spiritual state of people, but liberation from the temporal. The Kingdom is not of this world. It could be that in the restless questioning of all establishment that is noticeable in our time, some dynamism is at work, that is worthwhile if we can only recognize it.

Such an evangelic apostolate, pure of any alloy, demands constant readjustment. Putting the Church in a state of mission, now at the beginning of Lent, means leading all Christians to find out what are the dangers, within themselves, of alienation from spiritual values. Their collective effort to surmount these could help to bring about that great sign of grace which an adult world expects from the Church.

Welcoming the Word and the victory over temptation

The first Sunday of Lent summons the Christian to confront his daily activity constantly with the Word. Anyone who wishes to belong to the regime of faith, to build himself in that mold and share in Christ's victory over the Tempter, must be always receptive towards the Word which leads him, envelopes him, gives him some deep dynamism and drive. The community which believes in the Paschal mystery, if it is to be spiritually healthy, must be getting more and more involved in salvation history. Proclamation of the Word assures that involvement, provided of course that it is actualized in the living witness to their faith Christians must bear in the daily texture of their lives.

2. The Theme of Satan

Many Christians no longer believe in Satan. Their experience of temptation does not seem to them to argue the existence of demonic powers; sin is sufficiently explained by human liberty. Personifying evil was characteristic of an epoch, now past, when man saw himself as the pawn of cosmic forces. The popular mythology of yesterday is today rejected, and what used to be called diabolic possession has become just another malady to be explained in terms of depth psychology. Has not the Church itself undergone a similar change and become remarkably hesitant about the practice of exorcism?

There are others who do not take this view. Satan they say has never been more active. Is not his trump card making people disbelieve in his existence? Without opposition, he can work all the more effectively. If we allege that Satan is not active in the world, how can we explain the many scriptural passages about him? Was Jesus himself the victim of folk beliefs? Surely not.

Questions such as these make us reflect more deeply about what we believe. What validity do these traditional affirmations have, about Satan's role on earth? As we review the various stages of salvation history, we shall find that the affirmations are by no means gratuitous. Without them it does not seem possible to see the work of Christ, or the duty of the Christian, in adequate dimensions.

The adversary of Yahweh's plan

Pagan man saw himself under the dominion of a world of spirits who were superior to himself. Very early he made an attempt to explain good and evil by seeing two principles locked in combat. This sort of dualism has had very many manifestations in the religious history of humanity. The very creation of the world was often seen as a victory of good over evil.

In the climate of the covenant, and of Jewish monotheism, this dualist outlook was profoundly changed. There is but one God, Yahweh; the existence of everything else is entirely due to his benevolent creativity. Thus it is absolutely unthinkable that any creature, of whatever kind, should dispute his exclusive domain with Yahweh or jeopardize in any basic way his plan of love and mercy. Man is created to respond by fidelity to the loving initiative of God; but, because he is free, it is possible for him to be unfaithful and to betray his vocation.

In fact, man has rejected God and bears responsibility for that. But man's experience of sin leads him to the conviction that what takes place is capitulation by him to temptation. It is as if there were some evil inherent in the object of temptation, antecedent to his voluntary act. In other words experience seems to teach him that what happens when man sins is an awareness of involvement in some evil that existed independently of his sin, and embraces also spiritual creatures other than man. If God has created everything in love, everything he created is capable of rejecting him.

Such was the Jewish explanation. The result of human sin was expulsion from the terrestrial paradise. Man henceforward belonged in a world that was acquainted with death, and this world was the empire of spiritual powers who had themselves rejected God. These powers used death as their most potent instrument for confronting man with temptation, and when he yields he becomes their slave. The hope was for the advent of a man who would not yield, who would open himself to the action of God's victorious Spirit and Word. Then the power of death would be broken. For it is only by his own connivance that man becomes the slave of the demonic forces; he is not by nature the plaything of other spirits.

Christ's victory over the adversary

To ensure human salvation the dominion of demonic forces had to be destroyed; death had to be vanquished on his own ground. Of all this dread dominion Satan is the prince. He it was who at the very beginning took the form of a serpent in order to deceive the first Adam. He it is whom the Messiah must confront and conquer in a new combat. That is the object of Christ's mission "to take away all the power of the devil, who had power over death" (He 2:14).

We should not then be surprised when the evangelists present his public life as a constant combat with Satan: the encounter in the desert, the liberation of those possessed, the challenge to unbelieving Jews, finally the passion where, even when he seemed to be in control, Satan was overwhelmed. By being obedient even to the death on the cross, Jesus dethroned death and deprived Satan of the primary weapon whereby he built his earthly kingdom.

What is the basic meaning of this victory of Christ's? Affirmations about Satan's defeat really mean affirmation of the cosmic dimensions of what he did. We are dealing with something very fundamental indeed. Previously all creation was encompassed in the solidarity of sin. From now on there is a breach in the barrier. Christ, in a cosmic fashion, has opened up the way for a new cosmic solidarity, that of love. In other words, in Jesus Christ, the real creative plan of God breaks through; man becomes the ally of his creator in bringing to actuality his plan of love. Salvation-history, in the cosmic sense, has its real beginning. The day will come when Satan and death will be thrown "in the burning lake" (Rev 20:14). Then the solidarity of sin will have lost all consistency; there will be no kingdom of sin any more.

"He is the image of the unseen God and the first-born of all creation, for in him were created all things in heaven and on earth, everything visible and everything invisible, thrones, Dominations, Sovereignties, Powers; all things were created through him and for him. Before anything was created, he existed and he holds all things in unity. Now the Church is his body, he is its head" (Col 1:15-18). It is in such terms that Saint Paul reveals the cosmic dimensions of Christ's intervention in history, and delineates the basic role of the Christian.

The adversary of Christians

The Church's mission here below is constantly to widen the breach opened by Christ, the Head of the Body. Satan's empire has been undermined, but it is not yet destroyed; death in all its forms continues to lure sinful man into temptation. Christ has once for all defeated Satan; but each man is summoned to win the same victory in turn.

Membership of the Church by baptism means accepting the duty of working for the fulfillment of Christ's primacy, so that beginning with him the true creation may be shaped. It means undertaking a responsibility of cosmic dimensions. The baptismal rite itself dwells upon this aspect of Christian vocation. Time and again the Spirit of God is dramatically opposed to Satan. The catechumen is made aware that the sacrament is about to snatch him once and for all from the dominion of demonic forces and incorporate him with true humanity. In other words he is about to pass once and for all from the world of sin to that of grace and fidelity, set up by Christ to give real validity to God's creative plan. He is required to endorse personally the triple renouncement of Satan, and the triple confession of Trinitarian faith.

But the struggle with Satan does not cease with baptism; this is a triumphal beginning of something designed for the advancement of all creation. In any man's life it is the initial act of regeneration which equips him to join Christ's struggle against the sin of the world and against all powers that reject God. Christ made the definitive breach in the solidarity of sin: baptism summons us all to continue his work. Because the Kingdom of the Father must be expanded until it absorbs all creation.

Mission and the struggle with Satan

In mission comes the high moment of the struggle with Satan, the time when the Christian must summon all the resources of his baptismal state. We have mission in the strict sense when the Good News of salvation is preached to a new people, when there is question of planting the mystery of Christ in a hitherto untouched cultural *milieu*. Here one has a more proximate sense of the cosmic weight of sin. Not that God's Spirit is not active in such environments. On the contrary, the religious pilgrimage of any non-Christian people is invariably the result in some part of action by the Spirit. But because the mystery of Christ is not yet rooted here, the pilgrimage is tentative, without the key to fulfillment. Death retains its power; Satan's sway is formidable.

What is the work of the missionary? He leaves one cultural milieu already shaped by the Church to bear witness to the risen Christ in another where the Good News has not yet penetrated. His task is to make his own the religious pilgrimage of this people, to use it and shape it in every possible way towards culmination in Christ. This is a sharing pregnant with paschal meaning. He anticipates somehow in himself the experience the people are destined to have when the mystery of Christ is rooted here; he points the way that they must take in order to accomplish their true destiny.

All this, as we said, indicates a paschal rhythm and it is therefore imperative that the people should realize this truth. Their deepest aspirations will only be accomplished, when death, wherever it appears, above all in relations with others, is challenged in obedience. In this sense the object of mission is the overthrow of Satan's empire in an area where it is still jealously preserved, just because death here has never yet been shorn of its power.

The Eucharist, the meal of victory over satan

Baptism equips the Christian for the triumphal struggle with Satan, but only sharing in the Eucharist nourishes him for successful combat day by day.

First of all, reception of the body of Christ gradually nourishes the baptized person as a child of the Kingdom. It absorbs him more and more into the true creation built on Jesus Christ, not only for his own personal salvation, but for entry on his cosmic role. Did not Saint Paul say to the Corinthians that on entry to the Lordship of Christ they would judge the angels?

Then, beyond that, openness to the triumphal Word provides each member of the assembly with the impetus he needs for deeper and deeper integration into salvation history. He becomes aware of the concrete terms on which death must be challenged in obedience, or Satan combatted.

FIRST WEEK OF LENT

I. Leviticus
19:1-2, 11-18
1st reading
Monday

This passage is a portion of a collection of legal material put together after the exile (Lv 17-25) and known as the "Law of Holiness." The collection shows particular concern for the holiness of God and for the demands this makes upon the people who have made a covenant with him.

The demands are above all of a liturgical nature (sacrifices, ablutions, priestly character), but concern is also shown for the purity of the race by precise rulings about sexual relations. Like the earlier legal compilations, this collection brings together texts of different origins. Nevertheless it is somewhat surprising to find in a context that is mainly cultic and sexual a piece about brotherhood (vv. 9-18), the main thrust of which is a summons to love neighbors as oneself (v. 18).

The passage is mainly drawn from deuteronomic legislation (Dt 24:7; 14-15; 19:16-21) which was so concerned with social relations. Can the reason for its insertion in the cultic legislation of Leviticus 17-25 be the realization even at this stage that fraternal charity is just as important as proper sacrificial ritual? It is the veritable sign of the presence of the all-holy God among men.

a) It is interesting to compare Leviticus 19:13-14 and Deuteronomy 24:14-15. The latter is concerned only with the poor man who is humiliated, the former extends the law of charity to all *neighbors*. Yet where Deuteronomy takes account of the foreigner, Leviticus is too preoccupied with racial purity to do so.

It seems that the main purpose in one case is pity for the poor, whereas in the other solidarity of blood and relations with the "neighbors" takes precedence. In fact times have changed. Deuteronomy belongs to a period of profound sociological mutation; Leviticus to an era when nationalism seems the only bulwark against pagan influence.

b) Blood solidarity is clearly the main concern in the verses about "false witnesses" (15-16). Society in Israel seems to have been continuously bedevilled by the injustice of tribunals because the law constantly returns to the problem in the effort to institute proper dispositions, and the psalms and prophets are full of complaints about the venality of judges and witnesses (Ps 81/82; Jr 21:11-12; Am 5:10-15). However the argument for justice in tribunals brought forward by this Levitic collection is new. National fraternity ought to be sufficient to prevent legal proceedings among Jews ("your compatriot": v. 15; "your own"; v. 16). A simple brotherly reprimand should have the effect that people seek to gain before tribunals (v. 17b).

Evidently then the purpose of the collection is to create an awareness of national solidarity. The ethical norm is to be dictated by such a consciousness — one does not hurt one's blood relatives. Primitive Christians too display this mentality when they require that quarrels between the brethren be settled within the community (Mt 5:25-26; 18:15-22; 1 Co 6:1-8; Rm 12:17-19); but it is an idea that has been somewhat outmoded in our climate of universalism and pluralism.

Of course, even in the Church, there is no guarantee of irenic conditions among believers. If many Christians leave now because they find only challenge and conflict where they hoped for cozy security, they should be told that they misunderstood the situation in the world of the Church. Rarely do we notice the boss and his striking worker, the conservative and the liberal, being reconciled by participation in the Eucharist.

What the Church does is enable people to live under love; it does not obliterate human differences. When one group confronts another it does not resolve the conflict; it does unite them at the same table. Any suggestion of Church life, or eucharistic assembly, "in complete harmony" is altogether misleading. Many Christians indeed are troubled by opposition and conflict and hope it will be silenced by authoritative decision from above;

but that is often because they fear, not conflict itself, but the element of hate and contempt for one's brother which is introduced. There is however little point in deciding to follow an ostrich policy so that wrongheadedness will not have a free rein. It is more sensible to work at controlling personal feelings, and to do penance when the control breaks down. Conflicts within the Church will begin to have meaning when they add to the general sum of charity. This is the one sure sacramental sign of the unifying presence among his people of the Lord.

II. Matthew   Matthew has pointed out that the members of
    25:31-46   the chosen people must practice vigilance if
    Gospel   they wish to have a share in the eschatological
    Monday   kingdom. Now he is about to deal with the
                        matter of the Gentiles' destiny at this event.
Jewish ideas on the subject were quite naive: the judgment of God would confound all Gentiles (Is 14:1-2; 27:12-13). Matthew's description of the judgment however is more nuanced.

There can be no doubt about his final retouching of this passage. Verses 31, 34 and 41 are his. Jesus would not call himself king or attribute to himself the role of judge, which was reserved to the Father. The other verses certainly go back to Jesus, but it is very likely the evangelist who groups them. In fact we can distinguish a brief parable about the shepherd separating sheep and goats (vv. 32-33), and a collection of sayings where Jesus identifies himself with those who have received kindness (vv. 35-40, 42-45). Matthew 10:42 may be a primitive elaboration of the latter.

a) The division of sheep and goats is an image from pastoral life in Palestine where shepherds followed this procedure to secure better shade for the more fragile goats. In the parable Jesus, it is probable, merely wished to attribute to himself the judicial function of the shepherd in Ezechiel 34:17-22. He was reminding people that the *judgment* would not be a separation of Jews from non-Jews, but a separation of good from bad, within the fold as well as without. It will not be an ethnic, but a moral judgment.

b) Matthew adds to the parable sayings that must have been delivered in another context. Here there is question above all of welcoming the *little ones* (vv. 40 and 45). This phrase, on the lips of Jesus, indicates more than anything else his disciples (above all in Mt 10:42 and 18:6, probably in Mt 18:14 and 18:10). Those, that is, who have made themselves little in view of the kingdom, who have left everything to dedicate themselves to their mission, have now become great, are united with the Lord to judge the nations and discern among them the people who have welcomed them (cf. Mt 19:28; 11:1).

In associating the parable with these sayings Matthew is indicating the only criterion which will enable Gentiles to share in the kingdom. The welcome given a disciple, which extends to actual succor of his needs, and the witness borne by favorable reception of Jesus' message. This however, we note, is still a somewhat narrow view.

c) Is it possible to give a wider interpretation to the passage, to see in the little ones not alone Christ's disciples, but every distressed person loved for his own sake, without explicit reference to God? One could, I suppose, do so by establishing that the beneficiaries of the kingdom, according to the passage, do not have knowledge of Christ. But is this conceivable in the case of people who welcome the disciples and their message? The works of mercy enumerated in verses 35-36 are indeed precisely those proclaimed by scripture as signs of the advent of the messianic kingdom (Lk 4:18-20; Mt 11:4-5), and there is no attempt to confine them to disciples alone. *Charity* was the essential thing for the inauguration of the kingdom of God (1 Co 13:13).

From a purely exegetical standpoint though, the interpretation is somewhat hypothetical. Primitive communities were not wont to pose themselves questions about the salvation of non-Christians according to our pattern.

Of course, Matthew aside, a twentieth century Christian cannot possibly avoid this question. We remember that Christ presents himself not only as the Son of Man whom the Jews awaited, but as the pastor of Ezechiel 34 as well. It is not his view that the success of the kingdom of God depends on physical participation by the chosen people; he is determining conditions under which someone outside that category can be justified. Furthermore he does not take his stand on the knowledge of God and his Messiah that becomes possible for a Gentile, nor does he make such knowledge a sufficient criterion. For him the only valid criterion is the pattern of man's relationships with his brothers, and that criterion, with or without explicit knowledge of God, is in itself sufficient. What Jesus does then is put forward a profane concept of God's judgment, desacralizing on this point Jewish theology. The man who is brother to his fellow man accomplishes the messianic kingdom because his action, whether he knows it or not, is of God.

In a certain fashion then there are two standards in God's judgment, one for humanity in general, one for the chosen people. The former will render an account of their efforts for human betterment; the latter of their vigilance, their ability that is to see the presence of God in human relationships. This ability comes by faith only. Just like other men, Christians are obliged to love their brothers; but faith obliges them further to exhibit the divine dimension in such fraternity, to be witnesses in advance of what will become clear at the judgment. At that event God will reveal to all men how, in their mutual fraternity and solidarity, he has been always present.

"Vigilant" Christians are brought together in the eucharistic assembly, so that they may be aware of the duty they have before God and men. They must bear witness to God's presence in human society.

**III. Isaiah
55:10-11**
*1st reading
Tuesday*

Commentary on this passage will be found on the paschal vigil (Is 55:1-11) p. 375.

**IV. Matthew
6:7-15**
*Gospel
Tuesday*

The beginning of chapter 6 in Saint Matthew is an analysis of pious practice among the Pharisees translated to a Christian framework: almsgiving, that is, prayer and fasting. We have three paragraphs symmetrically constructed. In each instance an antithesis is set up by two phrases between the good and the bad procedures. They are introduced by the same conjunction: "when you give alms, when you fast, when you pray" (vv. 2, 5 and 16) . . . "as for you, when you give alms, as for you when you pray, as for you when you fast" (vv. 3, 6 and 17). Thus we are dealing with a primitive discourse (Mt 6:1-6, 16-18) in the middle of which a long piece on prayer (general principles: vv. 7-8; text of the Our Father: vv. 9-13; a catechesis on pardon: vv. 14-15) has been inserted.

To conclude all this, Matthew gives us a sort of catechism of prayer made up of different sayings by Jesus. This was meant for neophytes of Jewish origin who were already accustomed to prayer but were too often immersed in verbalism and routine. It becomes more evident when we compare Matthew's text with Luke's Lk 11:1-13). Luke gives us a catechism too, in his own particular mold. It is meant for Gentiles who still have everything to learn so far as prayer is concerned and who must be encouraged in the arduous enterprise.

Both Matthew and Luke give the text of the Our Father that is current in their respective communities, but it is very difficult to say which version is more likely to reflect the actual prayer of Jesus. While Matthew's text seems closer to the Aramaic, at least in the portions he has in common with Luke, one can scarcely believe that Luke would have suppressed important portions. The liturgical trend in fact was otherwise: a gradual accretion in prayer texts, a longer text always developing from a shorter. This would indicate that the portions proper to Matthew are later. The matter however remains extremely hypothetical.

a) The first part of the catechism is concerned with the *secret* character of Christian prayer.

Prayer is a natural human impulse and the different religions have tended to channel the impulse towards the greatest degree of efficacy. The manner and time of prayer, its content, proper prayer attitudes, have all been organized.

Jesus actually counters this concept. Prayer may indeed be a valid human reaction, but this of itself does not make it valid before God. God knows very well what we have need of (v. 8) and does not require our entreaties in order to provide it.

He rejects the pseudo-securities of prayer: the publicity of the street (and the publicity of ourselves we tend to set up for our own selves) (vv. 5-6), also verbal formulas (v. 7). But then, ought one still to pray?

The reason the Christian prays is not only because he needs to pray, but because Christ told him to pray, because he is in communion with Christ and his Father. The essential condition then for prayer is the sort of obedience and faith that links us with the Father (v. 6). No longer is it a matter of prayer attitudes or prayer content, but of unselfish and intimate confidence. This has nothing to do with the publicity of the street or the publicity of one's room, with longer or shorter versions of the *Our Father*, with longer or shorter prayers indeed in any sense, with individual prayer or community prayer. It is a firm conviction that we are communicating with the Father and a fulfillment of Christ's request that we ask in his name.

b) The only possible way of commenting on the *Our Father* is to take the petitions in order.

Invocation of the Father implies a communication of life, the possibility of imitating the fidelity of Jesus. The original Aramaic *Abba* was probably retained for a considerable time in the Greek versions. This would explain the difference of title as between Matthew and Luke, and the presence still of the word in Romans 8:15 and Galatians 4:6.

Two wishes follow immediately: the hallowing of the name and the coming of the Kingdom. The name signifies the person, and the prayer is that God be recognized for what he is, holy and transcendent. Nevertheless this holiness is communicated to the kingdom: the transcendence becomes immanence (Ez 36:23), and the Father's gratuitous gift meets human collaboration. Thy kingdom come.

There is a third wish added which may not, because Luke ignores it, belong to the primitive version. Thy will be done .... The divine will in this instance is the salvation of man by sanctification and entry into the kingdom (Ep 1:3-8). Thus the third wish would be no more than the repetition, from a different angle, of the first two.

After the wishes come requests: for bread, for pardon, for protection. We cannot really say whether Christ had in mind material daily bread or the bread of life eternal. But is there any reason for opposing one to the other? Was it not by giving material bread to the hungry that Jesus told us of the bread of life?

The request for pardon is clarified by the catechesis in verses 14-15. It will be discussed later on.

The request for protection is specific about "temptation" (and about "evil" personified). In the contemporary Aramaic context the phrase refers to the great ordeal which believers must encounter, the final assault launched by the Evil One before the establishment of the Kingdom. The petition then is one for God's help against apostasy (Mt 24:4-31; Lk 22:53; Jn 12:31).

The final part of the Our Father is a prayer that the manifestation of God and his Kingdom, the communication to men of his life, be fulfilled in the bread, the pardon, the protection with which he rewards the disciples' faith.

c) Matthew returns to the topic of *pardon,* a favorite one

where he is concerned (Mt 18:11-14; 9:10-13; 11:19; 26:28, etc.). His text of the Our Father (v. 12), and of the commentary (vv. 14-15) reflect Si 28:1-5.

Matthew's text indeed gives us an early stage in the development of Christian ideas about pardon. Like Si 28:1-3 they were still influenced by the concept of retribution. God pardons just as we pardon; he gives according to our measure (Mt 5:7; 25:31-46); his mercy will be tempered exactly by our mercy towards our neighbor.

It will take a later Christian insight to reconcile the two principles. We pardon according to the pardon we have received (Mt 18:23-25; Lk 6:36; Ep 4:32; Col 3:13). Here there is no question of retribution or merit: the only point emphasized is the advent, in a world of sinners, of the kingdom of God.

V. Jonah
3:1-10
1st reading
Wednesday

Our parable here tells of the preaching of Jonah at Nineveh, about the unexpected conversion of the population of this great city, once the message of Jeremiah had been clarified. Jonah was sent to Nineveh to proclaim the approaching chastisement, not to save, but to prepare the punishment. Jeremiah 18:7-8 however had pointed out that God could "repent" of the appointed punishment once it became clear that conversion was beginning (cf. further Jr 26:3, 13, 19; 42:10). Already he had instanced indeed the retraction of a divine decree as a result of a conversion (Jr 36). The teaching had evidently influenced the author of the book of Jonah to the extent of constructing his parable. He actually goes further than Jeremiah. With him, the king of Nineveh, a Gentile, repents (3:5-8) while the king of Judah refuses to do so (Jr 36:24).

Over and above this there are many phrases which indicate that the passage is a commentary on Jeremiah: "men and beasts" (vv. 7-8; see Jr 8:20; 21:6; 27:5, etc.); "from the greatest to the least" (v. 5; see Jr 5:4-5; 6:13; 44:12) "burning wrath" (v. 9; see Jr 4:8, 26; 12:13; 25:37, 38).

Thus it would appear that decrees of God launched against the Gentile nations may be rescinded by *conversion*. This seems to be the fundamental moral of the parable. We are dealing then with a new teaching. Previously the Jewish belief was that the prophets' maledictions against the nations were ineluctable, that only in the case of divine decrees against the Jews was remission possible. Indeed Jonah himself does not accept the new point of view. He is particularist in spirit (Jon 4) and objects to the pardon accorded Nineveh.

The author seems to have another point too. He reproaches the Jews because of the tardiness of their conversion (Jr 25-26; 25:4, 26:5, etc.), where Nineveh is converted at once. Consequently the whole thrust of the passage is the moral Jesus will draw (Mt 12:38-42). The prophets' maledictions against the nations are no more irreversible than those against the Jews because God's pardon is without limit.

It cannot be maintained that Jonah was a missionary, summoning the Ninevites to conversion. His mission is punitive and provides not the slightest evidence of diminution in Jewish particularism. The city's conversion was an unforeseen consequence of his preaching; the conclusion outstripped the premises.

Had Jonah been a missionary, his summons to conversion should have concerned himself in the first place. One does not invite people to change their central attitude without giving evidence that one's own central attitude has been changed.

The truth is that, at this time, it would have been impossible for Jonah or Israel generally, to imagine a conversion of Nineveh, or any other Gentile city, that would not be simultaneously a cultural deracination and Judaization. A genuine summons to conversion must take account of the real spiritual dynamism of the people in question, and not ignore it. The soul and the heart must be reached if we are suggesting any despoliation of the self. Have not Christians in their turn often played the part of Jonah? What of the conversion of Africa and Asia? On the principles we have just outlined, we might ask ourselves whether much of the effort expended has not been in vain. Given that a summons to conversion must be backed by witness of despoliation on the part of the missionary, the question must be raised whether a Church that is unduly rich or powerful can adequately perform that function.

VI. Matthew
12:38-42
Gospel
Wednesday

This is an extremely complicated passage. The collection of episodes and teachings appears contrived and there is no common theme. We shall comment only on verses 38-42 (the sign of Jonah and the fast of the Ninevites) at this stage. What follows (vv. 43-45, the return of the unclean spirit) is not really intelligible except in the context of Matthew 12:24-30. And the conclusion (vv. 46-50, the beatitude about those who hear) demands the context of Matthew 12:22-23, the cure of the dumb man. We have in fact a signal instance of the "inclusive" tendency in Hebrew style, and for a proper understanding of our text it is necessary to begin the reading at verse 12.

a) In the synoptic tradition we have four allusions to the *famous sign of Jonah* (Mt 12:38-42; 16:1-4; Lk 11:29-32; Mk 8:11-12). These different versions doubtless stem from sayings of Jesus himself, in a context where the reference that we today have lost was easily understood. In any case, it is quite certain that the Matthean interpretation of the sign is rather late.

Probably Jesus wished to tell the Jews that, for their conversion, they needed no more signs than the Ninevites had (Jon 3:1-10): The mere presence of God's prophet and his message ought to be a sufficient summons to conversion (Mk 8:11-12 and Mt 16:1-4). But gradually, as the primitive community reflected on the whole topic of the Christ, his manner of speaking in this instance was seized upon as a clue more or less to his personality. So Christ himself becomes the expected sign.

Thus Luke 11:19-21 already likens Jonah to the "Son of Man."

The more people pursued reflection in this vein, the more concentration we find on the paschal mystery. Noting the parallel between Jonah's three days in the sea and the three days of the Lord's Pasch, the "sign of Jonah" becomes for the primitive community the very sign of Christ's obedience and resurrection. This is the rather allegorized interpretation which Matthew takes.

The text then has actually a double nuance: first, the idea that the prophet's word is its own confirmation and needs no external proof; second, the idea that the veritable sign offered for men's credence is none other than the mystery of the man-God crucified and risen.

b) Thus today's gospel is an occasion for considering the signs of faith. The Jews take the exterior view: they demand wonders so that they may have faith and be converted. Christ goes to the heart of the matter when he proclaims that faith depends altogether on the trust placed in the person of the envoy.

For modern man there is little danger of excess in the Jewish manner. Miracles in the physical sense he discountenances and is more ready to believe indeed in spite of them than because of them. There is a sort of miracle-mongering which tends to find God only in something supra-human, whereas in fact he is present in man and in the works of man.

The true significance of a physical miracle is to be found in the fact that it is an expression of the personality of the one who performs it and a challenge to the person of the witness. So it is that Christ's miracles for the most part are cures, signs of his messianic function and of his goodness (Mt 8:17; 11:1-6), which is also true of his relations with the Father (the theme of the "signs" in the Gospel of Saint John). So it is too that they are generally a summons to interior conversion and to faith. They summon to faith, but they do not give it. First we must have the antecedent action of the Spirit in a man's heart, if he is to accept, as seeker, not as judge, the sign that God sets before him.

People wonder, I suppose, why God, or Christ, never smooths the path for the Pharisees, or atheists, of our day, by giving them the sign they want. Why is not his name so visibly writ in the heavens that doubt would become impossible? The further we move toward progress, toward secularization, the more we are "desacralized," the fewer the signs from God.

If God gave us "signs from heaven," he would not then be the god who chose to become men's servant so as to win their love and their spontaneous trust. He would be blazoned so publicly that no one could miss seeing him, and very probably there would be an end to all human hesitancy. . . . But would he then be witness to freedom, to the quest for a free and trusting love? In truth there is no other sign but that of Jesus, because God chose not to constrain man: he wanted, by dying for him, to win his love. Just because he is the God of love, this is the only sign we have.

The true believer, without indeed minimizing the role of miracle, does not any longer look for wonders; because, in the very person of Christ, the man-God, he discerns the quiet presence and intervention of God. Our greatest miracle is of the moral order: the human condition of Jesus, undertaken in absolute fidelity, obedience and love, so thoroughly permeated by the divine presence that, even at the moment of death, God was there to raise up his Son. This is the sign of Jonah towards which all the gospel miracles point. They summon us to conversion, to be open to God's salvation: they are signs of his presence with us in the war against sin and death.

VII. Esther   Esther is a book which derives from the
14:1-5, 12-14   biblical stories of Joseph and Daniel, and
1st reading   from other Eastern tales. The purpose was
Thursday   to strengthen the faith of Jews dispersed
                     throughout the Persian empire. Its very pop-
ularity was responsible for several interpolations, one of which
we have here, the prayer of Esther — a very late piece (1st

century) found only in the Greek bible. Though it is thoroughly saturated with Old Testament themes and piety, the prayer has certain original characteristics, principally a concern with individual justification.

It seems likely that during the first century Esther, for its 9th chapter, was read at the Purim celebrations, and that the prayers added were prayers recited during the festival.

Faced by her great responsibility, Esther is represented as penitent and recollected in a prayer° that is touching and humble. She turns to analysis of her own feelings (a novel procedure in Old Testament prayer: of verses 17^{vx}), and discovers only weakness in herself, but she realizes that God will give her the necessary courage (v. 17^r). The people are on the verge of decadence, and have never really recovered from the horrors of exile. Perhaps for Esther and her like there will be sufficient strength to encounter the challenge if God at least agrees to restrain them (v. 17^t).

VIII. Matthew	The probability is that Matthew himself in-
7:7-12	serted this text in the sermon on the mount.
Gospel	It is not linked in any way with the context.
Thursday	Furthermore the same text is better situated
	in Luke 11:9-13, where it appears immediately

after the parable of the importunate friend. The aphorisms in verse 7-11 have been taken by Matthew from a context where their meaning is well elucidated: God's manner of dealing with the seeker. He probably did so to avoid introducing a parable to the mountain discourse; he devotes a special chapter to the parables (cf. Mt 13).

a) Originally, at least in Luke's context 11:9-13, this teaching

°See doctrinal theme: *prayer,* p. 185.

was intended as a paraphrase of the fourth petition in the Lord's Prayer, "Give us this day our daily bread . . ." (Mt 6:11). The theme of *bread* appears anyhow in verse 9, and is found also in the parable of the importunate friend (Lk 11:5-8) which Matthew does not record. He chose rather to paraphrase the fifth petition "Forgive us . . . as we forgive . . ." (Mt 6:12-15). Here we see the total contrast between the two evangelists. As commentators on the Our Father, Matthew appears the catechist, anxious about the virtuous life of Christians; Luke appears as prophet of detachment where earthly goods are concerned and stresses the tenderness of God for his children.

b) When we take them as a commentary on the petition of the Our Father for daily bread, verses 7-11 have a very particular meaning. If a human father, sinful as he is, gives bread to his child, how much more likely to do so is the heavenly Father. What is emphasized is not so much the dogged perseverance of the petitioner, but the difference between the goodness of the human father and the very great tenderness of our heavenly Father. We should not hesitate to add: what a man will do reluctantly, God will do with joy.

There is emphasis on *perseverance* in prayer, but not with any purpose of recommending unceasing prayer. What is affirmed is simply the benevolence of God and the certainty of his constant tenderness. We must never forget that the verses are describing the generosity of the giver, not the pertinacity of the petitioner.

The text then conveys the optimistic character of the Christian notion of prayer. The efficacity, so far from depending on the petitioner's persistence, rests altogether on God's goodness. There is still an important element, however, not mentioned in this teaching — the paramount necessity of Christ's meditation. The reading of John 16:23-26, which may be inspired by these very verses, goes much further, and rightly finds the essence of prayer in the indispensable intercession of the Lord.

IX. Ezechiel
18:21-28
1st reading
Friday

Ezechiel is the individualist prophet *par excellence*. Our passage illustrates this very well.

Where the *individual* is concerned, as he sees it, there is no fatality. God judges the individual solely on personal justice or injustice. He does not want death or chastisement; he wants life for the greatest number possible. The new covenant is directed toward this end: man has only to become converted in order to bring the divine plan to accomplishment.

Conscience always tends to become submerged in the group. Is it not true that people who make groups, or God, responsible for what happens are generally looking for a means of palliating individual conscience? In order to realize, gradually, the challenge that freedom presents we sometimes need to undergo dramatic experiences.

X. Matthew
5:20-26
Gospel
Friday

This is an extract from Our Lord's teaching about the new justice, with a particular application to the fifth commandment. There is a general introduction (v. 20) after which it is possible to distinguish three sections:

Verses 21-22: Jesus goes beyond the prohibition of homicide by extending its application to simple injuries. The style is archaic and the vocabulary heavily Jewish, the reason probably why Luke does not bring the text to the notice of his Greek readers.

Verses 23-24: This is an independent text. It makes charity the essential condition for sacrifice, and takes up the theme, already known in the Old Testament, of spiritual sacrifice. The phrases linking it with the preceding text indicate that it too is archaic. Luke does not have it; his readers were not directly interested in temple sacrifices. Mark (11:25) gives us a different version.

Verses 25-26: These appear to be displaced from their original context, which is probably correct in Luke 12:58-59.

a) To understand the impact of Jesus' teaching one should be mindful of the refinements introduced by scribes and commentators on the homicide law. The scribes listed a catalogue of circumstances, one more extrinsic than the other, for determining whether homicide had taken place. Jesus establishes a new criterion: *personal intention*. This could be judged more severely than actual murder, even in cases where the external act was a mere injury.

There are in fact two distinct sentences in this first section. In the first one (vv. 21-22a) Jesus asserts that simple injury is matter for the "tribunal" just as much as homicide. The tribunal here is the community council, on a national (Sanhedrin) or local (Qumran, for instance) level, which had the right of excommunicating errant members. It enjoyed then a power of life and death as it were, determining who deserved membership in the community (Mt 10:17; Jn 16:2). It is certain that primitive Christian communities exercised power of this nature (Ac 5; I Co 5:1-4; I Tm 1:20; Mt 18:15-17).

The second sentence (v. 22b-c) is not a further statement. It merely repeats what has been said in different terms. The "tribunal" is neither more nor less formidable than the "Sanhedrin" or "Gehenna." There is question all the time of a community expelling the guilty from its midst. But where Jewish jurisdiction was exercised only on the basis of external circumstances, Christian procedure should, like God himself, take account of individual intention.

In the development of this new jurisprudence, two preliminary principles had to be agreed. First, that God "examines the heart" where man considers exterior things (Jr 11:19-20; 12:1-3; 17:9-11); second, that more can be demanded from those involved in the new covenant, because it "changes the heart" (Ez 36:23-30; Jr 31:31-34).

b) The second text (vv. 23-24) deals with the necessity of love in *sacrifice*. A Jew if he suddenly realized, before offering sacrifice, that he was impure (Lv 15-17), was obliged to undergo a series of preliminary ablutions. Jesus requires the Christian to react in similar fashion if he realizes that he is in conflict with someone. Here he is no longer concerned with prohibitions about homicide, but with the rules about ritual purity. Consequently the background of the two texts is different; but both reflect the desire to set up a new justice. It will be based on interiority and opposed to all formalism. It will underline the fact that, in the Christian assembly, the bonds between individual and community are interior bonds.

The eucharistic assembly, which does penance and appears before God in the celebration, should examine itself to see whether, even at this moment, there are not numerous accusing voices between it and God, interfering with its penitence and its offering.

The full meaning of the link between the Eucharist and charity is not generally appreciated. We tend to regard charity as an individual requisite for sharing in the Eucharist, a moral state of participants. We do perceive properly the actual coincidence between the Eucharist and charity, to the extent that collective charity becomes obligatory for the Church itself and for each of its eucharistic assemblies.

This profound cult to which the priestly people is dedicated is the pursuit of charity to the point of total self-giving, for the salvation of all humanity. When we call the Church a priestly people what we mean above all, in concrete terms, is that it is the leaven in the mass — that Christians, mingled among men, live the whole tenor of their daily lives in a mission of gathering together the scattered children of God. Too many Christians fail to see how very foreign such considerations are to the Levitic priesthood of the Old Testament. In the New Testament the priestly people is not a people gathered in a temple for prayer and sacrifice, a people segregated from the rest of humanity and dedicated exclusively to religious practices. On the contrary it is directly involved in the mass of humanity: men and women indistinguishable from other men and women except in their sharing of the Body of Christ, their cooperation in the act by which Christ, today as always, builds the Kingdom of his Father out of human material. Its priestly responsibility lies in extending love and Christ to the very frontiers of humanity.

It is precisely the function of the Mass to invest the Christian once again with the power of reconciliation that belongs to Christ alone. If the eucharistic sharing is seen by us merely as an expression of the love that is obtained by Christians, we are wrong. Its central position in the task of reconciliation between brother and brother is no more and no less, in terms of ordinary Christian life, than the central position, absolutely, of Jesus Christ.

XI. Deuteronomy Deuteronomy, the last book of the Pentateuch,
    26:16-19   despite the weighty legislative material it
    1st reading   contains, is nevertheless one of the least
    Saturday   juridical books. The purpose is more hom-
iletic than legislative, and the author's very highly developed sense of history as well as personal relationship with God makes his compilation above all religious. Our reading reminds us of the content of the convent and stresses its spiritual character.

The *Covenant* remains always actual. This is strongly emphasized by Deuteronomy ("today" in verses 16-18; cf. Dt 5:3; 6:10-13). There is no question then of living under an ancient dispensation; history merely serves to clarify the present, the wonders of the past continue to be displayed now. In each believer the drama of the desert is reenacted; its achievements, its murmurings, its blessings, the decisions to be taken. Each one must choose between God's antecedent love and the temptation to forget (cf. Dt 6:12). Happiness and glory (v. 19) are the recompense promised by God to those who serve and obey him (v. 16).

To stress the religious nature of the covenant, the author resorts to the image of a bilateral contract, the only way in his estimate of engaging themselves for two free agents (vv. 17-18). He sees the law not as a mere catalogue of precepts for man but as something which engenders a religious attitude "I shall be your God (v. 17) and you will be my very own people" (vv. 18-19).

A portion of Deuteronomy was written at a time when Israel became conscious of having abandoned Yahweh and was seeking to rediscover, in the original event of the promise and covenant, its faith and its sense of history. Accordingly the covenant linking it to God is presented not as something unilateral on God's part (a "testament"), but something mutual. The intention here is essentially religious; there is no question of placing man on an equal footing with God — the latter remains the primary, and the only, agent. But forgetfulness had developed on the people's part; response to God's initiative called for hearts of flesh, not stone (Jr 31).

Such a bilateral view of the covenant had its dangerous aspect, of course, which pharisaism was later to exaggerate. Yet it remains true that God, the sole architect, in respecting human liberty and inviting human cooperation is already preparing his incarnation. It is only with man that he will save man, with man's total commitment to the human situation.

The Christian in turn will display his faith by relating his conduct here and now to an original event. That event is the free choice of God in Jesus Christ, focus of the new covenant, and fulfillment of the promise. Under this light the Eucharist takes on meaning; each participant is summoned to live the events of his life as Christ lived his. The same fidelity to God's will is required, the same confrontation of death, the same proclamation of man's glorious destiny.

XII. Matthew   Here we have the last of six antitheses which
5:43-48   are grouped by the evangelist in the sermon
Gospel   on the mount (Mt 5:21-48). The concluding
Saturday   phrase — "be ye perfect" (v. 48) — refers not
                        alone to the final antithesis but to the whole
of the antithetic discourse.

a) Consequently we must beware of confining the interpretation of God's *perfection* (v. 48) to goodness only (the topic of the final antithesis). There was a very particularized Jewish meaning for perfection: it was looked upon as the fulfillment of all the legal prescriptions and of the tradition of the ancients. To such a formalist notion, limited to legal observance, Christ opposes a new type of perfection (Mt 5:17, 20; 19:21). We shall not be judged "perfect" on the basis of observance, but on the standard of free giving after the pattern of God's free gift to us.

b) Of the six instances of God's gratuity, our gospel gives only the last, love for others, above all for enemies. The law enjoined love for neighbors, and Matthew contrasts with that precept the *gratuitous* nature of love for enemies (vv. 43-44). The new commandment is formulated as a triad (there is a similar procedure in the 1st, 4th, 5th, and 6th antitheses: Mt 5:22, 34-35, 39-41). Then two examples are given (vv. 46-47). One is drawn from a Jewish environment (publicans), the other from a Gentile, so that we have stress on the independence of the new morality of legal or philanthropic climate.

This corresponds with the general tone of Matthew's gospel. The specifically Christian characteristics are brought in to focus: we must reproduce in our lives the Father's manner of action.

And we must do so spontaneously, unconstrained by any legal shackles.

So, when contrasted with the general rabbinic teaching of the period, the message of this new rabbi is set in a totally new framework. Instead of being preoccupied with commentary on the law, considered as the exclusive norm of God's will, Jesus deliberately makes individual conscience the ethical norm. Conscience should be acquainted with the law, but it should then plumb the depths of a self where communion with God is possible. After that comes decision.

For Jesus then, blind obedience to the law even when the law is "perfectly" fulfilled, is not obedience at all. Obedience in fact cannot depend on authority in the purely formal sense, though the statement of God's commandments is of course not such. We have true obedience only when a man himself decides what is laid upon him, decides indeed to transcend the letter of obligation, adopting as criterion the most profound thrust of his being, the search for God.

A very important area for the application of this doctrine is precisely that not contemplated by the law. When matters of this kind make their appearance, Jewish or ecclesiastical moralists are concerned to cover the area as speedily as possible. But the procedure is one of making new laws after the pattern of the old. Obedience thus becomes submission to new laws, instead of what it should be: the expression of the deepest self summoned to creativity by changing circumstances.

Men who regard obedience to the law as a meritorious thing (Mt 25:25-28) will always stand condemned by Jesus. The obedience he proposes is "light" (Mt 11:28-30) because it springs from a source unrelated to formal authority, or the judgment of men: the deepest self. But it is demanding too, not indeed because of the material precepts imposed, but because of the constant duty of decision it requires from the person.

Christ on the Cross did much more than obey an order of God. There was no question of any such order. In the depths of himself he laid bare in full freedom a communion with the Father and the decision enjoined by that communion. Likewise we too are summoned by the Eucharist we celebrate to the same liberating decision, valid unto death.

SECOND SUNDAY OF LENT

A. The Word

I. Genesis **Abram** came from Ur in Chaldaea (Gn 11:
12:1-17 31). His father settled at Harân, some 1500
1st reading kilometers north of Ur. Growing up in Ur
1st cycle meant exposure to the most elaborate culture
of the world at the time. Here were the
earliest tribunals and assemblies known to history, the first
social legislation: here agriculture had reached a technical excellence never known before. Scripture however is silent about
the prodigious influence of Sumarian culture on Abram. There
was a reluctance to allow the father of Israel to display pagan
traits, and a conscious effort to find the origins of the chosen
people in a radical breakaway from the pagan world.

A considerable movement northwards took place in Sumeria
in the 17th century, prosperous families fleeing a territory rendered insecure by constant conflict. The migration was joined
by Abram's family, who penetrated as far as Harân, a cross-
roads for caravans. A further journey would mean a change of
culture. The Armenian mountains barred the horizon. Harân
was the limit of Sumerian lunar religion, and of civil institutions
reasonably similar to the Sumerian.

The traditions about Abraham's call (vv. 1-4) and his entry
to the promised land (vv. 6-9) are of Yahwist origin. The call
and entry are linked by a reference, due to a priestly hand,
to another episode.

a) The purpose of the two first verses seems to be to furnish
the etymology of the name Abram. It is a word meaning: whose
father (Ab) is great (ram). Hence an explanation of the
promise: if you leave your father who is "great", you will
become a "great" people. Thus *greatness* apparently is a leit-
motif of the blessing of Abraham, one of the least detailed

blessings in the whole bible. The nations shall bless themselves (shall desire the good, that is) by using the name of Abraham (v. 3), an allusion possibly to those wish-formulas which contained the word "ram" or "great." The Jews on hearing such formulas would be inclined to trace the word "ram" to their father Ab-ram, and would find here proof of his greatness and his influence everywhere.

b) The second portion of the passage seeks to make Abraham the founder of two popular *sanctuaries*. Nevertheless Sichem cannot date from Abram because it was known one or two millennia before him. But Jewish tradition was fairly vague about this matter. We find the Elohist documents attaching Sichem to the memory of the patriarch Jacob (Gn 33:18-20). And Bethel, the other sanctuary, which was also much anterior to Abram, is also referred nevertheless by the Elohist sources to Jacob (Gn 28:11-22). In any case, as is clear from verse 7, these Yahwist sources only preserve the foundation narratives as traditions. The real point of interest for the compiler is that Abraham's presence at Sichem and Bethel is the first step toward possession of all the land. To emphasize this, the Yahwist author does not hesitate to associate with Sichem the promise of the land, which was not actually formulated until the 9th century.

c) Verses 4b-5 were added later by a priestly editor, who was concerned about chronology (v. 4b), and anxious to include in the context all the persons featured by the subsequent narrative. He had also a less obvious purpose, to show how Abraham brought *all the riches of the pagans* to enrich his own people, just as the nation did when coming out of Egypt (Ex 11:2). Here one detects traces of reaction against contemporary Jewish inferiority complex *vis-a-vis* the civilized and powerful nations surrounding them. It was not possible that they should have anything not available also to the Jews (cf. further Is 60:1-10)!

Thus the biblical presentation of Abraham is in some ways

incomplete. Nothing is said of the early pagan formation which was none the less the source from which Abram drew his experience of God. Authors preferred to find the origins of his call and career within the context of Jewish life. So thoroughly had the lesson of events been learned that these became the very Word of God intervening.

II. Genesis
22:1-2, 9a,
10-13, 15-18
1st reading
2nd cycle

The author of this narrative of Abraham's sacrifice makes fairly random use of both Yahwist and, above all Elohist sources (vv. 1-13).

a) It seems probable that before incorporation into the biblical saga of Abraham the narrative existed independently. As in the case of many ancient traditions, the idea was to explain the *origin of a high place* by describing the original sacrifice offered there. There should be explicit mention of the sanctuary, but an Elohist account would suppress or conceal it, and then a later hand, anxious to supply the omission, was responsible for the mention of Moriyya (v. 2), the old name for the mount of the temple (the mount of the "Amorrhaeans").

b) The original editors were likewise concerned with a liturgical motive: to persuade the people against the practice of infant-sacrifice (cf. Jg 11:10-30; 2 K 16:3; 21:6; Dt 12:31; Jr 7:31; 19:5; 32:35), which was apparently rather prevalent in the 8th and 7th centuries. In view of the fact that every first-born belonged to God (Ex 22:28-30), the law insisted on the obligation of redemption (Ex 34:19-20, Dt 15:19-23) by a substitute sacrifice. It would seem then that the description of Abraham's sacrifice is a way of enjoining this obligation of redemption: the first-born must be redeemed by the sacrifice of a ram (v. 14).

c) However the Elohist narrator glosses over the emphasis in the original account. He is at this stage under the influence of the liturgical teachings of the prophets, for whom obedience is more important than sacrifice (1 S 15:22; Mi 6:6-8). He manipulates the text so as to make verse 12 the central point, and Abraham becomes the champion of *spiritual sacrifice.*

Frequently the Elohist will be more concerned than the Yahwist with the psychology of the protagonists and their feelings. There is emphasis, for instance, with a great profusion of detail on Abraham's personal agony, the love he bears for his son, the faith in God he manifests by his prompt obedience.

The important thing is that Abraham be seen to realize that the promise depends not on Isaac but on God. That is why there must be a breach in his own father-son relationship, he must realize that the only really important relationship for him is that between himself and God. Then only can he recover his son, not as it was before, but as if God were ceaselessly bestowing the son. Between person and person there can be no true path except the one that leads through God. Between father and son everything will be as it was before. And yet it will be new, because God will be implicitly recognized as mediator.

d) It could be that more still is intended in the Elohist reading. When this account of the sacrifice is incorporated into a series of traditions about the first evidences of realization for the "multitude" promise made to Abraham, when there is such insistence on the fact that the sacrificed son is the very instrument of realization, the Elohist is making *trial and death* essential features of the covenant. No man responsible for the work of God can reap the fruits until he experiences in his own deep self deprivation and sacrifice, the despoliation of self which leaves room for God's gratuitous gift.

In any case, Jewish interpretation of this episode made of it a meditation on the meaning of suffering. It went further still. The sacrifice of Isaac, particularly in the "Book of Jubilees," became the exemplar for the investiture of the future suffering Messiah. In the liturgy of Tabernacles, which is strictly a liturgy of messianic investiture, the episode was read; and one of the most interesting aspects of the relationship is the faith that would in turn be manifested by the suffering Messiah. In consequence we understand why it was at the feast of Tabernacles (Mt 17 and 21) that Jesus revealed his suffering messiahship to his followers, and how vividly the theme is illustrated in the narrative of the transfiguration.

III. Genesis   Genesis 15 is one of the most motley passages
15:5-12, 17-18 of the whole Pentateuch. We have both
1st reading   Elohist and Yahwist traditions, but interwoven
3rd cycle   to such a degree that disentanglement is
                   extremely difficult.

a) The Elohist context is that of a contract between a king and his mercenary soldier. As king, Yahweh promises Abram a "shield" (Gn 15:1), that is to say his help, and an important "reward," the word here meaning the mercenary's pay (as in Jr 46:21; Ez 29:19). In the near-East this consisted of real property (v. 7), in Abram's case, Palestine. Abram, as mercenary, promises fidelity to his master (v. 6). Thus the atmosphere of the covenant is *military*. Abram however points out to Yahweh that he must go to war with no "servants" (not "child") except a single dweller in Damascus (v. 3). Can Yahweh possibly enter a contract with someone so poorly equipped, or can he in fact believe that Yahweh will really so bind himself? He further begs for a sign of authenticity (v. 8). The sign consists of ratification of the treaty according to the accepted form of the time: the dismemberment of three morsels (a more exact translation than the "three years" of verse 9a), a heifer, a she-goat and a ram.

After the conclusion of this treaty the warrior Abraham sees the realization of his wishes in a dream. But the struggle will be severe against the conquerors (symbolized by the "rapacious ones" of verse 11; cf. Is 46:11), especially against the Egyptians, whose symbol is the "falcon" Horus (cf. v. 13) and the Amorite Canaanites.

But, again, was it possible for God to promise so much to Abram, so poor and feeble? So again the patriarch, in a dream, is present at the passage of Yahweh, symbolized by a firebrand (v. 17), between the divided animals. This was a procedure whereby the parties to a contract agreed to become like the dismembered animals, if found unfaithful . . . Only Yahweh passes between the victims. His fidelity is sufficient for the maintenance of the contract; no similar procedure is required of Abram.

b) The Yahwist tradition about the covenant is altogether different. The direct interest is in Abram's *posterity*. There is question of a promise about descendants rather than a mercenary contract. According to this tradition Genesis 15:2 was certainly interpreted as a lament by Abram who goes to death (not war) without a child (not servants). It was responsible for the addition of verse 4 which prophesies a male heir for the patriarch, and for the description of Abram's dream which reveals a posterity as numerous as the stars (vv. 5-6). It is only then that Abram asks Yahweh to bind himself to his promise by contract. Verse 9 describes this procedure. Abram prepares two birds, a turtledove and a pigeon, but they are not dismembered (vv. 9b and 10b). Unlike the dismembered beasts in the Elohist version (v. 9a), they are not sacrificed. They should probably be taken as figures of the male and female posterity of the patriarch, symbolically placed under Yahweh's protection (cf. Ps 73/74:19; Dt 32:11). It is for this reason that Abram does not sacrifice them like the other animals.

The narrative goes on to describe the deep sleep (v. 12) of Abram, similar to Adam's sleep before the emergence of Eve and as a result his progeny, of Noah's before he becomes father of the multitude of men (Gn 9:20-29). Verse 18 gives us the kernel of Yahwist teaching: Yahweh reveals that he is bestowing the land, not upon a mercenary vowed to his service as in Elohist teaching, but upon the posterity of a patriarch.

In compiling the two traditions the author of the final

redaction suppresses his own personality. He shows respect for the most diverse data, and manages to combine them in a single account that is relatively simple. Doubtless he was anxious to demonstrate that all tribes, northern (Elohist) as well as southern (Yahwist), stemmed from the covenant that was made by Yahweh with the one and only patriarch.

IV. 2 Timothy   The second letter to Timothy, like the first,
  1:8b-10   has not escaped the critics who assail its
  2nd reading   Pauline authenticity. However, no argument
  1st cycle   advanced by this school of criticism is con-
vincing. It is true that since the first Pauline letters the situation has changed. There are new problems to be solved, and this is sufficient explanation for the change in style. Paul moreover has aged, his tone has grown more serious, not to say disturbed. But, in both 1 and 2 Timothy, there are sufficient indications of similarity in style and doctrine with the corpus of Pauline episodes to place authenticity beyond doubt.

a) At the time of this letter, the Church is scarcely organized. Paul has sovereign authority over the communities he has founded, and over some others as well. He is wont to delegate this authority to certain disciples, above all to Timothy. His "legates" are plenipotentiary *vis-a-vis* the local authorities, and enjoy a special grace which has been conferred by imposition of hands (v. 6; cf. 1 Tm 1:18; 4:14). A college of presbyters (I Tm 4:14), doubtless presided over by Paul (v. 6, more exclusive than 1 Tm 4:14), has performed this. In today's passage Paul is not very explicit about Timothy's powers; he restricts himself to stressing one particular gift — that of not being ashamed of the gospel (vv. 7-9). In general indeed there is vagueness about this matter. Timothy is to be the "successor" of Paul (2 Tm 4:5-7): he has the commission to teach (2 Tm 2:15), to adjudicate certain problems (1 Tm 5:19), to determine the liturgy (1 Tm 2:1-12), to recruit ministers in the Church (I Tm 3:1-13; 5:22).

Is Timothy then already a bishop? What is his exact relation to the presbyters? There are a great many questions to which answers will be vainly sought in the pastoral epistles. All we can say is that they reflect the mutation period in the primitive Church, just before the disappearance of the apostles, as precise dispositions are about to be established between the communities and their *hierarchy*.

b) There are however two essential elements which enable us to define the role of the hierarchy. The first is the *service of the Gospel* (vv. 10-11). In other words the authority of the leader in the community is proportionate to his responsibility (and his mandate) for proclaiming the gospel to the world. The second is almost identical. It is a matter of extending to all humanity the manifestation of the man-God (v. 10), who destroyed the alienation of death and gave unhoped-for access to the plenitude of life.

The leader of the community, that is, is not only he who is most capable of administration, of presiding at liturgy and catechesis, but he who has at heart above all the missionary proclamation of the good news: Christ become Lord of life. The function of the hierarchy is not *ad intra* only, but essentially *ad extra* as well.

**V. Romans
8:31b-34**
2nd reading
2nd cycle
Chapter 8 of the letter to the Romans culminates in a paean about the love of God. The first two strophes (31-32 and 33-34), which form today's lesson, celebrate that love: the other strophes allude to the forces capable of militating against it.

a) Like Job 1 or Zechariah 3 (cf. also Rv 12:10), Paul is

imagining Christians being accused before God's tribunal. It is only too true that the combat waged by faith and the struggle against evil are not invariably successful. Frailty and meanness often manifest themselves; there is no dearth of reasons for reproach.

But who will be the accusers? Three are possible: God himself (vv. 31-32), Satan (the "accuser" in the etymological sense of the word: v. 33), or Christ (v. 34). Paul is asking himself which of the three could be the accuser of Christians.

God? But he has already declared himself definitively on our side, in that he has not hesitated to give us his son (v. 32, inspired perhaps by Gn 22:16). Can he go back on his decision and deny us the benefits of Christ's death?

Satan? True, he is the accuser of men before God; he wants to persuade God against having confidence in man, who does not deserve such love (Jb 1). But Paul recalls the text of Isaiah 50:8-9, where the Servant of Yahweh challenges his accusers. Since God always pardons and justifies, who can accuse him?

There remains Christ. Can he condemn to death those for whom he died (v. 34a)? How could he, who was "raised up" as a savior, become the one to condemn (v. 34b)?

b) The final point calls for some explanation. The word "raise up," which refers in this verse to the resurrection, is regularly used in the Old Testament to mean the choice by God of a king or prophet who is destined to retrieve the situation at a particularly critical point in the history of the chosen people (Jg 2:16; 3:9; 3:15; 2 S 3:10; 1 K 9:5; Ez 34:23; Is 41:2, 25).

Thus the resurrection theology of the passage is still fairly primitive. God has promised to "raise up" a savior every time misfortune befalls the people. He has "raised up" Christ from the dead (cf. Ac 2:32-33; 13:23, 30) to make him a savior. Salvation then is linked to the resurrection and to baptism which enables us to share in the resurrection.

VI. **Philippians**
  3:17-4:1
  2nd reading
  3rd cycle

This brief extract is part of a long disquisition by Paul on Christian perfection (Ph 3:17-4, 3) where he attacks those enemies of the cross (v. 18) who make their belly their god (v. 19, a reference to forbidden foods).

Those in question are in fact circumcised Jews who put their trust in the flesh in contrast with those, Paul himself in particular, whose trust is in Jesus Christ.

In his analysis of Christian asceticism, Paul has stressed at some length the need for effort: one must know how to choose, how to seek perfection as he himself does (Ph 3:12, 17, etc.). He is not at all quietist: the "way" (v. 16) he delineates, by counsel and example, is very exact. It is punctuated by struggle, by passing beyond the horizons of selfishness (the stomach and pride).

Nevertheless the fundamental principle of Christian ascetism is rooted in Christ,* above all in the efficaciousness of the incarnation event. Every human being who believes in him (Ga 2:20; 3:27; 4:23; 6:14) is transformed, receives a *heavenly life* (v. 20; cf. 1 Co 15:47), that is to say a life transcending ordinary life, a gratuitous and unhoped for sharing in the divine life. Christian justice, even though conversion be required, and effort, is not a human justice, not the sort of thing sought by supporters of the works of the flesh, such as the Judaisers were (Ph 3:19; 2 Co 5:14; Ga 6:15).

To explain sanctification in these terms (or "transfiguration," v. 21) Paul sees Jesus, according to contemporary cosmology, as wresting leadership from the "powers" who hold the universe and humanity in thrall. Above all he means the powers of sin and death (2 Co 5:14) which prevent our wretched bodies from becoming glorious bodies by constantly forcing us back to our own resources.

---

*See the doctrinal theme: *asceticism,* 84.

Because it comes from Christ, the victor over death and sin, Christian life is a superior life. It is animated by the Spirit of God, and its goal is eternal life (2 Co 4:18; Col 3:1-4). Already "seated at the right hand of God," Christ substitutes heaven (divine life, that is to say) for man's terrestrial life, and he draws man towards the celestial city that is to be. Hence the duty of witnessing here below to that era which is the goal of our moral effort, which has indeed already begun, ever since the holiness of Christ has been communicated to mankind.

Delivering up one's "wretched body" to the transforming action of him who conquered death and subdued the universe, means, in sum, mortification. It is not only a matter of physical mortification, denying to the body means of expression and gratification. More radically, it means being ready to pass the bounds of self, experiencing the death of all that one was, and is. Not only physical death to which people are resigned – at the last possible moment – but the death of innocence too, the death of ideas and attitudes, the death of one's God, of one's truth.

The celestial life that Paul encourages us to anticipate he does not see at all as an apotheosis, the recompense for a terrestrial life that was distinguished by achievement and success. It is something which follows the "transfiguration" of a wretched body, something that must be preceded by a death. Nor is the transformation just one moment of our future life. Any experience one has had of passing the bounds of self in the business of living is sufficient to convince one that transfiguration of our being by him who went beyond death is something entirely possible.

VII. Matthew 17:1-9
Gospel
1st cycle

The primitive transfiguration narrative which is common to all the synoptics presents the event in apocalyptic style as a discovery by the disciples of the personality of Jesus, as an eschatological figure and source of salvation (verses influenced by Dn 10:5-6; Mt 17:2, 9; by Dn 10:9; Mt 17:6; by Dn 10:10; Mt 17:7; by Dn 12:4; Mt 17:9). Then this eschatological manifestation was interpreted in terms of the feast of Tabernacles and the enthronement of the suffering Messiah which it suggested. In the commentary on Mark 9:1-9 (p. 92) this will be the principal area of discussion.

a) Subsequent redactions probably stressed the connection between the theophany of Thabor (?) and that of Sinai with some idea of featuring more prominently the two great decisive moments in salvation history: the covenant and the coming of the Son of Man. In fact there is close parallelism with Exodus 19:16-17; 24:15-18; 40:34-38; 34:29-30. Already in Jewish circles, particularly by the orientation given the feast of Tabernacles, the Sinai theophany had been transposed to the eschatological era (Is 40:3-5; Za 14; Rv 7:9-11). Allusion then to the Sinai theophany and the feast of Tabernacles tended to emphasize the eschatological nature of the Messiah's enthronement.

Accordingly it was but a further step for Matthew to stress the parallel between Moses in Sinai and Christ in transfiguration.*

In fact his gospel is structured around five discourses of Christ (which correspond to the five books of the law). In each of the five portions a group of events is followed by a discourse. In the fourth (where the transfiguration is described) the series of events leads up to the discourse on the future life of the Church (Mt 18).

Matthew's whole purpose is to descry in Jesus the *new* Moses, legislator of the new dispensation. By this means he wants to convince Jewish Christians that the old law has been replaced by that of Christ. That is why, unlike Mark 9:4, he mentions Moses before Elias (v. 3). Furthermore he is the only one to speak of radiance in the face of Christ, (v. 2), corresponding to the radiance in Moses' face (Ex 34:29-35; 2 Co 3:7-11). Like-

*See the doctrinal theme: *the law and moral life,* p. 80.

wise the voice speaking in the cloud (v. 5) corresponds to the similar detail on Sinai (Ex 19:16-24). The injunction "listen to him" (v. 5) recalls the prophecy made to Moses of a future replica of himself "whom you will hear" (Dt 18:15). Where the others cite only Psalm 2: *This is my son,* Matthew adds a few words taken from Isaiah 42:1 "he enjoys my favor" (v. 5) alluding to the Servant as "light of nations" because he does the will of God. Finally, the detail about the transfiguration taking place "six days later" (v. 1) helps to associate the episode with Moses climbing Sinai (Ex 24:16-18).

Thus, over and above his eschatological character, Christ is seen as the new Moses, law-giver to a new people. He has the title because, already by obedience, he has entered the realm of suffering and death. The new Moses begins by personal obedience to the law he proposes. Unlike the first Moses, Christ is not a lawgiver who is satisfied with legislating: he simultaneously provides the interior method of following it.

b) The transfiguration does not lose, in Matthew's account, its basic significance as *investiture of the Son of Man* (notice for instance the reference to the feast of Tabernacle); but, if one may put it that way, the significance becomes crystallized in the magistral prerogatives of Christ the new master of thought. Just as the suffering Servant became the light of the world because of his obedience, so too Christ becomes master of thought and the new law-giver for the world, because he was the first to submit to his own new law, that of love and renunciation (v. 9). It is noteworthy that the transfiguration narrative introduces the discourse of chapter 18, where Christ establishes messianic powers for the Church, in particular giving to his apostles the right which he himself acquired by transfiguration, that of being heard (Mt 18:15-18).

How are we to compare the work that Jesus did and that of Moses? As he himself said, Jesus did not come to add to the law; he came to accomplish it, give it perfection. In the mind of the first law-giver, the law was meant to indicate the path of true fidelity to Yahweh. In fact it was in the person of Jesus that it found its first exemplary exponent of fidelity. Definitively and with exactitude he determined the balance between law and faith, a balance nowhere else achieved. Only his human nature, precisely because it was that of the man-God, was capable of the sort of fidelity demanded by the veritable covenant.

Brought to perfection in Jesus the very essence of the law is transformed; the limits of the old covenant give way: the old bottles are no longer adequate. From now on the evangelical law, based on universal love, is directed to all men. No longer is Jesus after any fashion slave to an exterior law, the essence of the law engraved on his heart is the Spirit. Just as the prophets said, renewal of the heart means renewal of the law.

Thus we are led to an understanding of the paschal rhythm of the new law by the mystery of the transfiguration. It is obedience even unto the death of the cross that marks the fidelity of Jesus. It is only by giving up one's own life that one can become the neighbor of all humanity. To triumph over death, death must be encountered on his own terrain.

VIII. Mark 9:2-9 In the second gospel the context of the trans-
Gospel   figuration is more closely linked with Jesus'
2nd cycle   presentiments about death and glory than in
             the other synoptics. He has just announced
his forthcoming Pasch (Mk 8:31-32), and Peter immediately recoils. He cannot contemplate suffering and death as the issue of the kingdom of glory and power foretold by the prophets (Mk 8:32-33). Accordingly Jesus uses the rite of enthronement for the suffering Messiah provided by the feast of Tabernacles to convince his followers that suffering will indeed be the road to his messiahship.

a) The first verse sets this context very obviously. There are some problems about text transmission in the verse; but it would appear that what Jesus says, rather sadly, is: "There are people so intensely expectant of a kingdom of power that not one of them is willing to pay with his life for the coming of the kingdom." Mark sees the whole transfiguration episode above all as Christ's disclosure to the elite among the apostles (the very ones who will be near him at Gethsemane: Mark 14:33) of the totality of the paschal mystery.

So it is that he gives Elias priority over Moses (v. 4), because if Elias is John the Baptist, it is clear that by his own suffering he foretells that of the Messiah (cf. the explanation by Jesus in Mk 9:12-13). Essential then to the whole gospel of Mark is the concept of a *suffering Messiah*.

b) The real transfiguration consists in the three apostles' becoming aware that Jesus is the veritable Messiah who is being enthroned at the *Feast of Tabernacles*. Mention of "six days" (v. 2) is an allusion to the classic duration of the feast, and the mountain and cloud are also traditional details, as is of course above all Peter's suggestion about living in tents (v. 5). In this respect the narrative is absolutely parallel to that of Jesus' entry to Jerusalem (Mt 21). Jesus is the Messiah awaited each year in the feast of Tabernacles, enthroned in anticipation by an aura of whiteness and radiance (v. 3), invested by the very word of God (v. 7). Already the Jewish book of Jubilees, practically contemporaneous with the gospels, had proclaimed that the Messiah of the feast of Tabernacles was destined to be a suffering Messiah. Christ has just told his followers about his approaching passion (Mark 8:31-38). It was very natural that he would use this occasion of investiture ritual in the feast of Tabernacles to point out to the apostles that the way of suffering was the indicated way. It was confirmed by the liturgy itself.

Thus the transfiguration amounts to being a strong exhortation, directed especially at Peter, to listen (v. 7) to what Jesus says about suffering and death, all the time acknowledging him as the authentic Messiah, the ideal Servant (Is 42:1).

The faith demanded from those who witnessed the transfiguration is a lesson to the Church of today that she must not
avoid necessary incarnations, or the despoliations they require;
nor must she seek incarnations that do not have corresponding
transfigurations. Her presence in the secular structure is for
the transformation of that structure; and the transformation will
be wrought at the price of renunciation on her side of comfort
and security. So it is that she experiences the ups and downs
of glory and humiliation. She realizes that victory will not be
hers until the day when, after being crushed by death, she
rises again in a world for the transfiguration of which she will
have labored.

IX. Luke   Luke, in his particular version of the trans-
9:28b-36   figuration, does not greatly stress the phe-
Gospel   nomenon itself. Doubtless he was worried lest
3rd cycle   readers of pagan origin should confuse it with
                 mythological "metamorphoses." Accordingly
he simply says that the countenance of Jesus changed, and he
attributes the illumination to Jesus' prayer (vv. 28-29). Furthermore with the glory illuminating Christ (v. 31), he associates
first Moses and Elias, and then the apostles themselves (v. 34),
thus tempering to some extent the uniqueness of the episode.
On the other hand he devotes more attention than the other
evangelists to the presence of Moses and Elias. He is the only
one to mention their particular glory, or to give us an explanation of the exchange between them and Jesus: the "exodus" of the
Lord, that is (v. 31, often badly rendered as the "departure").

a) It would seem then that the really important element in
Luke's narrative is Jesus' *prayer* to his Father (vv. 28-29). Luke
is wont to associate this prayer with the critical moments of
Jesus' life, and the transfiguration is one of these. Jesus has just
become aware in fact of a turn for the worse in his mission,

and, like any leader of a revolutionary band, a presentiment about approaching death obsesses him. He has a foreboding too that the disciples who are willing to follow to the end will also pay for their messianic enthusiasm with their lives (Lk 9:23-26). Perhaps here and now comes the moment to rejoin God? Even before being raised on the cross Jesus is already dead, dead to the mission he thought he was fulfilling, dead to all hopes of success or influence, dead maybe to the concept of a God who made everything succeed and enabled him to work miracles. His prayer then amounts to being an oblation of himself in his present state to God, and a new insight about God, the insight that comes after the death of the self, the collapse of all security. The outward change in his appearance could only come from a deep inner certainty: the realization that even after one dies to everything and encounters total failure God is still God. The more radical his renunciation, and that of his disciples, of all quest for human glory, the more ready will God be to glorify them.*

b) It is certain that Luke saw in Jesus the fulfillment of the prophecy of Deuteronomy 18:15, which promised Moses a successor of his own ilk. Frequently in his writing (v. 35b; cf. Ac 3:22; 7:37) the prophecy recurs. For him, as for Matthew (see gospel, first cycle, commentary above), Jesus is the second Moses (cf. Lk 14:27). But he goes further than Matthew in pointing out how Jesus inaugurates the *New "Exodus"* (v. 31). In the Old Testament the Exodus from Egypt was the classic example of divine intervention in salvation history. Such an intervention again could only be in the guise of a new Exodus (Mi 7:15; Is 11:11). Luke sees the new Exodus as a going out from the terrestrial Jerusalem, which is unbelieving (Mk 19:41-44; 13:33-34; 21:37) like ancient Egypt. It makes for the new Jerusalem (cf. Ga 4:25-26; He 12:22), the abode of the Father, and there is a "submersion" in the water (Lk 12:50) on the way. In actual fact, after the transfiguration, Jesus begins the journey

*See the doctrinal theme: *prayer*, p. 185.

toward "Jerusalem." It is only when he leaves the ancient capital for the mount of olives and that of the ascension (Ac 1:6-11) that the journey will be completed. It is remarkable too that all the principal stages of this Exodus, the transfiguration (v. 30), the resurrection (Lk 24:4; though the other evangelists speak of one person) and the ascension (Ac 1:10) are attended by "two witnesses." Perhaps, right through, this is the function of Moses and Elias?

So we have Luke placed midway between Matthew and Mark. Where Matthew sees in this episode the revelation of the new Moses, law-giver of the new covenant, and Mark is above all concerned with the events of the Lord's Pasch; Luke has both insights. He makes Christ the new Moses, but also the kind of law-giver who seals the new covenant by bringing to accomplishment his personal Exodus.

For humanity today the presence of Moses and Elias by the side of Jesus can convey a deeper lesson still. In ancient Israel these two patriarchs vainly tried to pierce the inner mystery of God (Ex 3; 1 K 19). Now, in Jesus, their quest is ended. Comprehension of the mystery is measured by the degree of God's self-manifestation in the flesh, for the service of mankind. Man's constant quest has its answer in this history of a search that led finally to Jesus. There can never be any question of turning again to Sinai or to Horeb. We can only turn to Jesus, fully man and God, fully at the service of mankind. It could be that the transfiguration is less the mystery of Jesus' personal divinization than the discovery by men of the kind of God who is not known to philosophers.

B. DOCTRINE

I. The Theme of Law and Moral Life

The transfiguration narrative should develop our insight into the unique nature of Christian moral life. Too many Christians are inclined to make their faith simply a moral ideal, reducing the gospel message to a rule of life, albeit a particularly noble one. Bearing witness to Jesus Christ, as they see it, means above all leading a life which conforms to the gospel ideal. It is as if Jesus of Nazareth were just another sage, as if grace meant nothing but a better alignment of one's life to his precepts.

Such a view of the Christian ethic, so very inadequate and distorted, has many unfortunate consequences. It is illusory indeed to anticipate from grace a direct effect in a domain which is not the domain of grace. But, from a missionary point of view, the consequences are more serious still. An exemplary moral life does not necessarily proclaim the Good Tidings of salvation. That Christians have no monopoly of goodness can be very early demonstrated among people devoid of any religious pretensions. Indeed basic human values like solidarity sometimes find more authentic expression in such groups, which are utterly untouched by the Church.

The Christian is faced with two questions. What is the meaning of the new law, revealed in Jesus Christ? And how precisely does the Christian bear witness to Jesus Christ by the quality of his moral life?

Moses, law-giver of the old covenant

The law of Sinai is closely associated with the regime of faith inaugurated by Abraham. Awareness of this association is of prime importance. At a precise moment in the history of the chosen people, the exact point of covenant between Yahweh and Israel, Moses intervenes. From the hands of a totally-other God he receives the Law, for transmission to the people, and he does so in full awareness of what the way of faith means.

The promulgation of the decalogue is not quite comprehensible outside the context of the first Jewish Pasch. Yahweh has gratuitously freed his people from the yoke of the Egyptians. He has freely chosen Israel as *His* people; but, the desert is a necessary preliminary to the land of promise; because Israel must clearly realize wherein lies the wager of faith. He will save Israel, but in return for fidelity. Fidelity in the desert, that is, not any sort of fidelity. In the desert there is no way of masking daily insecurity. Tomorrow is not predictable; from every angle one is thrust back upon the benevolence of God.

Accordingly the Law, at the deepest level, only makes sense as an exercise of faith. It is not possible to reduce it to an ethical code, without reference to the concrete wants associated with its beginnings. It is an exact expression of Israelite fidelity to a transcendent and unique God, a God who leads his people. and is always, in all freedom, a savior.

This close link between the law of Sinai and the regime of faith is a very clear vindication of Moses as the first of the prophets. Pagan sentiments are always recurring; they shun the law. The prophets reread events, and keep reminding people, who opt for illusory security as against fidelity to God, about the requirements of the covenant. The requirements are not arbitrary; whatever happens in people's lives has relevance in an ultimate analysis.

Once detached from the regime of faith the Mosaic law will be automatically degraded. Prescriptions will be multiplied, scribes will replace prophets, fidelity to the faith will yield to legalism.

The moral life of the Father's children

The basis of the Christian's moral life, its real and authentic source, is the decisive event of Christ's death and resurrection. No theoretic wisdom, however noble, explains the unique quality of the Christian ethic. It must be traced to an existential link with Christ's Pasch. It must be, in a veritable sense, an "imitation of Jesus": "As I have loved you, love one another." Always it is a matter of being able to discern God's will in the march of events, of realizing that, in Jesus Christ whom he has given us, we have the means of triumphing over the pall of death that encompasses all events. So it is that the Christian ethic is synonymous with a paschal life; divorced from an existential faith, it does not have a meaning.

On the selfsame principle it is a life in the Spirit. When the Spirit has free play in the human psyche, an inner law is established, woven into the very texture of events. Obedient to this law, the Christian finds himself ever more free. What he follows is no longer something external. Even when he is confronted by precepts that seem external, the reality for him has to do with the transfiguring action of the Spirit.

For this reason then, because of dependence on Christ and the Spirit, the Christian ethic will have, inevitably, an ecclesial dimension. It will be effective in proportion to its involvment in the Church's contribution to salvation history by transmission of the Word. It is this which challenges the believer, leads him to descry in the Spirit of Christ the vital and controlling principle of his daily activity.

Such a "supernatural" ethic does not, we should realize, detach man from his creaturely condition. On the contrary it leads him to more lucid acceptance of that. To put it another way, the Christian ethic fosters respect for rationality, and attracts by the very naturalness of its achievements.

The missionary significance of the Christian ethic

What has been said enables us to judge how the Christian ethic can be the sign of salvation acquired in Jesus Christ.

A Christian will bear witness to the risen Christ when his life has the fruitfulness of the paschal mystery. Evangelization is not furthered by the goodness of the Christian life as such, by the degree of perfection, to be precise, in terms of the gospel ideal. An exemplary moral life might make an impression; it does not necessarily manifest Jesus Christ. If that is so, when *does* a life bear witness to the Risen Lord? When, in the warp and woof of daily trials, it meets the challenge of death, above all where there is question of relations with fellow man. The confrontation, in obedience, of death demands annihilation of self, that sort of "poverty" which is within the capability of any man whatever his condition. A prostitute could become an authentic witness of the resurrection!

People say that in the world we know the witness Christians bear is negative. What is one to reply? Negative witness means blindness to the "signs of the times." The world we live in is one where the event weighted with the will of God assumes planetary dimensions. But Christian eyes are often closed. They fail to perceive the claims that actual crises make upon their responsibility — countries which are underdeveloped economically, the problem of hunger in the universe. The most frequent failing is one of imagination, inability to realize the full potential of collective Christian charity. The Christian confronted casually by a starving man knows what is required of him. Before the problem of hunger on a planetary scale, on highways that are remote, far removed from the limited horizons of his daily experience, he stands bewildered.

The eucharistic event in Christian ethic

For the Christian the Eucharist is the source of renewal in moral life. Here the Church offers him a living link with the major event in salvation history, Jesus Christ who died and rose again for all men. However, in the local eucharistic assembly the link with Christ is only real when the Christian is called upon to experience there God's today. Hence the importance of the liturgy of the Word where the reality of Jesus Christ in the world is celebrated. The homily then is crucial. It is the means whereby people can see the connection between the forces of evil that Christ conquered and those spawned by our sort of world. They are at once individual and collective. They are the forces that we, following Christ, must conquer in our turn.

2. Auxiliary Theme for Lent: Asceticism

For a long time asceticism and mortification have been of considerable importance in the religious life of mankind. The quest for happiness requires a certain mastery over the passions of soul and body. In pursuit of this goal some have gone against the most spontaneous and natural urges. Modern man is rediscovering asceticism on a very simple, very human, level. He sees it as a harmony and a balance, at once physical and psychological or moral.

When the Christian speaks of asceticism and mortification, what is he talking about? The very terms for many people suggest something old-fashioned and quite negative; they belong to an era when fear, not to say disgust, of bodily realities was rampant. Asceticism of that brand is not welcomed any more, doubtless for very good reasons. But can it be replaced by something that is more wholesome? Lent gives us the opportunity to return to the sources.

Jewish man and the mortification of sin

Mortifying means making something die. What, for Jewish man, should be made to die? Biblical tradition is quite clear. Not life, surely, whether it be that of the soul or the body. All manifestations of death in the human condition run counter to the happiness reserved by Yahweh for his people. What he wishes is life, not death. Death in every guise is evil, a consequence of sin. What should be made to die is wickedness, and only that. Yahweh's goal is "that (Israel) be converted and live" (Ez 18:33).

Jewish man is enamored of life. Terrestrial life, its richness, its warmth, its fruitfulness, he loves to distraction. This love is fostered by the regime of faith. Life in all its concrete forms is celebrated by the Jews; faith makes him see everything with the eyes of God, who says of his creation "all this is good." For Israel future salvation was conceived in terms of physical happiness. Once death in all its forms is made away with, abundant life will flourish everywhere. Yahweh's believers are wont to speak of a new *earth*. They never tended to subordinate life here below (as did some Greeks, for instance) to hopes of immortality for the soul.

The only thing that makes mortification necessary is the disorder introduced by sin. This temporary stage will pass; once sin has disappeared there is nothing that must be made to die. Mortification belongs to the time of trial that precedes the era of definitive salvation.

The asceticism of Christ, the source of life

Jesus of Nazareth is by no means the professional ascetic. With perfect naturalness he becomes involved in ordinary life, its difficulties yes, but its real joys too. The very first sign of his public ministry is set by Saint John in the context of a wedding, which in the East is a time of unlimited rejoicing.

Nevertheless, more than any person ever, he was a perfectly mortified man. Where he was concerned, sin never had any entry. Each time temptation presents itself he resists it. The war he waged day after day with sin, so deeply rooted in the human condition, was finally to wrest from death his power.

There is however, with Jesus, a new dimension to mortification. Jewish man's position was thus: once men cease to sin, straightaway over the entire earth life will supplant death. But Jesus too, sinless though he be, is touched by death. This death, an essential element of man's terrestrial state, is not made by him to disappear. The works of death he does destroy; death loses his empire, because in the case of Christ his was only a seeming victory. The true life of both soul and body, the gift of God conveyed by Jesus in obedience, is not of this world. So it is that it becomes capable of surmounting the crisis of death.

The meaning of Christian mortification

To the Christian community of Colossus Saint Paul does not hesitate to assert: "You are dead, and your life henceforth is hidden with Christ in God" (Col 3:3). This text can help us find a meaning for Christian mortification.

The Christian has a lucid view of death. It is something woven into the texture of daily existence. Always it hounds the projects of man, who is hungry for security. Its weapons are the unexpected, the unpredictable, failure and suffering. Those with sensitive insight will see the stamp of death in every human relationship, even the marriage-relationship, even the most closely-knit and successful marriages. Because ultimately all men are strangers to men.

But the Christian knows that it is from man himself that death derives all power. When man, that is, shuts his eyes to the presence of death in the human condition; when he attempts to divinize himself by basing everything on the existential, the security of here and now, individual and collective. It is when negated that death really goes to work. The gates are opened to pride of spirit, to the passions of the flesh, to division, to ruin.

If the members of his Body, the Church, confront death as Jesus did, they do not make it disappear. But they do hold its power in check. They affirm that despite appearances death is not the last word in human existence. They share here below in the only life that is real, that of the Risen Lord. It is this life that proves always impregnable before the onset of death.

Recognizing then that he can be struck by death in all its guises, the Christian will be enabled by his faith to withstand the enemy. In this sense he is called upon, day after day, to mortify himself, to make Christ's own death actual and concrete in the texture of his life. He is, in Saint Paul's phrase, indeed "dead"; but in reality he is always "returning" from this death which is forever shorn of power. His life is "hidden with Christ in God." Mortification then in the Christian sense can be, because of faith, the way to true life.

The missioner, a mortified man

Mission is carried out among peoples and cultural enclaves that have not yet received the Good News of salvation. The purpose is to graft on to their religious tradition the mystery of Christ. Little by little their religious ethos should be shaped towards the paschal rhythm; and in the domains where death manifested itself, signs of resurrection will begin to appear.

In this paschal process, the role of the missionary is of first importance because at every stage of his work death surrounds him. At the very outset it confronts him. Once he decides to share the fate of a region foreign to him he must leave his family, his friends, the whole accustomed ambience of security, individual and collective. Finally, one day he succeeds in crossing the crest of adaptation; he finds himself at home in his new life. But deep down he must always realize that he remains a stranger, a solitary. It is then that he is confronted by the temptation *par excellence:* to refrain, under the influence of pagan wisdom, from denunciation of the regime of death. It is here that challenge, not to say persecution, can present itself. The missionary must become as it were a dying victim (cf. 2 Co 6:9) who constantly intercedes for those he evangelizes, so that life may triumph where death was rampant.

When Saint Paul speaks of his apostolic life he stresses heavily the things that link him to the death of Christ. He knows that when face to face with death he is actually laboring to sow the mystery of Christ. He is ready to let death have its way with him, because that means life is burgeoning round him: "So death is at work in us, but life in you" (2 Co 4:12).

Eucharistic celebration as source of mortification

If Christian mortification consists in making the death of Christ actual in the whole texture of life, it follows that the Eucharist must be the great source which gives it impetus. It is eucharistic life which binds the Christian to the paschal mystery with an intimacy that is always being renewed. Each eucharistic celebration proclaims and represents the sacrifice of Jesus on the cross. Each believer, in the very bosom of his community, can make Christ's victory over death his own until it becomes actual for him. Sharing the bread cements the bonds of grace. Sharing the Word gives one a clearer view of the marks of death in one's own life and that of the world. A man discovers how, here below, he is "dead," how his life is hidden with Christ in God.

But over and above the link of grace that it forges between the Christian and Christ in the mystery of his death, the eucharistic celebration can give a particular insight into the meaning of mortification. The whole thrust of eucharistic assembly is towards the greatest possible catholicity. Despite all the divisive influences — men and women in the Church are gathered in the same place and bidden to the same repast. Christians gathered in this way should not be blind to what divides them; on the contrary they should face this. It is their business to confront the sign of death in the very heart of their assembly, proclaiming all the while the unity they have acquired by the death of Christ. That unity is not blind to all the contrary thrusts; in fact it acknowledges and accepts them. But it is the closest unity conceivable, that of the Father's family, and it enables the Christian, day by day, to combat the forces of death that appear along the way.

SECOND WEEK OF LENT

I. Daniel 9:4b-10
1st reading
Monday

This is a brief extract from Daniel's prayer to God in the name of the repentant people. As response comes the revelation about the seventy weeks which will be the prelude to salvation. The prayer should probably be dated about 165, during the reign of Antiochus Epiphanes. There is no great evidence of originality. Like most contemporary prayers, it draws considerably from the book of Deuteronomy (compare verse 4 with Deuteronomy 7:9, 21; verse 8 with Deuteronomy 28:64; verse 10 with Deuteronomy 28:15). In turn, it will be the inspiration for the prayer of Baruch 1-2; and it was only inserted in the book of Daniel at a relatively late stage. Despite its derivative character, it is one of the loveliest penitential prayers in the Old Testament.

The conventions of *penitential prayer* (cf. 1 K 8; Jr 32:16-25; Ezr 9:6-15; Ne 9:6-37) are followed. The speaker addresses God in the name of the entire people, acknowledges the sinful character of this people who are forgetful of their creator, and affirms the great majesty of God, who, in his mercy, is ever ready to reestablish the atmosphere of the covenant.

The Christian should reread such prayers with reverence, primarily because of the wholesome sentiments they contain, but also because it was such prayers that pleaded for, and hastened the advent of, the last ages in which he lives.

II. Luke 6:36-38
Gospel
Monday

The compilation of this particular gospel we owe to the hellenist communities in the primitive Church. Where Jewish communities always spoke of the "Father of the heavens" (Mt 5:45; other instances in 6, 9, 14, 26, 32), the hellenist Churches, influenced by some Greek books of the Old Testament

(Ws 14:3), rejected this in favor of the more direct "Father" (Ga 4:6; Rm 8:15; Ep 3:14; Lk 6:36; 12:30, 32). Then for Greeks such as these, unfamiliar with the mystique of the Law, an ideal of "justice" after the Jewish pattern, even when revised and modified as in Matthew 5, 6, 10, 20, was not really comprehensible.

That is why Luke alters the teaching about perfect justice (Mt 5:48) to teaching about mercy. The lesson however remains identical: Christian moral behavior is inevitably an *imitation* of God's behavior — the Christian acts "like" God. Luke's standpoint might perhaps be described as theocentric whereas that of Matthew is anthropocentric.

Subsequently Luke reproduces Matthew 7:1-2, but not without a certain personal nuance. For Matthew 7:1 "judge not that you may not be judged" (the theme of earthly retribution, the *lex talionis,* in proverbial style), he substitutes a triple parallel (Lk 6:37: judge not . . . condemn not . . . forgive), thus modifying the overly Jewish emphasis. His phrase is doubtless just as original as Matthew's, and he has preserved it because the three verbs indicate the character of God's activity and judgment. And God's manner of judging being what it is, it behooves man to conform to that in his own judgments. So that Luke's theocentric bias, as distinct from Matthew's, is once more emphasized.

Likewise, for the proverbial affirmation in Matthew 7:2 "according to the measure you mete out, it will be measured unto you," Luke has a whole passage made up of disjointed sentiments about the key-word "measure." The reason for the addition is obvious. Matthew 7:2 is emphatic about the exact correspondence between the measure we mete to others and that meted to us by God. For Luke, on the contrary, emphasis is placed on the total generosity of our giving, and in return we are promised not alone equivalent measure, but superabundant. This is a sentiment dear to Luke: a charity so large that it dwarfs all the calculated equivalence characteristic of Judaism.

In Matthew 7:3-5 this teaching is followed immediately by the parable about the mote and the beam. Luke has this too (vv. 41-42); but he prefaces it by the parable about the two blind men (v. 39), and the sentiment about the disciple and the master (v. 40), both items drawn from a different context. Why he does this is by no means clear, because the parable of the mote and the beam makes a very suitable conclusion to teaching about how others should be judged. The only possible explanation seems to be a pre-Lucan source, where the style followed was to group the teachings of Jesus around key-words. Thus in the preceding verses the key-word was "measure;" here it is "eye," and there are two distinct sentences: one about the blind, the other about the mote and the beam. Consequently, to preserve the continuity in today's gospel, it is reasonable to omit verses 39-40.

Thus the emphasis of the Lucan passage becomes concentrated on the quality of Christian morality. While Matthew bases it on the order of Jewish "justice" (the Christian merely surpassing the Jew in this), the basis for Luke is the order of charity and his standpoint is strictly theocentric.

But what constitutes this imitation of Christ? It should be clear first of all that for imitation a necessary preliminary is being conformed to his image, being qualified that is to act in his way. The initial intervention of the Church is required. That comes through baptism, which introduces a man to the Body of Christ, and enables him to act as adoptive son of the Father, in union with the only begotten Son, while accepting his earthly condition as creature. Nor does the function of the Church end here; her services will be constantly required for the exercise of the imitative capacity. Because, if we are to conduct ourselves as adoptive children of the Father, we must be always open to the action of interior grace; we must allow ourselves to be modelled by the sacraments and the Word.

Ecclesial influence of this kind protects the believer against various escapist temptations, and disposes him ever better for the challenge of the event, for what God wishes, through him, to say to others. It is these events of daily living, of whatever kind or provenance, which are always challenging the faith of a Christian and molding his acceptance of the creaturely condition. Imitation of Jesus Christ is not accomplished by putting into practice some predetermined set of rules. It means encountering the event with absolute openness, as he did; it means following him in his Passion, the event *par excellence.*

Imitating Christ does not mean conformism. It is not a matter of slavishly reproducing this or that trait of his character. It consists of confronting reality precisely as he did, being disposed as he was to meet the event as it came. Indeed it is more a matter of being inventive than being imitative. The event is always in some way particular; so too must be the performance of the believer. He will be always careful to adapt his attitude to whatever comes.

Just because modern man is not religious in the sense of former times, Christians when they bear witness now to Jesus Christ are perhaps tempted to emphasize the service they render to mankind as against their relation to the Father. There *are* colossal undertakings where the concentration and collaboration of everyone are needed: peace, progress, social and international justice, and so on. If we Christians want to be accepted as such, we must participate in the collective task that confronts mankind just now. Men realize that they have the tools to confront it.

There is here a subtle temptation that must be vanquished. If we yield to it, we are jeopardizing the very essence of our witness. Indeed it should be said that Christian witness loses all savor, even for modern man, when its original content is no longer operative. If the essence of our missionary witness includes imitation of the Father, we conduct ourselves as sons of God and we prove to the hilt our fidelity to the creaturely condition. We demonstrate that man in Jesus Christ can give his activity an eternal dimension, while remaining absolutely loyal to his condition as creature. Frequently enough people make the mistake of thinking that modern man, because of his preoccupation with terrestrial responsibilities, has turned his back upon the absolute. That is not so: the only difference between him and his predecessors is that for him the thrust towards the absolute penetrates right into the texture of human tasks. It is wrong then to describe as purely "temporal" the earthly projects that engage the united effort of men today. And when the Christian shares with other men of our time the responsibility for the immense challenges that lie ahead, one thing should be clear. As child of God he should demonstrate by his attitude, that far from being hesitant about the deployment of merely human resources, he is on the contrary admirably disposed toward the enterprise of civilization.

We must always remember that modern man is only impressed by the sort of Christian cooperation in human enterprises that shows scrupulous respect for the rules of the game. The good success of such enterprises depends not only on the inspiration which suggests them, but on the solid integrity and effort which go into their prosecution, in whatever domain, political, economic, social, etc. The Christian like every other man must submit to the necessary preliminaries. Without these, the central purpose will never be accomplished.

During the eucharistic celebration the Christian community is united in the charity of Christ, which is the perfect imitation of the Father. But the fruits of the celebration are never automatic. The proclamation of the Word is all-important; the scripture readings, and the celebrant's homily which demonstrates their living actuality. So too is the very make-up of the assembly. People should be aware that unity is being formed of diverse elements, that this is a microcosm, that openness is essential.

III. **Isaiah**   This prophecy belongs to the early years of
1:10, 16-20   Isaiah's ministry (before 735?), and, in the
1st reading   elevated style characteristic of Amos (Am
Tuesday   5:14-21), deals with religious hypocrisy among

the people. There is reason to think that it was pronounced during a liturgical celebration (v. 13), probably as the smoke of sacrifices (v. 11) ascended while the people stood around in an attitude of prayer (v. 15).

The chosen people think that Yahweh derives pleasure from the numerous crowds in the temple precincts who bring such rich offerings. But in fact the moral unworthiness of those who offer sacrifice is so repugnant to Yahweh that he truly cannot abide this *religion without faith*.

The sole condition under which such worship will prove acceptable to God will be a conversion on the part of the people that will induce them to welcome the poor and give them a share in the richness of sacrifices with which Yahweh could very readily dispense (vv. 16-18). A threat (v. 19) brings the passage to a close, a threat still based on temporal retribution – obedience brings abundance; revolt will bring punishment.

The liturgical reform undertaken by Vatican II is an indication of the extent to which worship, as understood by many, was tending again in the direction of religion without faith. A great many believers, seasonally practicing the faith, were under the impression that this was a matter of paying their respects to God and being done with it. They had no difficulty in submitting to bizarre and incomprehensible rites; it was the price that had to be paid so that God would protect and bless their lives.

The reform, by simplifying and in a way impoverishing, ceremony, gives us rites that absolutely depend on the faith and actual texture of the lives of participants, on the encounter that is between God and men. Such a sudden switch to ritual austerity discomfited people who could previously mask their real feelings and seek security by partaking of the sacraments. Henceforward rite will be designed to express both individual and communal conversion. It can only do so by respecting the particular character of individual consciences, the actual milieu

in which they are developed, the socio-cultural milestones that
mark the shaping of faith.

IV. Matthew   Here we have the preamble to the denuncia-
23:1-12   tion of the scribes and Pharisees (Mt 23:12-
Gospel   32). In the second verse Jesus makes it clear
Tuesday   who his adversaries are. They wrongly occupy
the chair of Moses because the law has en-
joined that priests alone should have the right of teaching and
interpreting the Word of God (Dt 17:8-12; 31:9-10; Mi 3:11;
Ml 2:7-10). By usurping that function the scribes have brought
about a change in religion that is profoundly important. For
faith in the Word they have substituted a brand of intellectu-
alism, for obedience to God's plan a juridical casuistry. In
denouncing them Jesus is rejecting such a purely human concept
of religion.

The words of Jesus quoted in verses 8-10 are peculiar to
Matthew. The keyword rabbi joins them to the previous text,
and the verses are constructed in a sort of triple rhythm with
successive featuring of the words "Master," Father," "Doctor"
(preferably "Director"). It is not so much the titles that Jesus
is condemning, but rather the religion of exegetes and professors
they suggest. He insists that one does not know God by having
recourse to professors.

The two final verses do not belong originally to this Matthaean
context (cf. Mt 20:26).

Thus what Jesus is stigmatizing in the passage is the *hypocrisy*
of the scribes and leaders of the synagogue. Their essential
crime is deception of others by religious posturing and usurping
sacral prerogatives. It is hypocrisy to take to oneself honors
that suggest one is God's representative (vv. 6-7). Such a person
pretends worship of God; what he is really doing is putting himself forward. This selfish ambition (cf. Mt 6:2, 5, 16) has

deprived genuine religious practices of their true significance. The hypocrite merely serves his personal ends by his theological knowledge. He uses casuistry to select those precepts which advance his interests, and imposes commandments on other people where he dispenses himself (v. 4; cf. Mt 23:24-25).

The crowning injustice of which these men are guilty is usurping the place of God by claiming powers to which they have no right (vv. 8-10; cf. Mt 15:3-14). Where they should be guiding people towards personal encounter with God, towards the delicate point of free individual decision, they have become immersed in arguments, conclusions and regulations that are too obviously human to have anything to do with God.

This very brand of hypocrisy which Jesus denounces remains a temptation throughout the long history of the Church: a subtle temptation discernible in the relation of priests to laity, and more generally perhaps in that of baptized Christians towards other men. We can all learn a lesson from today's gospel.

It is of paramount importance that the Church never regard herself as the definitive reality. She announces the Kingdom that is to be; but she is not yet that Kingdom. She herself must not be the center of her own preaching; the world must be guided not towards her but towards the Kingdom. Thus she must not lay insupportable burdens on believers: she must be always pointing towards a future that has to be shaped. She must avoid all vanity. Those responsible must take care that there be no avenues leading individuals towards personal power, diplomatic intrigues, political pressure, honorific titles, etc. The Church can never afford to forget that her business is to serve.

If she does, she is immediately hardened in heart. Her justice becomes her own merely; she is the harbinger of calamity and catastrophe, to be denounced in the same terms as the haughty scribes. The truth is that no one is altogether impervious at the delicate frontier of good and evil. Only the mercy of God has maintained the Church in continued existence.

V. **Jeremiah**   This reading describes the Jewish plot against
18:18-20   Jeremiah. For the name *Jeremiah* the liturgi-
1st reading   cal text substitutes the words *just one* (v. 18),
Wednesday   and it is a change that corresponds well with
the original sense of the passage because
Jeremiah is a type of the just man under persecution.

There are several passages in the book of Jeremiah which
give us information about these intrigues against the prophet:
Jeremiah 11:18; 12:6; 11:19-20; 12:3; 11:20b-23 (texts which
should probably be taken in this order). Today's reading is in
the same context. The prophet's enemies think that his death
will be no disadvantage; there are sufficient priests and wise
men to provide the "word" for the people without having recourse to Jeremiah (v. 18).

His prayer to God in this predicament, taken at face value,
is thoroughly marked by the desire for vengeance, a common contemporary Jewish sentiment (Ps 5:11; 10:15; 30/31:18,
53/54:7; etc.). The reaction is normal for one whose religion is
as yet a doctrine of temporal retribution. Only the New Testament will succeed in transcending this attitude (Mt 5:43-48).
However the large interest of the prayer is concerned with some
themes that are destined to be of fundamental importance in
delineating the character of the suffering Servant and of Christ.
The themes of *conspiracy* that is (cf. further Is 53:8-10; Ac
4:25-28; Ps 2; 70/71; etc.) and of retribution for the conspirators
(Ws 2:10-3:12, a passage which is probably the source of the
word "just" for our reading). From this aspect Jeremiah's prayer

deserves close attention from Christians. It is the authentic cry of the just man who is being persecuted because of the mission God has laid upon him, the authentic protest of a prophet whose word has no more weight in Jewish estimation than the most banal of human utterances (v. 18). The prayer will be purified by Christ, but he will disown neither the context nor the anguish.

VI. Matthew **20:17-28** *Gospel* *Wednesday*	The passage gives us Christ's announcement about his going up to Jerusalem (vv. 17-19) to die and to be glorified, and describes the immediate reaction to this among the apostles (vv. 20-28).

a) At nine different points in the synoptics we have this *announcement of the death of Jesus* (Mt 16:21-23; 17:22-23; 20:17-23; Mk 8:31-33; 9:30-32; 10:32-34; Lk 9:22, 44-45; 18:31-33). All three evangelists are meticulous about the exact terms of Christ's discourse, this being a characteristic of primitive kerygma and of the original *Credo* of the Christian communities (note for example the theme of the third day, in verse 19). There is moreover an important development in the three successive announcements of the approaching death. In the first two Jesus is still speaking as a rabbi concerned with the destiny of the Son of man. In the third it is no longer the rabbi who speaks. It is a faithful man who knows where his duty lies, who firmly contracts for the inevitable journey ("now we are going up . . .," v. 18) that will have its issue in the death reserved for prophets and trouble makers.

b) Jesus announces not only his death, but also his *resurrection*. This is the surprising detail. He could have found in scripture many texts which foretold the passion, and indeed the announcement of this is manifestly inspired by Isaiah 53 (hand over, Christ . . .). But nothing in the Old Testament pointed to a resurrection of the Messiah. In a few instances (2 M 7:9-29;

Dn 12:2) there is a suggestion of general resurrection, but tenuous only. Later when the apostles had to justify resurrection from Old Testament sources they could only find texts in the accommodative sense like Psalm 15/16 (Ac 2:22-32; 13:34-35).

But whence, one may ask, did Jesus derive this conviction that he would rise again? Principally of course deep in his own realization of the nature of the mission entrusted to him. The debacle was now imminent, and in order to pursue his mission beyond the confines of death he must return to the Father.

In addition to this realization he could have taken his own interpretation of Isaiah 53 where the suffering Servant is promised a triumph without precedent (Is 52:13; 53:11-12) which will follow upon his suffering and death. In certain versions Isaiah 53:11 can even be translated "he shall see the light again." Furthermore, Daniel 12:3 speaks of a glorious resurrection for those who justify the multitudes. He could also have relied on Ws 2:12-20 and 5:1, 15-16. If he found in such texts an announcement of his destiny, he could not fail to find in them too some hint of his triumph.

c) Where Mark 10, 35-40 expressly mentions James and John, Matthew, doubtless anxious not to hurt their reputation, mentions their mother only. When the apostles ask to sit on the right and left hand of the Lord in his Kingdom (v. 21), they are not thinking of eternal reward, but of assessorship with the Royal Judge (Mt 25:31). What Matthew is doing actually is recalling Jesus' promise about having his followers sit on twelve *thrones* judging the tribes of Israel (Mt 19:28).

Thus, at this point, Jesus is aware that he will be more than a Messiah; he will be the Son of man himself to whom God is to entrust the judgment and condemnation of pagans (Dn 7:9-27). Daniel's prophecy (Dn 7:9-10) envisaged this Son of man in the midst of a tribunal seated on thrones. Immediately the apostles, as the request of James and John indicates, became convinced that they would be the tribunal in question. They understood that Jesus would be delivered over to the pagans

(Mt 20:19). They thought the judgment by the Son of man would be the punishment of the pagans for their crime, and they wanted a share in this divine event.

Jesus then tells them that access to these thrones of judgment will be by the way of suffering; they must drink a chalice and be overwhelmed by trial (v. 22). It is only God who can fix the hour of judgment or determine the composition of the tribunal. In the last times the various functions of individuals are a matter of divine choice: the paschal mystery envelopes all.

d) But Jesus also uses the image of a *cup* to describe the passion. The image was used in the Old Testament of God's judgment on sinners (Jr 25:15-17; 49:12; 51:7; Ez 23:32-34; Ps 74/75:9; Is 51:17-22) and the cup must be drained to the dregs (Jr 25:28; Ez 23:32-34). It has too a sacrificial value (Mb 4:7, 14; 7:20; 19:17). Christ then sees himself encountering this judgment of sinners in a drama of liturgical import (cf. Is 53:10). Alone, rejected by the world, he wants nevertheless to die for the world, and so remove the barrier erected by incredulity that keeps men from discerning the will of God.

One person only may drink this cup, the suffering Servant, the Redeemer. It is a unique and incommunicable role which the disciples can never share. That is why the question in verse 22b indicates a negative response. And yet they will be associated in the Savior's role by drinking the cup of suffering, as well as that sacramental cup by which the Christian links himself with the passion and death of Christ.

e) What he has said to James and John Jesus goes on to repeat to the ten others, but now he stresses the theme of *service* (vv. 24-28). He discloses the awareness he himself has of his role, Messiah and Son of man, but also the suffering Servant who immolates himself for the multitude (v. 28; cf. Is 53:11-12). Conscious of his mission as leader and of the proximity of death which will impede that mission, he becomes aware that it is only when he has acted as servant of Yahweh that he will become leader in very truth.

But he must wait for the apostles to experience the same psychological development. He has revealed his vocation as suffering Servant; they in turn must learn the meaning of service (vv. 26-28).

So it is that this gospel presents the passion and the resurrection in the full dimensions of their meaning for the Christian life itself. To sit on the thrones one "must" drink the chalice; to judge the earth one must be baptized in tribulation; to be leader one must serve. Suffering will leave its signature on the life of the true disciple, not only that sort of accidental suffering which, moral or physical, is part of the human condition, but the suffering which arises from rejection and abandonment, which culminated, for Jesus, in the cross.

It could be that the Christian's isolation in an atheist and secularized world is here and now a sign of our rejection, a reason for carrying the cross with Jesus when we celebrate the Eucharist.

VII. Jeremiah   Here two different texts are juxtaposed. Fur-
17:5-10   thermore they are probably not from the hand
1st reading   of Jeremiah, but belong to wisdom literature.
Thursday   The first text (vv. 5-8) is a psalm, probably the source of Psalm 1; the second combines two proverbs of which we are given the first only in today's liturgy.

The psalm contrasts the just man with the wicked in a series of very suggestive comparisons, one of which is the *tree*. In the proverb emphasis is laid on the extraordinary depth of the human heart, which only God can fathom.

The source of the theme about a tree and its fruits is the ancient myth of the tree of life (Gn 2:9). However, Jewish tradition had modified this pagan myth by making fruitfulness depend on moral attitude (Gn 3:22). Wisdom literature was to make frequent use of the tree of life image, making it a figure of the moral life of man, where fruits of long life and happiness are produced (Pr 3:18; 11:30; 13:12; 15:4).

The prophetic tradition however was to apply the image to the entire people, according to the measure of fidelity to the Covenant (Is 5:1-7; Jr 2:21; Ez 15; 19:10-14; Ps 79/80:9-20). God destroys the tree that fails to bear good fruit.

Yet another strain of prophetic tradition would compare the King (and thus the Messiah too) to a tree (Jg 9:7-21; Du 4:7-9; Ez 31:8-9). It is a commonplace of all Eastern literatures, and had the advantage in this case of rendering the theme personal, indicating that the people as a whole might benefit by the life of a single individual. The central trunk is the life of the king, whence something is communicated to branches and foliage.

Applications of the image finally coalesce when the just man becomes the tree. Where other trees remain barren he bears luscious fruit (Ps 1; 91/92:13-14; Dt 2:1-3; Si 24:12-27). He must be watered by God; for Ezechiel (Ez 47:1-12) this fecundation is part of the eschatological future. Before planting his own tree which will bear eternal fruit, the cross, Christ firmly denounces the Tree of Israel which has borne no fruit (Mt 3:8-10; 21:18-19). John the Evangelist makes Christ himself the fruit-bearing tree (Jn 15:1-6) to which all of us, if we would bear good fruit, must be grafted.

The fruits we produce in these conditions are those "of the Holy Spirit" (Ga 5:5-26; 6:7-8, 15-16), works that is that indicate the presence of new life. We are partners with the new Man.

And, finally, the tree of life will be reestablished in Paradise, surrounded for all eternity by fruit-bearing trees (Rv 2:7; 22:1-2, 14, 19).

VIII. Luke	Luke is our only source for the parable of
16:19-31	the rich man and Lazarus. As distinct from
Gospel	the other evangelists, he seems to have drawn
Thursday	on some source where there was considerable

preoccupation with problems of riches and poverty (Lk 6:30-35; 16:13-14; 19:1-9; Ac 5:1-11). However the parable itself at the time of its insertion in this context had undergone some changes in original emphasis.

That is the reason for the two distinct parts of the present narrative. In the first (vv. 19-26), the sole example of such a procedure in the parable literature of the gospels, one of the protagonists gets a name, Lazarus ("God enables"). This could be a Christian adaptation of an Egyptian story introduced to Palestine by Jews from Alexandria. The story that is of the different fates of the publican Bar-Majan and a poor scribe. The second part (vv. 27-31) is more original, but the point is a different one. Lazarus has a secondary role only; the main attention is centered on the five brothers of the rich man, who fail to be converted by the threat of the Day of Yahweh (cf. Mt 24:37-39).

a) What we have then in the first part is an application, as in the beatitudes, of the Jewish theory of the *reversal of situations* between poor and rich (Lk 6:20-26; cf. further Lk 12:16-21). The question is not whether the rich man was good or bad, or Lazarus good or bad. In the parable there is no interest in the moral quality of their lives; the main interest is the proximity of the Kingdom for a world that is sociologically determined. We are in fact seeing things with the eyes of the primitive Jerusalem community which is made up of poor people who have little sympathy with the rich (Ac 4:36-37; 5:1-16). For them, the rich were incapable of opting for the new life. They were too attached to life, to their property; the poor were more open, for them the Kingdom was accessible in some way.

Subsequently come the nuances. Matthew speaks of poverty "of spirit," and will not allow us, according to the beatitude, to take poverty in the purely sociological sense or richness in the purely economic. Thus the eschatological theme of reversing the two situations is a literary device that should be interpreted with caution. It must always be seen as a means of proclaiming the imminence of the last times.

b) The second part of the parable is heavily colored by the atmosphere of *eschatological expectation,* and reads remarkably like correction of overly sociological or materialistic details in the first. The matter at issue is not richness or poverty, but the irreligion and selfishness of men who cannot interpret the signs given by God. For them death means the end of existence (v. 28). Not even a proof of the resurrection of the body will convince them because they have lost the insight to perceive in their own very lives the signs of survival. Asking for signs is only a false pretext; man is not saved by apparitions and miracles, but by hearing the Word (Moses and the prophets).

There is no point in turning to this narrative for information about the pains of hell, about purgatory and the "intermediate state." And it would be wrong also to find here a categorical judgment about sociological poverty or riches. The purpose is to condemn selfishness and unbelief. The affirmation made is that the unbeliever, if he is unable to recognize the signs wrought by Jesus in life, will not be able to recognize such signs of survival as resurrection of the dead.

IX. Genesis
37:3-4, 12-
13a, 17b-28
1st reading
Friday

Though the principal source of this narrative is Elohist (vv. 6-10, 14, 18-20, 22), the Yahwist version of the facts is nevertheless faithfully reproduced. The opposition of the eleven brothers to Joseph is fostered in the first version by his dreams of glory; in the second the aggravating feature is Jacob's particular affection for him. For the Yahwist it is Jude who prevents his brothers from killing Joseph (vv. 25-28), advising them rather to sell him; the Elohist gives the credit for saving his young brother's life to Reuben (vv. 21-24).

There are many etiological features about the Joseph story. His dream for instance (vv. 6-10) serves to explain the predominance, for a period, of the tribe of Joseph over the other tribes. But, for all the light it throws on the vicissitudes of tribal history, the general lesson in the narrative is a doctrinal one. The tribes were learning from experience that glory is only achieved after *trial* has been successfully encountered. It is only the cross which leads to life. Joseph in fact sees the fulfillment of his dream of glory, but only after he has been betrayed by his brethren, after exile and prison.

X. Matthew   The primitive version of the parable about
21:33-43, 45-46 the laborers in the vineyard was apparently
Gospel   on a considerably simpler scale. By com-
Friday   paring the synoptic narratives with that of
    the apocryphal gospel of Thomas, we can
certainly determine the actual words of Jesus. It was subsequently that primitive Christians, anxious to elucidate Jewish history and the roots of Christology, "allegorized" the parable with details about Israel the vine, and the stone that was rejected.

a) The primitive version depicts for us the owner of a vineyard (v. 33) who by reason of absence is compelled to deal with the workers by using his servants or his son as intermediaries. This corresponds to the economic situation just then, the land being divided into huge estates, of which the owners were, for the most part, foreigners. Peasants in Gallilee and Judaea who rented the estates, influenced as they were by zealot propaganda, felt extremely hostile towards the owners.

Thus killing the heir was a way of getting possession of the land because according to law vacant land fell to the first occupant. But the workers in the parable miscalculate: the owner will return to claim his property and will entrust it to others (v. 41).

What was the purpose of Jesus when he told this parable? Without doubt, so far as the zealots are concerned, he is withholding any sort of endorsement. If there is injustice in the world, the kingdom of God is not destined to come by means of hate and violence, but rather through death and ressurection. But, besides the zealots, he is addressing himself as well to the leaders of the people (Mk 11:27) who were so ready to see themselves as "keepers of the vineyard." He is letting them know that they have not proved equal to the task, that the land will be given to others, in particular to the poor (cf. Mt 5:4). He has often affirmed that the Good News, if not accepted by the leaders and the notables, will be directly communicated to the little ones and the *poor* (Lk 14:16-24; Mk 12:41-44).

b) The primitive Church was quick to allegorize the parable. To verse 33 was added an allusion to Isaiah 5:1-5, and another to 2 Chronicles 24:20-22. The idea was to attach to the story the *history of Israel as vine.* Israel constantly rejected the prophets; it rejected the Messiah (this was the meaning given to "Son" in verse 6; cf. Ps 2:7; Mk 1:11; 9:7). Then the prerogatives of the leaders, the keepers of the vineyard, are accorded not to the poor (as in the version of Jesus) but to the apostles.

c) Then Matthew, in turn, changes the primitive version of Jesus (which probably finished with verse 39) into an allegory designed to explain the reasons for the *death of Christ* and the repercussions it had. He achieves his object mainly by introducing Psalm 117/118:22-23. The citation is apt because, a few hours previously, this was the precise psalm used by the crowd to acclaim Christ (vv. 25-26 are quoted in Mt 21:1-10). What he is doing is pointing the lesson that Christ's glory is the result of suffering and death. Psalm 117/118 was indeed considered messianic by the primitive community (cf. Ac 4:11; 2:33; Mt 21:9; 23:39; Lk 13:35; Jn 12:13; He 13:16). For this reason it becomes possible to give "Son" in verse 37 the messianic significance it so often has elsewhere (Ps 2).

Thus Matthew is explaining Christ's death by pointing out that the messianic prophecies foretold it. He is also stressing the repercussion, the building of a new kingdom. The stone that was rejected becomes the cornerstone of the definitive temple. For Matthew the themes of the rejected stone and death outside the city (v. 39, cf. He 13:12-13) are combined with an ecclesiological motive. He wants to show that the new vineyard keepers, the new people, have the backing of a new sacrifice.

It is only when man fails to put it in its proper context in the creaturely condition that death acquires strength. If we refuse to face it, it begins to do its work; the way to spiritual pride is opened up. If, after the example of Jesus, we confront it, its power is held in check, no longer does it have the last word in human existence. True, it does not disappear; but man becomes capable not only of loosening its grip, but of making it the springboard of a new existence, just because he accepts it in loving obedience. The stone that was rejected becomes the corner stone.

The Christian realizes that the power of death is due to man himself. He will not place it in its proper context. He attempts to divinize himself, just as if death were not there. He leans altogether on the security he finds in individual and collective living.

The members of Christ's body, when they meet death as he met it, do not make it disappear: they contain its power. They proclaim that despite appearances it is not the last word. As Christians they share, here below, the true life of the Risen Lord; and this is a life which rejects by its nature the slightest contact with death.

When death in its various forms strikes, we recognize and accept that, but our faith is the bulwark against its power. Day after day we are summoned to mortify ourselves, to make actual in our lives the death of Christ. In Saint Paul's phrase we are "dead," but always "returning" from death in reality, because it is now bereft of its power. Our life is "hidden with Christ in God." Under faith, Christian mortification can be a source of veritable life. In the eucharistic celebration each believer is given an opportunity of proclaiming Christ's victory over death and making this his own. He is summoned to a deeper awareness of the signs of death in his own life and throughout the world.

XI. Micah
7:14-15, 18-20
1st reading
Saturday

The book of Micah concludes with a series of tests that probably date from the return from exile (Mi 7:8-10). Today's passage is a psalm-type prayer addressed to God who pardons the faults of his people.

From its beginnings the Yahwist religion was one of fidelity to the Sinai covenant: fidelity on man's part, manifested by scrupulous observance of the Law; fidelity on the part of God who bestows the blessings promised to those who avoid all transgression.

Man had very soon proved inadequate, nor was the situation redressed by rites and ablutions. He had to confess himself incapable of the fidelity required. The exile was sufficient to convince the most hardy and self-confident.

God showed his anger with the sinner, and expelled the unfaithful spouse: sin was something so grave that it had to be dealt with seriously. But, though far from being indifferent to sin, God remains faithful to the covenant and does not cease to love his people. For the Jews the most important insight during the exile was this realization. God was still faithful and funda-mentally benevolent. His fidelity is now seen in terms of mercy, pardon and grace (v. 18). So the leit-motif of our psalm today becomes the enduring love of God for a people that proved unfaithful (cf. Ex 34:6-7; Jl 2:13; Ps 50/51:3; 102/103:

8-14; Lk 7:36-50; 15:1-31). The words grace and fidelity, pity and pardon are in fact interchangeable.

Men today do not like to speak of God's mercy. The word is too suggestive of sentimental paternalism; but, more important, an impression is given of religious alienation. Is it not a way of escaping conscience when we rush to the arms of a merciful God whose pardon is limitless?

But in fact the mercy of God is a challenge to conversion and return: its effect is to make the recipient in turn merciful (Lk 6:36). There is nothing alienating here; rather a summons to precise responsibilities.

XII. Luke 15:1-3   Commentary on this gospel will be found on
11-32   p. 177, the gospel for the fourth Sunday of
Gospel   Lent, third cycle.
Saturday

THIRD SUNDAY OF LENT

A. THE WORD

I. Exodus
24:12, 15-18
1st reading
1st cycle

The ascent of Sinai is an important scriptural theme which the successive traditions have described according to their particular fashion. Old Elohist sources (Ex 24:12-15 and 18b) recount the events, making the tables of the law the focus of interest, and the length of Moses' sojourn on Sinai (forty days). Another tradition of prophetic origin which appears in 1 Kings 19:3-8 features, with Moses, Elias the prophet, indicating thereby that prophecy, equally with the law, springs from the covenant. Yet a third tradition, priestly this time (Ex 24:16-18), is found in today's reading. The theme of the law is actually ignored in order to emphasize themes like the cloud of glory and the sabbath (seventh day). Sinai takes on the essential lineaments of the sabbatical liturgy in the temple, where the presence of God would be symbolized by the cloud and the glory (1 K 8:10-12; Is 6:4-6; Ez 10:3-22; 2 M 2:8).

It is quite likely that the *cloud* motif begins with the passage of the Red sea. There could have been meteorological disturbances during some sort of storm which cut off the Israelites from their pursuers (Ex 14:19-31). Similar phenomena might have signalized the conclusion of the alliance on Sinai (Ex 19:16-20). Both experiences would have reinforced the impression that the cloud was a sign of God's presence.

In the temple the priests made a ritual of this. The cloud would be represented by the incense smoke made iridescent by sunlight pouring through apertures in the wall; and so the temple became the place of God's presence. The whole cultic procedure was then reciprocally associated with the original Sinai event, and it too took on a liturgical character.

b) There was always an interval of *delay* before the approach of God. The old Elohist account reckoned forty days, the priestly tradition the length of one week (cf. Gn 1). These two intervals, above all the one of forty days, precede all the great theophanies. A deluge of forty days ushers in the first cosmic alliance (Gn 7-9) as man's creation is prepared for by seven days (Gn 1). The theophany of Sinai is preceded by Moses' fast of forty days, or his wait of one week, depending on the tradition followed (vv. 16 and 18). So too it takes forty days for Elias to accomplish his journey to Horeb (1 K 19:8). In turn the evangelists will use these measures of time to describe Christ's preparation for his ministry: the sojourn of "forty days" in the desert (Mt 4), or the inaugural "week" (Jn 1:19-2:1). Thus man does not immediately step towards God. Before faith reaches sufficient maturity there must be a time of trial and purification. Interiorization must be continuous, conversion more and more lucid.

For Israel, in this regard, there was that remarkable period in the desert, forty years, which prepared her for the promised land. But this progressive deepening of faith is never uniform in all instances. Man being what he is, stress will be required now on one aspect of the pilgrimage, now on another. For believers now Lent is precisely this waiting time, the time to consider seriously the sort of adjustment that has become necessary for the progress of our faith.

II. Exodus
20:1-17
1st reading
2nd cycle

We have two versions of the decalogue. The first (Dt 5) comes from Josias' reform; the second (Ex 20) goes back to primitive Yahwist and Elohist sources; but it has been reworked by the priestly tradition, not to mention subsequent reformulations like that of Ezechiel 18:5-9 and Psalm 14/15.

It belongs to a very distinctive literary genre: the apodictic. A precept is formulated in the second person (you shall not kill) and forms part of a series of such precepts, grouped in tens or twelves with an established rhythm of phrase. The genre differs from the usual juridical style of the East, where it is customary to phrase conditionally in the third person (if a man kills . . . he shall be . . . ; quite a common formula in Israel).

The apodictic precept is proclaimed absolutely, proposing the decision of someone (God or legislator) which is not open to discussion. So absolute is it that there is no question of sanctions, particular cases, exceptions, or consequences as is the case with the other sort of formula.

a) Because the form is apodictic, both in Deuteronomy 5 and in Exodus 20, the decalogue is easily presented as the Word of God (cf. Ex 20:2; Dt 5:6), even though the probability is that the manner of linking the precepts with a formula for God (I am Yahweh) is relatively late. In certain treaties between suzerain and underling in the ancient East a decision is proclaimed in similar fashion. The Hittites for example had a formula for their oath of allegiance which the Jewish decalogue had only to copy:

(1) Preamble, with mention of the suzerain (Ex 20:2 and Dt 5:6).

(2) Preliminary statement about the historical circumstances entitling the suzerain to impose his will on the underling (Ex 20:2 and Dt 5:2-4).

(3) Proclamation of the principle of absolute loyalty for the underling, with a prohibition about any contacts with foreign powers (Ex 20:3-6 and Dt 5:7-9).

(4) Particular dispositions about goods, frontiers, military assistance, tribute, etc., in a word, all secondary obligations (Ex 20:8-17 and Dt 5:12-21).

(5) An injunction about placing the text of the treaty in the temple and reading it regularly (Dt 5:22b).

(6) A formula of malediction and blessing (Jos 24:35 and
    Dt 27).

Consequently the decalogue places the Jewish people in the
position of an underling nation towards its suzerain; the treaty
of *alliance* is the exclusive decision of the latter. This is something far more than a proclamation of a simple natural law.
Jewish faith is not just an elaboration of some sort of universal
ethic. The decalogue for this people is the means of interpreting
the personal will of God in order to live in union with him.
Even though most of the precepts are found in the laws of
contemporary peoples, what makes it a religious code challenging the faith of its observers is the manner of formulation.

b) It is conceivable too that the origin of the apodictic
formula is to be traced to the exercise of authority in the family
and clan. Here too the elder or father, who were guardians of
the child (as in the wisdom books: Pr 22:17-24, 22) gave
absolute precepts. Thus the people at Sinai would have been
substituting a higher authority for the elder of the clan, Yahweh
himself that is, father of all the clans. He begins by declaring
his decision, as the *father of the family* did hitherto. He adopts
the father's apodictic formula (you . . .) and reserves to himself
the power of life and death which the father had before.

c) In the course of history the text of the *decalogue* was
undoubtedly reworked. The 6th, 7th and 8th commandments,
so brief in phrasing, lead us to suppose that all the others were
originally brief too. Likewise we may suppose that originally
all the formulas were negative (only the 4th and 5th are
exceptions, at least to some extent, as we have them now; but
their negative form is known in Exodus 35:3; Leviticus 22:3b;
Exodus 21:15; Leviticus 20:9). Conjecturally, the primitive
decalogue might be restored thus:

You shall not have other gods before you

You shall not make sculpted images

You shall not take the name of Yahweh in vain

The seventh day being the sabbath, you shall not perform works

You shall not "dishonor" your father or your mother
You shall not kill
You shall not commit adultery
You shall not steal
You shall not give false witness against your neighbor
You shall not covet your neighbor's house

The killing contemplated in the 6th commandment is killing outside the community or legal framework. Adultery (7th commandment) includes all sexual acts which violate the marriage of another. Using the name of God (3rd commandment) alludes of course to the sort of magic mentioned in Exodus 20, and to the false oaths of Deuteronomy 5.

It is above all the form of the decalogue that is important, not only its content. The content does suggest a natural law, a simple ethical structure; but the form is personal — the expression of a will. Such too is the basis of Christian moral doctrine. It is God's commandment which lies at the root of Christian moral behavior; because our behavior can be governed by ten commandments or by the single commandment of love. We may use the law or use our conscience. The lesson is that our moral standards can never be delimited by general ethics or by a philosophic concept of God.

They do of course correspond to natural ethics and include them; but the standards are set in the deep recesses of the Christian person, the one who lives in communion with the God who was revealed in Jesus Christ.

God's commandment is always a word addressed by a person to a person. It is only under a regime of covenant and communion that it becomes livable. All the vicissitudes of life are contemplated, not analytically or casuistically. They are contemplated globally, as the source from which true fulfillment can spring.

III. Exodus Doubtless, at the royal school of administra-
3:1-8a, 13-15 tion in Egypt, Moses had received the sort
1st reading of training that fitted him for a position of
3rd cycle leadership among the Jews (Ex 2:11-15).
His early experiments however in leadership
had proved unsuccessful. He had to flee Pharaoh's vengeance
precipitously for having slain one of his agents, and he had to
flee the hatred of the Jews, who did not recognize the authority
of Pharaoh's functionaries even when they were, like Moses,
Jewish (Ex 2:14). Subsequently we find him in the Sinai desert
with the tribe of Madian, the daughter of whose chief he weds.
The religious and legal training there was probably according
to ancestral nomad tradition. It is even conceivable that, with
Jethro, he actually found the name of the God of his own
ancestors, together with certain rites like circumcision (Ex 4:24-
26). This experience must have proved highly important. His
previous juridical and administrative experience in Egypt was
now being reinforced by association with a social structure
and ethos more related to the nomad life he was destined to
share with his own people.

a) From these early developments in the life of Moses, came
a highly crucial religious experience. As he tends the flocks of
his father-in-law, at a stage doubtless when he was still imper-
fectly acquainted with Madianite religious customs, and unaware
of where the sanctuaries were located, he inadvertently stumbles
upon one of these latter. It was beside Horeb (where he was
destined to return one day in order to seal the covenant — such
premonitions are dear to the narrator), and he may have been
sheltering in a storm. The enclosure surrounded a sacred tree
that is suddenly blasted by lightening (vv. 2-3).

As he meditates on these mysterious events he realizes that
the ancestral God of Madian is also the *God of the promise*
(v. 6).

His reflections open his eyes to the misery of his people's lot in Egypt, and convinces him that if he prolongs his sojourn far from his own he will be making a liar of Yahweh. The certainty grows in his mind that Yahweh is about to succor the descendants of those to whom he promised a country and a numberless progeny (vv. 7-8).

The encounter with God is real. But the presence of God is more actual in Moses' heart as he ponders the meaning of the things he sees than in the burning bush.

b) No envoy had a chance of being accepted unless he gave the *name* of the author of his mission (v. 13). The name Moses reveals to his brethren is that of Yhwh — Yahweh (v. 15), perhaps the name of some of the contemporary pantheon, worshiped on Sinai under the form of a bull, whose bellowing resounded among the rocks like the voice of God's thunder. The main thing is that it is the half-forgotten God of the patriarchs and the promises who is meant.

The text however gives a new derivation to the name "Yahweh," in order to convince the people that this is a totally-other God, who cannot be likened to others: "I am who am" (v. 14). There is no question of a metaphysical definition of God's nature, but of double affirmation: evasive to begin with: God, that is, is beyond all naming and cannot be contained in a name, but then a historical affirmation too, so that a better rendering might be "I shall be what I shall be." That is to say — you will know me by what I shall do for you: "it is history which will reveal me."

Accordingly the name safeguards God's mystery and transcendence, but reveals at the same time his imminence in Israel's history and Moses' mission.

Modern man gets no further in naming God than Moses did. Indeed he may be coming to feel again how futile are the efforts of myth and metaphysics to find a meaningful title. God is not to be at the mercy of mythmakers, of the ups and downs of metaphysics. We must always realize that it is only in the human condition he can be recognized, particularly now when the goal of that condition and its key are made manifest in Jesus Christ.

IV. Romans   In the hands of exegetes chapter 5 of the
5:1-2, 5-8   letter to the Romans becomes either the
2nd reading   *finale* of the first four chapters or the intro-
1st cycle   duction to the following ones. Our space is
perhaps too limited for making choices. The chapter does indeed prolong, and carry a stage further, the preceding material, while indicating at the same time what follows. The first eleven verses, of which we have a sample in our reading, give us the trend of Paul's thinking. As he considers our present experience (vv. 1-2), peace, grace and hope, he finds there two signs of God's eternal love (vv. 3-8): the indwelling in us of the Spirit, and the death for our sake of the Lord Jesus. Following this meditation he goes on to describe future salvation (vv. 9-11).

a) His first affirmation is that of our *justification* by faith (v. 1). He uses the aorist tense, as of an event already accomplished the results of which one continues to experience. In the earlier portion of his letter the idea of justification was central to his whole discussion. There he saw the most decisive initiative on the part of God for human destiny. But with verse 1 he passes from a consideration of the topic that is outside time (its principles: Rm 3:21-26; its universality: Rm 3:27-4:25) to the concrete assertion of its actual realization in us now, since Jesus Christ.

For the Jews however justification had to do with the eschatological future, it was something which demanded a future tense. When he uses the aorist Paul is demonstrating the vast difference between faith in the Christian sense and in the Jewish. Justification is not now a matter of hope: it is an accomplished fact, a living reality which kindles a new hope, undreamt of by Israel. There is no point now in looking to the future for a solution to actual difficulties. They can be settled at once.

b) Among the actual fruits of justification acquired in Christ he mentions *peace* and *grace* (v. 2a). Peace replaces the era of enmity towards God and among one another that engulf mankind, both pagan and Jewish, before the advent of Christ (of the somber picture presented by the first chapters of the letter). Grace is the counterpart of divine anger (Rm 1:18-3:20): it enables those who had gone astray to live in God's friendship.

One of the leitmotifs of the whole letter is peace between Jews and Gentiles. Everything indeed leads us to think that just now there were in fact two distinct churches at Rome: the Judaeo-Christian, made up of original Jewish refugees from persecution, and one of Greek or Roman provenance. They must have been completely separated (the letter to the Romans is the only one indeed not to be addressed to "the Church of Rome").

So the object of the letter is clear: the two churches should become one. Jews and Gentiles should remember that they are both sinners (chap. 1-4), both gratuitously reconciled to God by Christ (chap. 5 and following). They do not need to await their peace: they should begin to live it.

c) But our enjoyment of the blessings here and now arising from justification is really eclipsed by hope. The emphasis of verse 5 suggests that faith itself is eclipsed by hope, so eschatological is the view Paul takes of faith and justification. The faith within us, an act of God, amounts to certitude of glory.

d) And yet this hope of glory throws into sharp focus the distance between the Christian's condition here and now in the world and the glory of which he awaits the manifestation. It was normal for Jews to see this gap between the states as a time of *trials* and persecutions that prepared the way to the new state. Deep down is the realization that transcendence can only be achieved by painful purification. The trials of this life, when one attempts to live by an elevated ideal, can seem to jeopardize the very existence of one's faith in the ideal; and the virtue of constancy will be needed to sustain it (v. 3). When the firmness of our faith is challenged by the sheer tedium of time, "perseverance" comes to the rescue of hope and carries it through to the end (v. 4). Simple virtues like constancy and firmness will avail us little, however, if the Spirit of God himself does not dwell in us to nourish our faith, if we are not joined in indissoluable union with the Father by the love of God (v. 5).

Roman Christians are split into two separate churches who cannot find peace with one another. Doubtless tension was increased by putting off reconciliation until doomsday, when the justice of God would be accorded to men. Paul reacts against such an overly Jewish mentality. There is no point in waiting for the justice of God and the peace ought to have been sought already and be now a living reality. Peace consists in the awareness on both sides that all have been justified in Jesus.

We have still Roman Christians among us. We too are inclined to postpone until doomsday reconciliations that would inconvenience us now. We pray for instance for unity among Christians, forgetting that the gift of unity is already ours. Our business is to make it actual, not to keep postponing it or making it the business exclusively of God. The same holds for peace generally among men and among nations. It ought to be worked for in the same spirit. Hope does not mean delivery from the obligations of the present.

V. 1 Corinthians
1:22-25
2nd reading
1st cycle

Paul is convinced that the factions in Corinth are due to a misguided enthusiasm for philosophy, for reducing the gospel message to systems of human thought. Our passage today contrasts the pretensions of such human wisdom with the wisdom of God's plan, and points out how inadequate is the former when we are dealing with the history of faith. To understand the passage properly one should begin with verse 18.

Here we find the basic proposition. In terms of human wisdom the language of the cross is *folly*, but this is the only language that can lead towards faith and thus salvation. He supports this affirmation with a series of arguments.

An argument from scripture to begin with. The quotation (v. 19) from Isaiah 29:14 reminds us that Yahweh saved Jerusalem by his own power, irrespective of any considerations about national or public interest.

Next, a challenging observation. In fact the sages, the learned and the scribes have not been converted. There are very few such in the Church (v. 20; cf. 1 Co 1:26), which indicates that their wisdom is not aligned to that of God.

The final argument is a diatribe (v. 21). Originally God had so disposed things that man could recognize him in creation, which was a product of his wisdom. But man had so far abused this as to turn it from its object (cf. Rm 1:19-20). Consequently he was forced to communicate in terms that lay outside the vocabulary of human wisdom, by means of the cross that is. It is folly precisely because it brings its message in a manner that transcends philosophic thought and definitions. To Jews who sought God in miracles (Mt 12:38-40) and Greeks who believed they could define him by philosophy, Paul points out that he is only accessible through the gospel of the cross (vv. 22-24). There what the Jew will find is a suffering Messiah, a being whose passage to his throne is through the way of death: the pagan will find a religious leader indistinguishable, on the cross, from a common brigand.

The order of faith differs from the order of reason. We can have a reasoned faith of course, or at any rate a reasonable one; but the appeal of faith to man is on levels other than that of intellect. People's real trouble, especially the average products of Western civilization, is that they have been formed in a Cartesian and conceptual framework that is difficult to shed. Consequently, when they are told that faculties other than reason are in question, they don't seem to comprehend. Part of their capacity for love and trust has been strangled; the transcendent is a closed book to them. In this atheist twentieth century the message of Paul is needed more than ever. The business of the Christian is to exhibit a better balance, to develop in himself those areas that seem, at a casual glance, less rational, foolish the apostle would say. Yet they are the source from which more balanced and more liberating human thrusts will spring.

VI. 1 Corinthians 10:1-6, 10-12 *2nd reading* *3rd cycle* Troubled with the problems that beset the eucharistic assembly in Corinth, Paul reminds his readers of chapters 13-17 in Exodus, and offers them some commentary. His discussion is based on an incontrovertible fact as he sees it: the continuity between the situation of the Israelites in the desert and the present state of the Corinthians. That is what he means by speaking of "our fathers" (v. 1) and about the "examples" for "us" (v. 6) to be found in their lives. The whole passage rests on this assumption.

a) His first point is about the *baptism* of the people into Moses by the sea and the cloud (vv. 1-2). We do not know of any Jewish tradition that drew a parallel between the baptismal rites known to Judaism and the Red Sea experience. The idea is exclusively Pauline. The sea reminds him of the baptismal water, the cloud of the Holy Spirit (possibly suggested to him by Is 63:11-14); and, obsessed as he was by the implications of Christian baptism, he sees in the relation between people and

Moses elements of the relation of the Christian to Christ. He thus introjects into the biblical episode involving Moses the role that Christ plays in the Christian sacramental economy. The crossing of the Red Sea, thanks to Moses, was already an initiation into Christ and the Spirit, because here they were already at work. Thus there is for him a structural unity between the original historical event and the sacrament that came to be.

b) The other points (vv. 3-4) concern the *manna* and the *water from the rock*. He speaks here in precisely the same way of "spiritual nourishment," "spiritual beverage," "the spiritual rock," because he sees a manifest reference to the Eucharist. In fact the manna and water were given to the people, like the Eucharist, by Christ ("the rock was Christ," v. 4). This Eucharistic insight (bread and wine = manna and water) about the desert miracles is altogether his own: Judaism had never made any such association. Numbers 20 and Isaiah 43:20 speak of water but not of manna, Wisdom 16:20-22 of manna but not of water: Psalms 77/78, 20 and 104/105:43-44 associate manna and meat, but have no allusion to water. The only text to conjoin the elements of manna and water is Deuteronomy 8:15-16, and here their order is reversed. It took experience of the Eucharist, the meal whereby the Lord nourishes his people, to bring about a realization that the happenings in the desert pointed already towards the person of Christ, that the sacramental economy casts a new ray of light on their meaning.

c) There is a final point (vv. 5-6), the *chastisement* of Israel in the desert. Here, likewise, Paul sees a figure of the punishment which threatens the Corinth community now. Of "all" the fathers "the majority" were chastised. That was because, all "sacramentalized" though they were, they yielded to covetousness (1 Co 10:7-10; cf. Mb 11:4-34; 13:32-33; 21:5-6; 25:1-5; Ex 32), the very thing with which Paul has to reproach the Corinthians. In the case of the fathers, the anticipated presence of Christ they experienced was insufficient to ward off the chastisement.

The conclusion follows. If our fathers were baptized because one day there would be a baptism in Christ, if they were spiritually nourished because one day there would be a Eucharist; and if despite these premonitions of sacraments to be they proved inadequate; the Corinthians like them will be punished, if they are guilty of similar murmuring (vv. 10-12).

Thus the sacraments are not magical rites; apart from the free cooperation of the recipient they do not assure salvation. There can be no question of automatic effect, everything depends on the encounter of two free agents. If we isolate the sacrament from the faith or performance of the recipient, we make the same mistake that was made in the desert and can anticipate a similar setback.

God's initiative in the salvation process should never be interpreted as automatic reassurance. Mere acceptance of his grace is not enough: he demands the response of faith, a lasting conversion which aligns us with him. The sacrament is more a beginning than an end in itself, some sort of insurance. It should foster in us the urge that leads towards the boundless horizons of love.

If Christian corpses are strewen along the path of humanity's pilgrimage now, as those of the Jews were (vv. 5-6), it is because many Christians receive the sacraments but fail to make these reverberate in their lives.

VII. John 4:5-42   Four separate strands of Jesus' teaching are
    Gospel   woven into the texture of this narrative. He
    1st cycle   is tired and asks his disciples for bread (v. 8).
                    When they bring it to him he makes them
realize that there is another kind of nourishment (vv. 31-34). Likewise he asks the Samaritan woman for water to quench his thirst (v. 7), and when she gives it to him he tells her about another kind of water (vv. 13-14). We have similar transposi-

tions when he turns from the mention of the Samaritan and Jewish material cult to speak of a cult in spirit and truth (vv. 20-24), and when he bids his disciples contemplate the material harvest to prepare themselves for the spiritual harvest (vv. 35-38).

It is wrong then to speak of a single theme in this passage: that of running water. It is criss-crossed with the themes of bread, cult and harvest. In fact the themes of bread and wine serve to illustrate the personality of Christ, his mysterious union with the Father (vv. 10, 26, 34), while those of cult and harvest indicate how the work of the Church transcends the bounds of Judaism. Her business is to gather into a spiritual cult, and harvest in the future kingdom, all men who are so disposed, beginning with the Samaritans (vv. 35b and 30).

a) The nomad patriarchs travelled from one watering place to another, and those among them who could drill the best wells for their families and stock achieved the greatest celebrity. Such were Abraham (Gn 26:12-22) and doubtless Jacob too, as the tradition mentioned in the gospel suggests (vv. 5 and 12). So it is that Jesus presents himself to the Samaritan woman as the new purveyor of a well of *living water*. This water however does not spring from the earth. It is a gift of heaven, to be found in Jesus, an eternal life (vv. 10, 14). He is very likely thinking of Amos 4:4-8; 8:11 (well symbolizing the word of God), Isaiah 12:1-4 (well representing the deliverance that God brings) and finally Jeremiah 17:6-8 (where the well of living water is the well of wisdom and of God's law).

However, without doubt John's thought goes further still and discerns in the well of living water the Spirit, of whom he is to speak explicitly later on (Jo 7:39). The Spirit has been linked to Christ's teaching throughout his earthly life, but was destined to be manifested above all in Christ's glorification, when he would build the new spiritual temple and send the apostles on their mission throughout the universe.

b) The purpose of the themes of water and bread in the

narrative is above all the revelation of the *personality of Jesus*. In the new world the only sacred place is to be his very person. The fourth gospel is the one most concerned with considerations about the person of Jesus (Jn 7:27; 19:9; 1:38; 13:36; 16:5; 8:14; 9:29). His fatigue (v. 6) and thirst (v. 7) demonstrate how real his humanity is; but at once there is a hint of transcendence too. That is because Jesus had integrated perfectly into his personality that deeper area of his being, which partook of the absolute and was in communion with the Father. He discovers too for each human being a way of plumbing his own personality (v. 14), because each human being is enabled, thanks to Christ, to find in himself this same area which partakes of the absolute and is in communion with the Father. This living water which Jesus gives is nothing external merely: by it a man is revealed to himself, discovers the mystery of his personality, the point of contact with the living water in himself (Jn 7:38). When Jesus gradually lets the Samaritan woman know who she is (vv. 17:19) the process of self-discovery, open to everyone, is as it were acted out in mime.

c) It is noteworthy that he speaks of living water only to a person whom he has asked to give a drink of real water to an enemy. He mentions eternal bread only to followers whom he has already sent looking for material bread to appease hunger and allay fatigue.

The lesson is that it is only those who seek bread and water for their brethren who gain insight into the personality of Christ. People who are not thoroughly *involved* in the profane cannot comprehend the mystery of Jesus. Where tasks like these are concerned, he is not an outside agent, detached: he is part and parcel of them.

d) There is some mysterious lack of comprehension (not necessarily in any pejorative sense however) where the revelation about the person of Jesus being the only sacral center is concerned. *Incommunicability* is very widespread in the human condition; and Jesus' acceptance of his human role resigns him to the fact that his person would be misunderstood just as human persons are misunderstood by one another. The mystery of Jesus is repeated in the world itself. It is composed of those who understand, who understand badly, and who do not understand at all. It is rather futile to inquire whether Christians are better than others in this respect. We have those who realize, and those who don't, particularly well; but all endure the same inability to communicate, of which God in the end will take account (Mt 25). That is the whole reason why both the Samaritan woman (v. 15) and the apostles (v. 32) fail to understand.

The link between water and the salvation event is at its highest intensity in Saint John. As he sees it union has been effected between the self of the man who is faithful to God, and God's anterior initiative in his regard. All that was ever attempted hitherto Christ brings to completion; on the profane level (water, bread) and on the historical level (water from the rock, manna, cult). He does so in order to set man free. And, transcending nature and history, the person of Christ becomes for mankind the only link with the sacred.

Linked to the Christ-event, water takes on sacramental dignity. In itself it is not a sacred thing. But it is a fundamental element of our world, which now, in Jesus Christ, is locked upon its course for the great return of all creation to God. Every Christian, baptized in Jesus Christ, is likewise carried forward by this sacred power.

The event which sets each one of us up as persons and as Christians has to do with water. And the living water which God gives us through Jesus Christ leads us to undreamed-of heights, where our person is fully realized by encounter with the absolute which animates us, and by communion with the life-giving Father.

VIII. John   By contrast with the synoptics, the temple
    2:13-25   cleansing narrative in John has a distinctive
    Gospel   quality. The doctrinal import is more stressed,
    2nd cycle   and above all the placing is different. He puts
the incident at the beginning of the public
life, something that could very well be the historical fact.

a) In the synoptic account we see Christ as prophet, anxious
to invoke the authority of other prophets (Mt 21:13) in proclaiming the real purpose of the temple. In John the significance
of the gesture is quite frankly messianic. Coming as it does
immediately after the reference to John the Baptist (Jn 1:19-34),
the cleansing indeed is like a fulfillment of Malachi 3:1-4. Again,
in John, Jesus does not cite any prophetic text, thus acting more
obviously by his own *authority*. And finally Jesus regards the
temple as "the house of his Father" (cf, previously, in Luke 2:49).

b) The second portion of John's narrative (vv. 18-20) is not
paralleled in the synoptics.

It begins by quoting Psalm 68/69, which has by now in the
primitive community a clear messianic meaning. Frequent use
was made of it for meditation on the passion (Ac 1:20; Rm
15:3; Mt 27:48; Jn 15:25; 19:28). In Christian eyes it was
Christ's "zeal" that cost him his life (Mt 26:61-63). And so
over his narrative at this point John sheds the clarification of
the *Lord's passion*.

There is yet another detail. Christ's words derive from an
ancient cliche of prophetic literature: "destroy-rebuild" (Jr 1:10;
18:7-10; 24:6; 42:10; 45:4) a motif very dear to Jeremiah. What
Jesus is affirming is that, as Messiah, envoy of God, he has the
power to destroy and rebuild the temple, even in three days,
because his power is not of this world.

c) A third portion (vv. 21-22) gives us the Christian interpretation of the episode. After the passion and resurrection it
was not only Psalm 68/69 that suddenly disclosed its meaning;
the point of Jesus' own statement became quite clear. Not only
is he a Messiah capable of "destroying and raising up again", he

is the Son of the Father, his rebuilding of the temple will be
of another order. The "three days" too take on a precise *paschal
meaning*, hitherto unsuspected. John goes on to observe, keeping
the doctrinal aspect in mind, that the incident took place as the
feast of the Pasch was approaching (Jn 2:15).

We have them in the Johannine account a priestly concept
of Christ's role that is absent in the synoptics. The new temple
is Christ's humanity, the new dwelling place of the Father, the
place of perfect sacrifice (He 9-10) and the source of abundant
blessings (Jn 7:37).

It might seem at first glance that Jesus does not see his
ministry in the tradition of Jeremiah 7. There is no question of
purifying an existing priesthood and temple; they must be replaced. Two affirmations are central to his preaching. The true
temple is his own person; and it is only by destruction and
being raised up again that it will fulfill that function. The
whole fourth gospel is structured with a view to verifying
these. At each feast Jesus goes up to the temple, but on each
occasion his attitude is that the object of the feast is being
accomplished in his person.

And yet there is a sense in which the substitution of Christ's
human person for the temple sanctuary is in accord with the
trend of ancient prophecy. It was their theme that the value
of sacrifice should be measured not by the dignity of rites and
their scrupulous performance, but by the inner sentiments of
the offerer.

It was with this mind that Jesus, in obedience, made a filial
and loving offering of his body so that he could take it up
again, in the plenitude of divinity, and by his Spirit communicate it to all men. It is with this mind that our eucharistic
offering today should join the filial act of Jesus to the faithful
love of believers.

In all then John's narrative of the temple cleansing conveys
a doctrinal lesson much deeper than the synoptic version. It is

not merely a matter of purifying the cult by restoring the central purpose, or of opening worship to the nations and to groups of people hitherto excluded. It is a matter of centering worship, in an altogether revolutionary way, about the Spirit "indwelling" in Christian man and thus giving all his attitudes and involvements the quality of divine sonship.

IX. Luke 13:1-9
Gospel
3rd cycle

To those who ask him for signs Christ answers that for people who can see and understand them there *are* signs. Death in fact is the clearest sign of all (vv. 1-4), one that can be read by all, one that is most efficacious in leading to conversion (vv. 3, 5). Conversion is a slow process because men are slow where their liberty is concerned; but God is patient and concedes the necessary time to people capable of penitence.

The signs of God that Christ indicates are both instances of premature and sudden death, the first in punitive action (v. 1) the second in an accident (v. 3). All had died unexpectedly . . . a similar fate might well have befallen others . . . (vv. 2, 4b). Death came like a thief, like the master of a house who unexpectedly comes home (Lk 12:35-40).

That is the way the judgment of God will come, unexpectedly, striking the one who least anticipates it.

The prominence of death in the proclamation of the Kingdom is sometimes rather surprising. Many people, irreligious as well as religious, are shocked by ecclesiastical complacency when the threat of death is brandished in order to bring about conversion. We hear talk of the poor creatures who are forced by fear of death to this decision, which can scarcely, it is alleged, with such unworthy motivation be a genuinely human one.

And yet in reality death is anything but a bugbear. On the

contrary it is the most compelling sort of "sign," which every man must at all costs read aright. When we are recommended by Christ to repent, it is not a matter of making a hasty preparation for entry to the other world. The conversion in question is that assent to death which is the most decisive test arising from the human condition. We consider every angle, and accept our lot.

B. THE WORD

1. The Theme of Living Water

Always hitherto water symbolism occupied a prominent place in the religious history of mankind. In Judaism and Christianity above all it was pervasive.

For modern man though water has become desacralized, on the surface anyhow; doubtless the fundamental symbolism where the old qualities persist has retreated to the subconscious. In general nowadays it is the profane signification that becomes obtrusive. Man today of course like his predecessor needs water, but it is a natural element of which he gradually gains more control. Is it possible under such conditions for water to retain its salvific significance? The symbolism we use in catechumenal and baptismal liturgy, is it not perhaps irrelevant for people?

The truth is that far from destroying the sacramental symbolism of water modern ideas about it ought in fact challenge us to deepen our Christian notions in this regard. The scriptural readings for this third Sunday of Lent can help us do so; because the themes of water and faith are closely interwoven.

The symbolism of water in Israel

Water is an essential element; man needs it to live. Not only that, but if it is not supplied according to some established order basic security is jeopardized. All nomads know that without wells the desert is uninhabitable; all agricultural communities that fertility is regulated by the seasonal rhythm of floods and rains. The quantity is important also, not too much water and not too little. But it is an element outside his control; his labor cannot produce it and the forces governing its supply are beyond him. Small wonder then that men naturally saw it as a gift of the gods, and saw the creation of the world itself in terms of functional disposition of the waters.

Under the regime of faith Israel recognized God's absolute mastery over the waters. He imposed a precise law upon them in creating the world (consider the biblical cosmogony, with the "waters above" restrained by the firmament, and the "waters below" on which rests the flat disc of the earth and from which come wells and rivers). Nevertheless he retains the power of withholding or releasing the waters as he wishes, and can cause drought or flooding.

He is master of the universe, and he is master of Israel's history. In the desert he makes a covenant with his people, choosing this terrain of insecurity in order to put Israel's faith to the test. When the unbelieving people grow thirsty, at the instance of Moses and Aaron, themselves not quite believing, he gratuitously gives them water from the rock. And so the theme of water is forever part of salvation history, linked as it is with the historical event that more than any other claimed Jewish attention.

Water is granted or withheld by Yahweh in accord with the behavior of his people. If they are faithful water comes as the source of life and fruitfulness. But if Yahweh brings drought or gives rein to devastating floods, where water, far from being a divine blessing, becomes the sign of malediction.

With the gradual interiorization of faith, awareness grows on the part of Jewish man that the water he so needs is not alone material water, but the water that cleanses the heart. Without the latter God cannot be approached.

Because infidelity continued to manifest itself, more and more, attention turned towards the eschatological future. With the definitive advent of salvation purifying and vivifying water would flow abundantly. In that new exodus of which the exiles in Babylon used to dream the desert prodigy would be repeated with such splendor that the desert itself would be transformed into a verdant paradise. The Jerusalem of the future would have inexhaustible water, a stream issuing from the temple. Paradise would be regained, fruitfulness beyond all telling. Nor were these imaginings altogether material; they indicate a profound change of heart, hearts that were now watered by the Spirit, by God's Word and his Wisdom.

Christ, the dispenser of living water

The association between water and the salvation-event reaches its greatest intensity in the New Testament. Just because it stemmed from the man-God, Christ's fidelity to God matched the initiative of God in regard to man. In his person he fulfilled the messianic hopes. He is the rock from whose side water gushes, the Temple from which the stream issues to make fertile the new Jerusalem; he is the living water that assuages thirst for all eternity. And the water that Christ gives is none other than the Spirit.

Thus linked with the Christ-event, the sacramental character of water becomes manifest. In itself it is not sacred; it is a basic element of our universe. But that universe is now, in Jesus Christ, locked firmly upon the course of great return by all creation to God.

When talking with the Samaritan woman Jesus leans with growing emphasis on the theme of faith. Yet the initial exchange about water from the well of Jacob is more than a simple strategem to lead the woman towards exchange on a higher level. As he guides this sinner towards clear insights about adoration of the Father in spirit and in truth, he also leads her to regard all things, including the water she draws from the well, with the eyes of a child of God. Man needs water to live; but God's crowning gift to man leads him to heights of infinitely greater dimension. When man receives this greater gift in faith, it means that his structure of values is radically transformed. His thirst becomes thirst for the Kingdom, and he realizes that all other things will be given to him in abundance. When she has recognized the Messiah, the Samaritan woman leaves her pitcher there and runs to the city to tell people what Jesus said to her. John's account goes on to inform us that Jesus, despite his disciples' insistence, refused earthly nourishment in order to demonstrate that his real nourishment was doing the will of him who sent him.

Water symbolism in the Church

The Church is the new Jerusalem as we see it here below. Its members have been wrested from sin. They form the temple of the Spirit and can adore the Father in spirit and in truth. They bear witness to the fact that the material universe is embarked upon its course of great return to God: that its real destiny can only be found in the ecclesial pilgrimage.

In the Church, material creation becomes the area of that dialogue which always, from all eternity, it is the will of God that he should hold with men. Under the aegis of the Church material creation is God's gift; it kindles faith. And, seen with the eyes of faith, it depends altogether on Jesus Christ, in whom all things are to be recapitulated. United with their head, the members of his Body have the duty to pursue his great task of "consecrating" the world. The task is not separable from that of humanizing the world; indeed this latter project is of its essence.

Of all the natural elements water, in the Church has particular dignity because of its integral part in the sacrament of baptism. There where it is linked with the Word, and indeed with salvation history, its deeper significance is emphasized. It is cleansing: baptism is the bath which washes away man's sins by virtue of Christ's redemptive blood. But in our world too water is also ominous, a symbol of death; because sin is still with us. When the neophyte enters the waters and emerges from them what is signified is the theme developed by Saint Paul, his burial with Christ and his resurrection.

Water as a sign in missionary witness

The gospel narrative of Jesus' encounter with the Samaritan woman is concluded by a direct allusion to mission and to the conversion of the Samaritans. This is by no means accidental.

For Jesus the water from Jacob's well was the means leading to a gradual revelation of the new religion in all its perfection and novelty. Henceforth adoration of the Father in spirit and truth is not confined to any one particular center. In missionary activity this universalism finds its natural expression.

But it would be wrong to think that the only lesson to be derived from such universalism is the vocation of all men to practice the new religion. There is more. Jesus means to convey that his work has to do with the entire universe, including the material universe. In him it reaches proper stature; in him it is restored. If one bears witness to his resurrection, one is pointing simultaneously to the signs of its restoration.

It is consequently of great importance for mission that the relation between Christians and all creation should be a lived relation, one deepened by faith. That action of the Spirit, whereby from the stuff of this world the new world is shaped, is not separable from his action in man's hearts. Mingled with the praises of humanity is the praise of all creation; the glory of God is celebrated by creatures and men in unison. Faith in Jesus Christ has adjusted man to his creatural condition, and his thanksgiving will be the more perfect the more he exerts himself in furthering the cause of humanity. The sign of the restoration of all things in Christ is a world more in conformity with man's dignity, a world seasoned with the salt of the gospel.

Eucharistic celebration of creatural praise

The eucharistic celebration, just because it is, in Jesus Christ, mankind's thanksgiving *par excellence,* is also the praise rendered by all creation. Various domains of sacred art express this cosmic dimension of Christian liturgy. A church is more than a mere center for worship; it should give some foretaste of a world transformed in the risen Christ. The hymn of all creatures, mingling their voices with that of the paschal lamb, should be heard there. The true purpose of material creation is indicated in this consecrated structure, made of stories, because it too has passed from death to life. But it acquires this meaning only through relation to the glorified body of the Lord. Space or time cannot be sacred of themselves; the sacral is inherent, not in things, but exclusively in Christ's humanity. This is the source of all consecration. So, in this church of stone everything should point towards the altar, where the eucharistic sacrifice is consummated. It is precisely here that Christ comes among his own, to give meaning to their spiritual sacrifice, and to augment their power of consecrating the universe.

Ideally speaking, the Christian should never enter or leave a church without being conscious of the fundamental tension between creation already transformed, and that creation, in its birthpangs, which yet awaits redemption. He carries this awareness into the texture of daily living, and, when it is constantly nourished by the eucharist, he is enabled to be fully faithful to his vocation as child of God.

2. Fasting: Auxiliary Theme for Lent

Fasting, whether it be fasting in the collective sense or that of private devotion, is no longer fashionable in the West. Even Lenten fast that is, though that means no more than restricting one's food to the necessary quantity. There is no question of fasting till sundown from all food and drink. People are ready enough to see the need for moderation, but fast in the strict sense is thought to be bad for health; there is little understanding of its spiritual usefulness.

Has not the Church too perhaps adapted herself to this trend? Collective Lenten fast amounts to very little nowadays. And as for eucharistic fast, which until recently was the only complete fast, it too has over the past few years been so modified that it is liable to lose all meaning for the vast majority of people.

On the other hand, in Germany and several other countries, the custom of "Lents of sharing" has been recently proving popular among Christians. There is a regular Lenten renaissance.

The connection between privation and almsgiving (under new collective forms, which answer special contemporary needs) seems to be naturally understood as an implication of Christian faith.

In any case the celebration of Lent continues to be, for all of us, an occasion for reflecting about the Christian significance of fast. Does the deprivation of nourishment in itself have any meaning? Or is it perhaps something of itself very marginal which can be fitted into the organic structure of Christian life?

The practical meaning of fast in Israel

In most traditional religions fasting has been of great importance. The reasons for it were various: ascetic belief, ritual purification, mourning, supplication. Sometimes indeed a form of Manichaean dualism gave impetus to the practice. Food was avoided as far as possible, because matter rejoined one to the evil Principle, any contact with which invariably meant pollution. To this very day such an important religious tradition as the Islamic lays particular stress on the Ramadan fast as a means of insight into divine transcendence.

For the Jews, as for their neighbors, fasting was an essential act of religion. The regime of faith however brought about an interiorization which tended to modify ideas about fast. To begin with there is no trace of Manichaeism in Israel. The Jew saw food and drink as a gift of the unique God, whose goodness is manifested in all creation, material as well as spiritual. No longer was fasting regarded as an ascetic practice or a preliminary to some sort of mystic exaltation. Only in the order of faith could it have meaning, as a demonstration of dependence or total abandon before Yahweh, so that one might prove more receptive to his action. It is an important preliminary to encounter with the living God, as the desert fasts of Moses or Elias indicate.

There were numerous occasions of collective or individual fast, with concomitant risks of perversion in fasting theory. Purely formal practices were constantly denounced by the prophets. If fasting were necessary, it could only be for love of God and one's brothers. Genuine fasting could not be divorced from prayer and almsgiving. The only thing pleasing to Yahweh is the search for "justice": if fasting does not improve authentic relations between God and man it is useless.

Jesus' attitude to fasting

In the sermon on the mount, the theme of fasting is closely linked with the new law of universal love and revelation about true prayer to the Father, Jesus is in the prophetic tradition, but his insights about interiority are still deeper. He warns about fasting that could prove the occasion for pride or ostentation. "But you, when you fast, put oil on your head and wash your face so that no one will know you are fasting except your Father" (Mt 6:17-18). For him fasting had to be an expression of abandon to the Father, and of hope in Him, a demonstration of religion in spirit and in truth.

But Christ's teaching about fast goes further than this. On the one hand we know that before the beginning of his public life he went to the desert and fasted for forty days, as Moses and Elias did before him. On the other hand during his public ministry he seemed very liberal about fasting, for his disciples, and where he himself was concerned. When criticized by the Pharisees his answer was: "Surely the Bridegroom's attendants would never think of fasting while the Bridegroom is still with them? But the time will come for the Bridegroom to be taken away from them, and then, on that day, they will fast" (Mk 2:19-20). How are we to reconcile these two apparently contradictory attitudes?

In fast Jesus' attitude is a simple demonstration of the close link, in the Christian view, between time and eschatology. His sojourn in the desert and his fast is a kind of replica of humanity's long preparation for the coming of the Messiah and the inauguration of the Kingdom. Fast is related to the time of waiting. After the public ministry has begun, he can say with good reason that the Kingdom is already here. The Bridegroom has come, and it is not fitting that the friends of the Bridegroom fast while he is with them; in the time of accomplishment fast has no more meaning. Once Christ is risen, fasting will only be appropriate in so far as it marks the road of faith, the dimension of preparation and construction in the Christian life.

The meaning of fast in the Church

In the Church we find the very same principles at work. On the one hand, fast derives its Christian meaning from charity: there is a long tradition to reassure us about that. On the other hand, the meaning is only valid so far as the Church here below remains at the stage of construction. She is in the time of trial, is not yet the heavenly Jerusalem, the full eschatological Kingdom.

Our first point can be illustrated by two texts, drawn from Church tradition. The first is from the Pastor of Hermas (*Similitude* V 1, 3): "Thus then you will carry out this fast. . . . On the day of your fasting you will take nothing but bread and water. Then you will calculate the amount you would have spent that day for your nourishment, and you will bestow that on a widow, an orphan or a poor person. In that way you will be depriving yourself, so that another may benefit by your privation, and be satisfied and pray to the Lord for you. If you fast according to the manner I prescribe, your sacrifice will please God." The second is chosen from among a number in the sermons of Saint Leo: "We prescribe for you this fast (Quartertense in September), reminding you of the necessity not only for abstinence, but for works of mercy of such nature that the amount you save by a holy economy from ordinary expense be rendered into nourishment for the poor" (*Sermon 89 on Fast*, Sept. 4).

For the first millennium the Christian attitude is absolutely precise: fast is never an end in itself, but is essentially bound up with the exercise of charity and can never be divorced from prayer and almsgiving. It does of course have value as an ascetic practice; but, because the chief enemy to be combatted is always pride, it must be somehow oriented towards the brethren. It is a useful means of elevating the soul to God; but the nourishing life the soul derives from God consists of divine love for all mankind. The attitude can be summed up in the close association between fast, prayer and almsgiving, always with the understanding that fast gives way before the higher claims of charity.

In later Church history doctrine about fast underwent considerable impoverishment, when the practice began to be considered an end in itself. Up to quite recently manuals of moral theology suffered from this defect.

Consequently recent relaxations in Church precepts about Lenten fast are relatively trivial considerations. What continued to be essential, in the keeping of Lent, is more intense community effort in charity towards God and towards less fortunate brethren. Modern life offers people a wide range of goods of all kinds. If we economize on these during Lent and bestow the equivalent on the poor, we are demonstrating the Christian spirit of fast. The Lenten renaissance then indicated by the practice of Lenten sharing belongs to the authentic Christian tradition in this matter.

Yet we must not neglect the ecclesial meaning either. The Church on earth is in the position both of awaiting and of possessing what it awaits. Day by day she advances towards the Kingdom, while being at the same time the manifestation of that Kingdom. Such is the rhythm: what she has gives what she builds its true meaning, and what she builds revolves always about what she has. Fast fits into this rhythm: the days deliberately set aside as times of waiting and preparation are for the Church the days of fast. In the primitive liturgy there was no Eucharist on such days, or it was celebrated in the evening, the reason being that the Eucharist is the ecclesial moment of "possession," of expectation fulfilled. Fasting was never permitted on Easter Sunday.

Fast and mission

Bringing the good news of salvation is the supreme work of charity towards God and man. Thus the missionary, by his word and by his life, must be a witness of love, if his mission is not to collapse to the level of mere propaganda or proselytism. The interconnection we have mentioned between fast, prayer and almsgiving is equally valid of fast, prayer and mission. This is borne out by the Acts of the Apostles: the mission of Paul and Barnabas is preceded by fast and prayer: "After fasting and prayer they laid their hands on them and sent them off" (Ac 13:3).

One question arises. Could collective or individual fasting, at least as an expression of charity, be made a visible testimony to further one's mission? There are people who regret that the Christian Lent does not make the same spectacular impact as the Musulman Ramadan. They should reassure themselves by recalling that when Jesus spoke of fast, he recommended that we should do so in secret and anoint our heads. The question could be pushed further. In that Christian fast consists of depriving oneself to benefit those in need, could not community service to the poor become a useful method for missionaries of indicating God's plan of love? But here also the situation is the same. Jesus' statement is clear: "When you give alms your left hand must not know what your right hand is doing; your almsgiving must be secret" (Mt 6:3-4).

Consequently certain methods of Lenten sharing can be contrary to the spirit of the gospel. Such is the case when attempts are made to give publicity to Christian charitable projects, as for instance a collection made in a particular Christian church for distribution in this or that needy area. The very same discretion should characterize both community and individual almsgiving.

Nowadays, furthermore, collective charity demands a great

deal more than mere almsgiving. Giving alms will not solve the problems of world poverty: they require a total economic reconstruction and a thorough reexamination of the relations between rich and poor countries. A primary obligation of Christian charity is cooperation by Christians in this gigantic task. Almsgiving acquires meaning when it becomes part of such a task; otherwise it becomes merely an inexpensive method of lulling our consciences.

The meaning of eucharistic fast

What we said earlier about the proper rhythm of ecclesial life, awaiting and possession, time and eschatology, is something that is verified in each eucharistic celebration. To borrow a lovely phrase from our Eastern brethren, the Eucharist is heaven on earth: it is essentially festive, stamped all through with the joy of the resurrection. It is by definition a breaking of fast, because fast belongs to the time of waiting and preparation.

But if it be a breaking of fast, that is because fast prepares us for it. And the Christian who experiences the true meaning of sharing in the Eucharist is the one who takes a serious view of time, of all the tasks that earthly life imposes, in the smallest detail. During our preparation, which is illumined by hope, fast can be a means, but only a means. For a considerable time the Church was very strict about eucharistic fast; under grave obligation it had to be observed from midnight to the moment of communion. No one objected; but very few understood the real meaning. The meaning is still there, even if there is a change in the law. What counts is not the deprivation of all food and drink before sharing in the Eucharist. It is the seriousness with which, in faith, hope and charity, we undertake the tasks that life imposes, because they can become an authentic expression of service to God and men. If our eucharistic fast is like this, the celebration itself will crown our time of waiting; it will be the Kingdom here and now in our midst.

THIRD WEEK OF LENT

I. 2 Kings   This narrative concerns the doings of Elisha.
5:1-15a   He succeeded Elias, but differed from his
1st reading   master. He was less isolated, less fanatical,
Monday   and exercized his charism in an organized
             fashion. He maintained a sort of bureau of
consultation with assistants who did the necessary screening
of his clients.

The cure of Naaman is set in a time of chronic wars between
Israel and Syria. We have mention of captives (v. 2) and of a
provocative letter (v. 7). During these conflicts the Jews were
often outclassed by their adversaries in the cultural and technical
sphere, as well as in battle. As a compensation many biblical
traditions attempted to redress the balance by stressing the
superiority of Jewish wisdom. So we have the international
repute (a bit exaggerated) of Solomon's wisdom, the triumph by
Joseph and Moses over Egyptian seers, by Daniel over the
Babylonian magi, by Esther over Vasthi. Our passage is of
similar character. Stories of magical procedures used by Syrians
to effect cures had penetrated as far as Israel (v. 12), and
frequently involved the latter in idolatry. To combat this tendency, the story of Elisha emphasizes the superiority of Jewish
methods of healing, which derive efficacy from the word of God
himself. It is true perhaps that in the procedure adopted for
Naaman by Elisha (immersion seven times, in the water of a
particular river: v. 14) the element of magic is not altogether
absent; but here the practice is spiritualized because the sick
man follows the prescriptions of one who bears the word of
God. The whole tension of Naaman's struggle with himself is
concentrated on one thing: being ready to subordinate the
particular rite to confidence in the Word.

Naaman's progress towards the healing rite is an illustration of what should be our proper approach to the sacraments. If the sacrament is to be fully effective its happening must be part of a dialogue between the God who reveals himself and the man who obeys. And the Church of course should recognize that it takes time for people to dispose themselves properly.

The truth is that we are just emerging from a period when, both in Church discipline and in the attitudes of the faithful, proper motivation in regard to the sacraments was inadequate. In the first place there was too much reliance on the principle of *opus operatum* and on the ineffaceable sacramental character, in deciding when sacraments should be received. These notions reassured us about God's part, so to speak, in the contract; but of course it takes two to make a contract. Then there was a definite tendency to accept what was really inadequate motivation (need for reassurance, for public ceremony, religious feeling, etc.), as if all inadequacies could be compensated by *opus operatum*.

Today we are coming to realize that a sacrament in the proper sense of the term requires a period of preparation that is not merely nominal. During that period the Church should exercise its prophetic ministry by proclamation of God's Word and interpretation of events, while the candidate renews his faith and measures the intensity of his conversion.

II. Luke 4:24-30 Gospel Monday   This episode comes immediately after Jesus' first preaching in the synagogue at Nazareth (Lk 4: 16-21). He had selected as text Isaiah 61:1-2 so that he might describe his mission.

a) By comparing himself with the Servant of Isaiah he was able to indicate that he was giving priority to the poor and preference to the unfortunate (Lk 4:17-20). But he avoided reading an important verse in Isaiah, where the prophet had proclaimed a "day of vengeance" on the Gentiles (Is 61:3). This indicated his anxiety to avoid condemning the nations. The audience was at first astonished at his "words of grace" (v. 22); but afterwards they were scandalized when they realized he had chosen to live at Capharnaum. This motley and commercial town had a mixed population of dubious provenance (v. 23), and among these he was accomplishing a work of salvation that he refused to carry out for nearer neighbors (v. 24).

His reply is a clear indication of his *missionary* intentions. The great prophets of Israel had not always given Israel the benefit of their miracles; on the contrary, there were times when they turned to the Gentiles only (vv. 25-27). He proposes to do likewise (cf. Mk 5:1-20; Lk 7:1-10; Mk 7:24-30; Lk 17:11-19).

b) It is clear though from Luke's redaction of the episode that he was concerned with another angle. It is indeed quite evident that Jesus' words in verses 23-27 are too strong for the context, and are not really an answer to the misgivings expressed by the people in verse 22. However, his discourse is perfectly authentic (it is indeed full of Aramaic expressions). But it was delivered at a later period in his life. Verse 22 mentions the miracles wrought in Capharnaum. In fact Jesus' sojourn in that city was subsequent to Luke 4:31. Then his discourse contrasts Jews and Gentiles, whereas the people in our passage contrast Nazareth and Capharnaum. The latter city, for all its mixed population, could scarcely be considered Gentile.

At the end (vv. 28-30) we have something from Luke himself, a description of the people who wanted to lay hands on Jesus. In all, what he is doing is casting over the first episode of the public life the aura which was to invest all that life; the mission to the Gentiles that is, the unbelief of Israel, and the *persecution of Jesus.*

The missionary encounters challenge sometimes in one quarter, sometimes in another. Paul received snubs from Gentiles as well as from "false brethren." Elisha was challenged by Naaman the Gentile, Jesus by his own compatriots. By definition the missionary must be associated with the actual Church of his time. And yet his horizon is the whole world. This situation demands limitless love. It is also terribly embarrassing. The non-Christian world will not regard him as belonging, especially when he is of alien culture. The Christian world looks askance on him too because his style of life, his challenges, his questions are all generally unsettling. He distrusts accepted values, he rocks the boat, he is a threat. Even ecclesiastical authorities may become uneasy, and he has to do some very painful rethinking.

Challenge like this can make the missionary an immeasurably deeper person. If he has given his life to Jesus Christ, challenge purifies him, makes him more and more in the image of the crucified Christ. He is a savior according to the measure of persecution he has endured.

III. Daniel Here we have an extract from a confession
3:25, 34-43 of the people's sins. Doubtless it was com-
1st reading posed at the same time as the book of Daniel
Tuesday (165 B.C., the persecution by Antiochus), and
later, under the pseudonym of Azarias, in-
serted in this collection. The speaker begs God to fulfill his promise of making Israel a numberless people (vv. 36-37). But to be heard, must not the prayer be uttered during liturgical sacrifices or with a prophet as intermediary? Now in these times of persecution (v. 38) there is neither prophet, nor leader, nor sacrifice. Is all prayer vain then? No, on the contrary the speaker points out the sacrificial value of repentance and con-trition. The prayer of a persecuted man is as valuable as any sacrifices of goats and sheep (v. 39). Spiritual sacrifice then includes in its ambit persecution. The suffering Servant was a sacrificial victim: so too in their turn are the martyrs made by Antiochus, and all such people.

Gradually God led his people from their original bloody sacrifices to the *sacrifice* of spiritual oblation inaugurated by Christ. A number of stages in the process can be distinguished.

There was the "quantitative" stage, when the Jews offered holocausts of the pagan kind, tithes and first fruits of their goods (Lv 2; Dt 26:1-11). It was a matter of sacrificing riches, because the extent of one's riches was displayed in the magnitude of the sacrifice; one's importance (and consequently one's religious status) was increased (2 Ch 7:1-7).

But sacrifices of this kind were carried out without really engaging the person of the offerer. The Jewish peasant brought along his victim, which was duly disembowelled according to rubric by the priest. Only the victim was engaged, and that unwittingly. We are very far from the ideal concept of sacrifice, where priest and victim are one and the same person.

Against such cult, wherein the ultimate spiritual and moral attitudes tended to be discounted, prophetic reaction was destined to be sharp; but it was often unavailing (Am 5:12-17; Jr 7:1-15; Is 1:11-17; Os 6:5-6). It was only during the exile that a dawning awareness of what spiritual sacrifice was began to take full shape.

In the expiation sacrifice of course, which was becoming prominent during this epoch (Nb 29:7-11), it is true that the quantitative aspect was yielding place to sentiments of humility and poverty. It is in the psalms above all that we notice this tendency towards spiritualization (Ps 39/40:7-10; 50/51:18-19; 49/50; Jl 1:13-14; Dn 3:37-43). So, bit by bit, people were coming to realize that the essential element of sacrifice was personal attitude; and the suffering Servant became the type of the sacrifice that was to be (Is 53:1-10).

The sacrifice of Christ clearly fits into this framework. It is constituted by his obedience and his poverty (He 2:17-18; Rm 5:19; He 10:5-7; Mt 27:38-60; Lk 18:9-14). His oblation was like that of the suffering Servant (Jn 13:1-15; Lk 22:20; 23:37; Mt 26:3-5).

The sacrifice of the individual Christian too follows the pattern of Christ's: a life of obedience and of love, which derives liturgical value from association with Christ (Rm 12:1-2; He 9:14). We must always be reminding ourselves that worship, which is not the expression of "spiritual sacrifice" in this sense, tends to lose all meaning.

IV. Matthew   The parable of the unforgiving debtor belongs
18:21-35   to Christ's fourth discourse, which is con-
Gospel   cerned with the relations of Christians towards
Tuesday   one another. He has already spoken of the
                     attitude that should be taken towards the
sinner (Mt 18:15-22), and of common prayer (Mt 18:19-20). Now, responding to a question by Peter (Mt 18:21-22), he takes up the matter of mutual forgiveness.

a) Judaism was already aware of the obligation to *pardon* offenses; but as yet it was a relatively recent awareness, interpreted in terms of precise calculation. Thus rabbinic schools were wont to require their adherents to pardon a wife, children, brethren, etc., a precise number of times, the number varying from school to school. Peter wants to know Jesus' ruling on the matter, and is anxious to see whether it is as demanding as the school which requires pardon seven times for a brother (Mt 18:21).

The response is a parable which lifts the theme of pardon out of all calculation, and makes it a sign of the pardon given by God. The original parable was probably very simple and straightforward. A sheik's servant has his debt remitted by his master, but refuses to remit a debt owed him by a companion. The sheik reproaches him for failing to remit, *precisely as* he had been treated himself.

The characteristic quality of Christian pardon is this: treating others as one has been treated, having pity because one has been pitied (vv. 17 and 33; cf. Os 6:6; Mt 9:13; 12, 7). True pardon arises from the realization that one depends oneself on the pardon of another. It is not a matter, as in Jewish teaching, of a moral duty that is precisely measured. It stems from an awareness that we ourselves have received pardon. Thus it becomes as it were a theological virtue, an extension to our neighbor of the pardon conceded by God (Col 3:13; Mt 6:14-15; 2 Co 5:18-20).

b) But Matthew makes an allegory of the primitive parable. The "man" of the original he changes, awkwardly, to "king" (v. 23), in order to suggest to his readers the king of heaven (note the similar procedure in Mt 22:2). The debt of the first man he gives as ten thousand talents, in order to stress the overwhelming insignificance of the sinner before God (v. 24). He makes the tribunal scene heavily religious in character (falling at the feet of the king, prostration, begging for pity) in order to suggest the last judgment. He highlights the disproportion between ten thousand talents and a hundred pennies (like the disproportion between the beam and the mote: Mt 7:1-5), to indicate the radical difference between divine and human concepts of debt and of justice. Finally he tells us the exact punishment of the wicked servant: torture to be prolonged until he has paid off a really inconceivable sum (v. 34). This could indicate eternal punishment (Mt 25:41, 46).

His whole procedure places the duty of pardon in an *eschatological* context. The last times have come, in the form of a sabbatical year (Dt 15:1-18) during which God cancels the immeasurable debt of mankind, and offers man justification. But some people refuse to participate in the sabbatical year and benefit from divine justice. They are condemning themselves to everlasting misery.

c) Confronted by man's sin Yahweh might have immediately exacted vengeance, broken the covenant and brought about the eschatological judgment. In fact the lesson of the parable is that God substituted pardon for that judgment, and postponed the judgment to a later date. The servant's life is cast between

two sessions of divine judgment (vv. 25-26 and 31-35). The
first ended in acquittal; the second will be dictated by what
takes place in the interval. If man wishes to be justified again
in a definitive fashion, he must take advantage of the intervening period to exercise pardon and justice himself. Christian life
is a sort of acquittal on probation: the acquittal will not become
absolute until the final judgment. What we have in the parable
is the theology of delay. The *time of the Church* is conceded
to man in order that he be converted (cf. Mt 13:24-30). In
fact throughout the life of the Church the history of the pardoning of man is being unfolded. That pardon comes not alone
through the sacramental ministry of the apostles and their
successors, but also through the ability of each baptized person
to make God's pardon manifest by his love for others.

In the Old Testament we have only one or two examples of
pardon; David pardons Saul (1 K 24 and 26), and Joseph
pardons his brothers (Gn 50:15-20). But the general trend was
towards a concept of pardon where unlimited vengeance (cf.
the *vendetta* of Cain; Gn 4:24) was controlled by the *lex talionis*
(Ex 21:24). In the new order (Mt 5:38-42) the true nature of
pardon is revealed, and examples of pardon are multiplied.
Christ pardons his executioners (Lk 23:34): Stephen (Ac 7:
59-60) and Paul (1 Co 4:12-13) their persecutors.

With Christ indeed pardon becomes one of the requirements
of the new law; the evangelists stress it in all his great discourses
(Mt 18:21-22; Lk 6:36-37; 17:3-4; Mt 5:23-26; cf. Ep 4:32).
Generally the duty of pardon is related to the last judgment.
We hope that God will pardon us at that time; accordingly we
pardon others (thus the petition in the Lord's Prayer: Mt
6:14-15; see too Lk 11:4 and Mk 2:13). Here there is still a
Jewish nuance, because retribution is the basis. But very soon
comes the essentially Christian concept: we pardon because we
ourselves have been pardoned (Mt 28:23-25; Col 3:13). For-
giving others is no longer merely a moral duty; it becomes a

demonstration of our dependence upon God and others. Pardon in this sense is not really conceivable in an order based on God's strict justice and his retribution. It belongs of necessity to an order where God's generosity is paramount, it is the hallmark of the new covenant where God reconciles man to himself.

The theology of reconciliation (2 Co 5:18-20) then is the proper setting for the duty of pardon, reconciliation in the final times of the return of peace (Ep 2:14-17; Col 1:20; Rm 5:1-11), of growth together by all men, hitherto estranged, in the one and only Body of Christ (Col 1:20-21; Ep 2:18).

V. Deuteronomy
4:1, 5-9
1st reading
Wednesday

This passage is the highpoint of the first of the great Deuteronomic discourses (Dt 1-4: 40). We find in it all the principal themes of that composition.

a) The discourse itself was written at a time when the exile loomed on the horizon. Was not Israel, like Canaan before her, about to be deprived of her territory, for similar reasons, her unfaithfulness and impiety? All the bonds (v. 5) uniting God with his people would have to be renewed.

The first step should be intensified teaching of the law and the traditions (v. 6). Fidelity to these will distinguish the people's behavior from that of other nations and mark them out as a people joined in a particular manner to their God (vv. 7-8).

The second step is the grace of God himself. Only he can sustain his people and give them the happiness they seek (v. 1). Commissioned by God, the legislator strives to touch the heart of the believer, and make him discern the deep connection between *law and life,* teaching and happiness.

b) It is only by existential awareness of this relation that God's merciful choice can be made manifest, and his *nearness* realized (v. 7). The latter concept has particular importance.

For the first time a legislative text is stressing nearness, as distinct from distance and separation in previous texts (Ex 33:20).

VI. Matthew
5:17-19
Gospel
Wednesday

These verses belong to one of the most manipulated passages of the sermon on the mount. Matthew is concerned to clarify the deepest meaning of the new religion, and uses the verses to introduce a series of great antitheses between legal justice and the new justice (Mt 5:21-48). Verse 17 is certainly original, and belongs to the tradition Matthew consulted. But it is interpreted in the light of a theme that is dominant throughout the first gospel: fulfillment.

Fulfillment, for Matthew, is an absolutely essential notion (Mt 24:24-35; 26:56). As he sees it, fulfillment of the law is not just a moral concept. Everything written there has prophetic import, and must be "fulfilled" down to the smallest detail, in the historical sense, during the eschatological era.

It is in pursuit of this idea that he borrows from the synoptic tradition (from another context: Lk 16:17) the beginning of verse 18. It is a saying of Jesus which indicates that no detail of the law is without usefulness (Mt 23:23; 15:6). But he adds a phrase: "until all is achieved," thus relating it to his over-all preoccupation (Mt 1:22; 2:15-17; 4:14; 8:17; 12:17; 13:35; etc.). The coming of Jesus, for him, is meant not alone to perfect the law in so far as it was previously inadequate, but also to ensure its fulfillment (taking law in the Old Testament sense, as a prophecy of the nearness of God). Consequently the Christian in his moral behavior (v. 19) cannot rest content with fulfillment of the broad precepts of the law. Even the tiniest detail he should attempt to realize, because all of the law has value as a sign of God's nearness.

It may seem surprising that in the New Testament, where we are accustomed to the diatribes of Christ and Saint Paul against the law (cf. also Jr 9:23-24), there should appear so precise a eulogy about its observance. The explanation lies in Matthew's eschatological treatment of the theme of fulfillment.

Pharisaic justice is limited to observance of the law. It is otherwise with Christian justice. It does not really depend upon observance, but on the fact that it proclaims the presence of Jesus, "prophesies" it in some way. Having verse 17 placed where it is, before verses 18-19, indicates a truth. Between the Christian and the law there is a process of mediation, the justice or nearness which Christ bestows on his own. When the Christian obeys the law, he does not seek there his justice: he "prophesies" Jesus Christ, and the last days in communion with God which Jesus has inaugurated.

Thus one of the prerogatives of the law is in fact removed: its capacity to bring God near, to justify man. This is now to be found in the communion with God which Jesus brings. It is the claim that was regarded as blasphemous by the Pharisees, who brought Christ to the cross. But it is precisely here that fulfillment of the law reaches perfection; because Christ carried out the law's precept in the most perfect communion with his Father. For us, the justice of the cross which replaced the justice of the law comes through the Eucharist, because it enables us to fulfill the law in communion with the Father.

VII. Jeremiah   During the reign of king Joachim (609-598)
7:23-28   Jeremiah delivered a series of oracles against
1st reading   the formalism of the temple. In these verses
Thursday   we have the third of the oracles.

As he sees it, the priests have become so preoccupied with rubrics and with the *formalism of sacrifices* that God can no longer recognize them as carrying out his will. He has never enjoined sacrifices of this nature (vv. 21-22). On the contrary, obedience to his will is what he requires from his people, not any precise routine of sacrifices (v. 23; cf. 1 S 15:22). The sign of such obedience should be acceptance by the people of the prophet's message. The prophets have not been heard (vv. 25-26), with the result that God's word no longer resides among a people who have grown deaf (vv. 27-28).

Christian worship guards against the formalism that overtook Sion by giving primacy to the Word. The essential content of Christ's sacrifice is obedience, and it is through obedience that each Christian can be linked with that sacrifice.

Yet Christian worship is beset by dangers as great as that which stifled Jewish cult. The Word may be proclaimed, or sung, with great dignity; it may be the material for skillful homilies. And of course the Word of God proclaimed in readings, in the celebrant's homily, or in the hallowed formulas of the Eucharist, is never nugatory. Yet if the words are those of someone who is a mere specialist in the "Book," without perception also of the Word in the events of life, of the presence of God in the actual world, what is the ultimate result?

True all these are liturgical renderings of the Word of God. But why do they have such difficulty in reaching certain elements of the laity? Why do as many find them so esoteric that they cannot find a way of responding? Why do people fail to find there the God they sometimes do find in ordinary walks of life, the God they converse with in absolute simplicity?

The inspired Word itself, but particularly the Word constituted by preaching, depends really upon the Word in a deeper sense, manifested in the person of Christ, and revealed to everyone in his innermost depths. The gospel accounts of the resurrection for instance are Words of God, as are, on another level, the sermons of priests. But the real Word of God is the resurrection itself, the event by which God has spoken that is knit into the tissue of man's lives.

Likewise the whole corpus of biblical traditions about the Exodus fall short, as Word of God, of the actual Pasch, the actual sojourn in the desert, the actual change that it wrought in the people who experienced it. So it is that the Word of God goes deeper than the language in which it is framed. And obedience to the Word means communion with the God who is present in our lives and actions. All the language used about the Word serves to demonstrate the truth of this.

VIII. Luke
11:14-23
Gospel
Thursday

These verses are part of an ensemble where the thread of unity is very tenuous (Lk 11: 14-32). We have in order the cure of a dumb person (v. 14) which is linked with the beatitude about those who hear the word (vv. 27-28). Next, the request for an extraordinary sign (v. 16), linked with the proclamation of the sign of Jonah (vv. 29-32). Then, a discussion of the relations between Christ and Satan (vv. 17-20) and the parable about the strong man (vv. 21-22), linked with a description of the return, with others, of the unclean spirit (vv. 24-26, not included in today's passage.) Inset amidst all this material is a saying of Jesus (v. 23), "he that is not with me is against me."

a) The more primitive portion of this material derives from the Jewish concept of *two spirits*. The world is under the sway of the spirit of evil and mankind follows his downward path; but in the last times a new spirit will appear, the spirit of good, who will redirect man towards good. The Qumran documents are frequently concerned with these opposing forces, who do battle for the world. Jesus, by expelling a devil, shows that the spirit of good has made his appearance. The two forces are now locked in relentless combat, and it is for men to enlist definitively under one or other banner. In Matthew's narrative attention is immediately concentrated on the opposition between the Holy Spirit and Beelzebub, and on the sin against the Spirit. This consists in denying the advent of the Spirit in the world, and denying his ability to create a new world.

Luke however modifies the intensity of antagonism which characterized the primitive version. He omits the reference to sin against the Spirit, and even replaces the word Spirit by "finger of God" (v. 20). It is clear that he had in mind an audience less familiar with the theme of two spirits.

b) To this primitive material about the two spirits, gospel tradition, concerned about particular interpretations, added some elements. To begin with, the cure of the deaf-mute (v. 14) and the beatitude about those who hear the Word (vv. 27-28), with which it is associated, belong to a context that appears to have been influenced by some catechumenal rite (cf. the use of "finger" in verse 20). The meaning doubtless is that the Christian must choose between the spirits, the one that leads to evil, or the one which, *by obedience to the Word*, leads to new life.

Luke's second addition tells of the victory of the "stronger" (the primitive version had "strong" only) (v. 15), and relates the parable of the return of Satan when expelled (vv. 24-26). He is anxious to impress upon Christians that their choice of life must be characterized by a certain firmness.

c) The substitution of *finger of God* (v. 20) for Matthew's Spirit of God (Mt 12:28) is quite surprising, because Luke has a devotion to the Spirit and likes to mention his action as often as possible. He must have had a very precise reason. The phrase is taken from Exodus 8:15, where the context is the contest between Moses and Pharoah's magi about miracles. The issue is that Yahweh's adversaries recognize his presence in the signs wrought by Moses. Luke (as in Ac 3:15, 20, 22; 5:31; 7:17-39; Lk 9:28-37) is making of Christ a new Moses.

IX. **Hosea**
14:2-10
1st reading
Friday

Hosea's prophetic ministry was exercised among the Northern tribes a little prior to the fall of Samaria (721). It was a time when Israel tended to deviate more and more from Yahwist traditions. His message was centered about two themes, an appeal for conversion, and a description of the prosperity reserved by a loving Yahweh for his people, if only they return.

a) Chastisement is already at the gates: before long Israel will be in exile. Let her not forget the love of God; let her be *converted*, and good days are yet in store for her. The essential nature of the conversion he proposes is recognition of the hopelessness of purely human endeavors. The alliance with Assur (v. 4) and the recourse "to horses" (v. 4), in the case of Israel, were human measures. Despite the protests of the prophets (Is 31:1-2) she had resorted to these in search of salvation. And she was deceived. Her political and military alliances bore no fruit, and, worse still, they had been entered without any attempt to see in the event of God's generous initiative. On the contrary, as they had developed, these measures were simply means of absolutizing man.

Their failure should be an occasion for some rethinking by Israel. Conversion did not mean changing policy; it meant that whatever policy was pursued should be pursued in communion with God who is the author of events. The God to whom Israel had to be converted was not one who dispensed with all human effort and human policies. Nor did conversion to him mean interruption or dislocation in that domain. It meant that his initiative should be recognized, that people should live in communion with him.

b) The account of promised *prosperity* derives much imagery from the autumnal rites common in Canaanite religion, which had been absorbed into the Jewish feast of Tabernacles. We have the themes of winter death and spring resurgence (vv. 6-8), of reaping and harvesting (vv. 8-9).

It is true that conversion is never altogether disinterested. Israel returned to God, but because of her passionate quest of abundance and prosperity. Such a mentality of course has its dangers when it issues in an ethic of merit and reward. Nor did Judaism altogether escape the dangers. Nevertheless there is a valuable lesson to be drawn from the idea of reward for merit. When we say an action will be rewarded what we are affirming more than anything else is the solidarity of the present with the future. We assert that the dimension of history is always present, that nothing is ever isolated, but always part of a future that is being shaped by God.

Hosea really changed the ideas of his compatriots about culpability. As he sees it, the fault is not one of violating the sacral traditions of ancestors which could be expiated, as among neighboring Gentiles, by penitential rites of some sort. It is the refusal to see God in the daily event. Sin means not seeing God in history.

Consequently the notion of conversion is changed too. It is not a matter of ritual ablutions, more or less efficacious. It means that sort of interiorization by which a man silences his pride and sees the event he is experiencing in a particular way. The focus of God's initiative, that is, and of his benevolence.

The Christian is converted to God, he is one of that group who make the Church. He is so in order that he can share in the great plan of God as shaper of events, in order that he can cooperate in the deployment of the human resources that flow from one great source, God who animates all things. Seen in this light, the Christian who is thoroughly involved in the contemporary world is the truly converted one.

X. Mark
12:28b-34
Gospel
Friday

Jesus has just dealt with the attacks directed against him by Jewish sects. In particular he has escaped the trap laid for him by the Pharisees concerning payment of tribute (Mk 12:13-17). Now he is approached by a scribe with a question about the greatest commandment. Where Matthew gives an aggressive tone to this episode (Mt 22:

34-46), Mark, curiously enough, depicts the scribe as well-disposed and anxious for enlightenment. Furthermore he is the only one to put in Jesus' mouth a eulogy of the man (v. 34). Possibly there was a general attempt in the synoptic tradition to gather different polemical episodes in one context. Mark may have done this less skillfully than the others, and thus allowed some details to stand, which are no doubt authentic, but in this context not appropriate.

Jesus answers the scribe's question by repeating the two commandments of *love* (vv. 29-31), though he was asked for one only. The first derives from Deuteronomy 6:4-5, but the version is the one used in Jewish morning and evening prayer. The formulation of the second is from Leviticus 19:18.

Mark gives us the two commandments juxtaposed, but treated as of different orders (v. 31). Matthew and Luke go the length of uniting the two texts, or speaking of a single commandment. Mark has not reached this stage, and follows the Jewish practice of conjoining the precepts as an epitome of the law. He is the only one to give us the scribe's comment on the precepts; and while Matthew's main point is that love is the key to worship that is pleasing to God (v. 33; cf. Am 5:21; 1 S 15:22).

Love of God and man is the essential core of Christian liturgy. And the eucharistic assembly is that ecclesial focus, where, over and above all other moments, the indissoluble bond between the love of God and the love of all men becomes real in the Christian consciousness. Our initiation is renewed, and, at the point where we render thanks to God for his loving initiative, we feel ourselves called to brotherhood in Jesus Christ with all men. Our thanksgiving in fact is expressed by a fraternal sharing the same bread, and consequently has a missionary import, because mission is nothing other than intense expression of love for all men.

So, each time the Church assembles her members or those

who are going to be members, she is putting them in relation with God and with all men. There are always the two objects of love, and they constitute the essential "framework" of all ecclesial activity. Whether it be a eucharistic celebration, a simple liturgy of the Word, or even a Catholic action meeting or the like, there is never question of meeting to give thanks to God at this time, and at that of turning towards men. The moment for both is the same; those gathered together are asked to rededicate themselves to a single ideal: love for God and love for all men.

XI. Hosea 6:1-6   The prophet is describing a ceremony of ex-
  1st reading   piation and repentance (vv. 1-3 and 5), or-
  Saturday   ganized by the people. They hope to obtain
          God's pardon and some sort of renewal of
spirit, all in the space of three days set aside for this ceremony (Ez 37).

It was customary to compare the grace given by God on this occasion to a rain which penetrates and renders fruitful the parched countryside (Ps 71/72:6). But the prophet stresses the hollowness of the ceremony: the repentance of the people is like dew which evaporates. That is why God is punishing Israel (v. 4); empty sacrificial ceremonies do not please him; what he wants is love (v. 6) and knowledge.

He is contrasting *knowledge* of God with ceremonies enacted without faith, and also with the idolatry which makes God what he is not, and reduces him to the level we want. Intellectual knowledge of God, unless accompanied by realization of his love as he reveals himself to us, and firm attachment to that love, amounts to nothing (Ho 2:21-22; 4:2).

Of how many liturgical ceremonies could not this be said? Nothing happens; we leave without encountering God, without knowing him. We experience the same weariness that Hosea did. Is there any way of changing this, of making every eucharistic assembly another felt experience of God?

XII. Luke
18:9-14
Gospel
Saturday

There have been very many different interpretations given to the parable of the Pharisee and the publican, which, while not being altogether wrong, fail to touch the heart of the matter. In the first place, an eschatological import has been detected, above all because of the last verse (v. 14b). At the last judgment we shall witness the elevation of the lowly and humiliation of the proud. This phrase however is so often put in the mouth of Jesus (Lk 14: 11; Mt 23:12) that it can be regarded as a sort of refrain, punctuating all the principal teachings.

Likewise the parable has been seen as teaching about prayer. Prayer must be humble, should not be based on personal merit, but on the initiative of God. Luke, it is suggested, combines two texts on prayer (18:1-8 and 18:9-14) to form a little euchological treatise. It is not impossible of course that Luke "reread" these texts in that light; but then how explain, in verse 9, his stress on the changed audience? He seems anxious to distinguish the two episodes.

The parable of course is first and foremost a moral lesson. A penitent sinner is more pleasing to God than a proud person who believes himself justified (Lk 16:15). Behind the two characters of the story, one can see a contrast between the two types of justice. On the one hand we have the man who, because he believes he has perfectly performed the necessary works, awards himself an acquittal, on the other, the justice granted by God to the converted sinner. Here already, in germ, we have the Pauline doctrine of justification by faith (Am 1-9 and Ep 2:8-10).

The prayer that Jesus puts in the mouth of the Pharisee

is paralleled by sentiments sometimes found in contemporary rabbinic sources. There is no petition (that would be undignified), simply words of gratitude for the assurance that one is on the road to eternal happiness. Among those who heard the parable some must have recognized themselves. What was there to criticize in such a prayer?

The publican's prayer is inspired by Psalm 50/51. Again the listeners could comprehend very well the note of profound despair. For them there really was no solution to the publican's predicament. How could he be pardoned unless he changed his occupation, and reimbursed all those from whom he had exacted tax? Here was a veritable hopeless case, who could never be justified.

Against such views the conclusion is directed. God is the God of hopeless cases, and the man to whom *justice* is accorded is precisely the one who has no right to it (v. 14), since he has not even made good his fault.

The parable contrasts the "just man," who thinks he can justify himself, with the man who can only obtain justice by confident faith in God (cf. Lk 16:15; 14:15-24; Mt 9:10-13). So does it prepare the way for the Pauline doctrine of justification given by God to people who cannot justify themselves (Rm 3:23-25; 4:4-8; 5:9-21). Justification in these terms is obtained by means of the cross of Christ (Rm 5:19; 3:24-25; Ga 2:21), and the instrument is baptism (Tt 3:5-7; Rm 6:1-14; Ep 4:22-24).

Justification is something already present among us. It is not the product of human justice, of resources that are merely creatural. But on the other hand it is not an exclusive eschatological reality, that must await God's direct intervention. By faith in Jesus Christ man is justified in the real sense. Jesus is at once the substantial gift of the Father, and the one man among men capable of responding to God in a pleasing fashion.

When we understand it in this way, justification illustrates very strikingly the meaning of our adoptive sonship in Jesus

Christ. Because we believe in him and can approach the Father as adoptive children, we are justified. The salvation which comes to satisfy man's expectant yearning is an absolutely gratuitous gift of God. But it makes to grow in us a filial activity, in which our obedience to the new law of love is brought to fulfillment.

In the eucharistic celebration Christians come to experience particularly the justification their faith has brought them. At that moment they realize they are answering a divine summons to salvation, and that the thanksgiving for which they assembled would have no meaning apart from the ecclesial link that makes them members of Christ's body. Sharing the Word and the Bread is concrete evidence that the grace manifested once for all in Jesus Christ, and very particularly in his death on the cross, is at work. Christians realize the overwhelming dignity of their sonship. They are the partners of God in building the Kingdom. They are the sign of justification which ought always to be resplendent before the eyes of men.

FOURTH SUNDAY OF LENT

A. THE WORD

I. 1 Samuel
16:1b, 6-7,
10-13a
1st reading
1st cycle

This account of David's anointing by Samuel undoubtedly belongs to a prophetic tradition that is without corroboration. There are in fact two other anointings which are more plausible and more frequently recorded: that of the Northern tribes (2 S 5:3) and that of the tribes of Judah (2 S 2:4). Those who could have been witnesses of an anointing of David, as for instance Eliab, the king's brother, appear to be unaware of it (1 S 17:28). The likelihood is that subsequent prophets were concerned that the davidic dynasty, so rich in messianic promise, should be made to stem from a prophetic gesture like Samuel's. Its prestige would thus be strengthened. Indeed the account could also be considered an attempt to whitewash the memory of the old prophet. The mistake made in Saul's case would be obliterated by an anointing of David.

It was because God wished it that after Saul, instead of his descendants, David took power. This *choice* by God is what the account of the premature anointing is designed to demonstrate. Verse 7 gives us the key to interpretation: God's ways are not man's. And Samuel finds himself forced to reject all David's brothers.

This is a well-known literary procedure, designed to stress God's liberty in choosing collaborators for his plan. We have for instance Esau and Jacob, Ishmael and Isaac, the two sons of Joseph.

II. 2 Chronicles   This passage concludes the second book of
36:14-16, 19-23   Chronicles. Verses 19-20 are taken almost
1st reading   verbatim from 2 Kings 25:9-10. Verse 21
2nd cycle   is borrowed partly from Jeremiah (Jr 25:11;
29:10: cf. Lv 26:34), and is designed to convince the reader that Jerusalem's fall was due to neglect of
the sabbath (an important topic for the author of Chronicles).
The last two verses are identical with those which introduce
the book of Esdras (Esd 1:1-3). They were added to the
account of the temple's downfall, lest the conclusion of the book
should seem too discouraging. A note of hope is introduced.
The suffering will not have been in vain, but will be the
harbinger of the Lord's presence once more among his people.
The davidic institutions, which are under threat, will not be
utterly obliterated.

The fall of Jerusalem, the *destruction of the temple,* and the
abolition of the davidic dynasty are part of salvation history;
they were foretold in Jeremiah and Leviticus. But God does
not interrupt his plan. He raises up Cyrus and guides him
towards a benevolent policy where Jews are concerned. They
are destined to rebuild a new temple and God will be once
more present with his people.

Thus the people will now have an absolute theocracy instead
of the dynastic regime; henceforward God himself will dwell in
Sion to govern his people (v. 23). The house of David will
no longer play a role in the earthly realization of this theocracy.
This latter affirmation is quite remarkable in the mouth of the
author of Chronicles; because, throughout the work, he tends to
associate Yahweh's theocracy with davidic institutions (1 Ch
17:10-14; 28:4-7; 2 Ch 13:4-8) to the point of forgetting the
Sinai covenant. He retains doubtless sufficient objectivity to
perceive that, while David and Solomon presented the perfect
kingly image of service to the theocracy, all their successors
have debased the ideal. The theocratic prerogatives claimed by

the davidic dynasty he transfers to the temple of the future and all it represents. This temple is not the work of David and Solomon like the former one; it is the product of God's own will, which is expressed by means of the decree of a Gentile king.

The temple he envisages then is independent of dynastic structures. But many more destructions and purifications must be undergone before God, as Lord of humanity and the universe, finds in the man-God his completely adequate sign.

III. Joshua   The Hebrews have just crossed the Jordan
   5:9a, 10-12   (Jos 3-4) and are preparing to reduce Jericho
   1st reading   in the land of Promise (Jos 6). They halt at
   3rd cycle   Gilgal, which up to the time of the davidic
                       dynasty was destined to remain one of the
most important sanctuaries in Israel. Chapter 5 of Joshua gives us different traditions concerning this center, the ancient custom there of circumcision (Jos 5:2-3, 8-9) and its inauguration as sanctuary (Jos 5:14-17). Verses 10-12 are a priestly composition, later than the rest of the chapter. Note the reference to the Babylonian calendar (the first month of spring), the anxiety about precise chronology, and the allusions of paschal ritual.

These verses do not give an exact description of Joshua's paschal ritual: they are a theological fragment. The Gilgal *Pasch* corresponds to the Egyptian one (Ex 14), and brings to a close the Exodus inaugurated by the latter. A new epoch is marked by the substitution of the fruits of the earth for manna. The desert existence, where gifts of Yahweh had always to compensate for the pitiless sun, yields now to a life when the luxuriant earth itself offers the things previously given by Yahweh. The people are now being called, after the era of wonders, to see God's presence in the fruits of their own labor. Likewise, in the future, the sacraments will be more than signs, like manna, of God's gratuitous initiative. They will be, like bread and wine, signs of human toil upon an element that is a gift of God, toil undertaken in profound communion with God himself. The Gilgal Pasch marks also the transition from the infantile stage where the people depend totally on their Father, to adulthood where they can experience communion with the Father in their own labor and their own freedom.

IV. Ephesians   This passage comes from the parainetic part
    5:8-14   of a letter which was written about 61-63, dur-
    2nd reading   ing the captivity. Paul has just enumerated
    1st cycle   those strands of pagan living which continue
                 to complicate the lives of the recent converts.
Baptism has introduced a definite break; their present life has nothing to do with their past. There can be no question of looking backward.

a) The contrast between *light and darkness****** is a classic one in primitive Christian circles (Rm 13:12; 2 Co 6:14; 1 Th 5:5; Jn 12:35; 1 Jn 1:5) and is frequently used to describe the gulf which separates Christian life from previous pagan behavior. The image itself is of biblical origin, darkness indicating misfortune, light good fortune. Paul however lifts it to the moral plane: Christians have emerged from night, and live in the light of the final times (Rm 13:12) so that they can accomplish there the "works" of light.

A whole vocabulary then, recovered in the Qumran documents, in Paul's handling becomes concentrated round the theme of light, with emphasis on the moral applications ("fruit of the light"; v. 9), and on the fact that this light is God's gift ("son of the light"; v. 8). Among the fruits of the light he reckons above all moral goodness, justice (right relationship with God, that is) and truth (fidelity, that is, to God's will). The three terms do not designate particular virtues, but rather the whole spectrum of moral attitude towards others (goodness), towards God (justice), towards oneself (truth).

b) Nor is he satisfied with merely requiring baptized persons to break with the works of darkness. They must denounce these latter (v. 11), brand them as guilty. It is not sufficient to break with evil; it must be challenged face to face and guided towards the light.

He has in mind here pagan sexual practices. He tells Christians that they must be unmasked publicly even though they are performed secretly. The reason is, he argues, that if these excesses are brought to broad daylight, their pardon and *justification* (v. 14) will come about. The worst excesses, once judged in God's light, cease to belong to darkness and share in justification. He wants to convince Christians that if they display firmness where such pagan practices are concerned they are destined to be victorious. This is the pledge of the spread throughout the universe of the kingdom of light.

He concludes his discussion by referring to a primitive liturgical hymn (v. 14). The pagan world as yet shrouded in darkness is invited to enter the domain of Christ's light.

V. **Ephesians**   Having contemplated the supremacy over the
   2:4-10   forces of evil gained by Christ at the Ascen-
   2nd reading   sion (Ep 1:15-23), Paul now takes the oppor-
   2nd cycle   tunity to utter a eulogy of this power of God
                     manifested in Jesus Christ and henceforth at
the disposal of men.

In contrast with this he depicts the weakness and death which characterize the sinful human condition. In no other New Testament passage have we such a depressing picture of the demonic element in human existence (Ep 2:1-3). But it only serves to emphasize the hope introduced once the power of God has made of Jesus Christ the Lord.

The first manifestation of the *power of God* is in the person of

Christ, who is risen, seated on the throne of Lordship (v. 6). But it goes on to be verified in God's attitude to us. Although dead in sin, we rise again because of his love, which will one day enable us to share the glory of his love. This is the same insight which we had previously in Romans 6:3-11 and 8:11-18; we are destined to be saved by the power of God.

But here, in Ephesians 2:4-7, Paul is affirming that the power of God has already made us rise again, already given us, in Christ, a share in divine glory. Of course it is only in the "ages to come" (v. 7) that the power will be fully revealed. But it is at work already, through the grace that wipes out our sin and guides our lives provided we receive it "in Jesus Christ," that is to say, with faith in his person, sharing his fidelity to the Father, through the mediation of his sacraments. All human pretensions to self-glorification are obliterated: there is no glory except the glory of God.

VI. 2 Corinthians This is certainly the most important passage
    5:17-21 of the long apologia for the apostolic ministry
    2nd reading to which Paul devotes the first chapters of
    3rd cycle the second letter to the Corinthians. Two
significant themes are treated: the role of love in the ministry, and the content of the gospel.

a) *The constraint of Christ's charity* (v. 14) is the basic thing in Paul's ministry. There is a question not only of Paul's love for Christ, but of Christ's love for him. As Paul sees it there is nothing sentimental about this love; it is the result of a considered judgment ("thought" in verse 14). To begin with he failed to understand Christ's love for all men when dying on the cross (v. 15); but once comprehension dawned he could no longer resist the "constraint" of this love and felt impelled to devote his life to Christ (v. 15ᵇ).

The "constraint" does not destroy freedom because he took

the time to consider. It is a new human experience (vv. 16-17) which made it no longer possible for him to act with the reserve and calculation of the "flesh." He was a "new creature." There was a fervor and dynamism, not controllable by the flesh (Col 3:14); a yearning for sacrifice like that of the cross (v. 15). All one's life received a new unity and equilibrium (*sunechei* is used in this sense in contemporary philosophic writing.)

b) His concrete manner of responding to Christ's love was to consecrate himself to the "embassy" of *reconciliation* (vv. 18:20). We have here a very favorite Pauline notion whenever he is concerned to describe the redemptive work of the cross (Rm 5:10-11; Col 1:20-22; Ep 2:16). It is equally important for modern theology, because it enables us to present the doctrine of redemption in terms of interpersonal relations between God and man. But we should be careful to understand it only in its psychological sense. Paul explains himself well. God does not change; he does not become reconciled to the world; he reconciles the world to himself (v. 18). So, the ministry of Paul among men does not only consist in reconciling them to God, but above all in proclaiming the accomplishment of reconciliation (Rm 5:10-11). God has made a change in man's state; the relationship to himself has received a new dimension. Thus it is proper to speak of a new creation (v. 17).

The whole concept is somewhat original. Previously prayer for reconciliation had a place in Jewish worship (2 M 1:5; 7:33; 8:29), but the prayer was that God would *be* reconciled, would change his attitude. Divine transcendence is better safeguarded in the Pauline view. He does not see God changing his attitude towards the world, but the world changing its attitude towards God.

For personal conversion this change must become actual in the individual life, and apostolic ministry is charged with this task. Once man has been made aware that his relation to God has been changed, the apostle invites him to modify his attitude accordingly. The very term embassy (v. 20), which he employs, carries the suggestion of conflict ended and restoration of normal relations (cf. Lk 14:32).

c) The reconciliation is the fruit of Christ's death, considered above all in its *sacrificial* aspect (v. 211 cf. Rm 5:9-10; Col 1:20-21; Ep 2:16). This sacrificial aspect of the death is prominently featured in the New Testament from the very earliest texts: the sacrifice of the new covenant (1 Co 11:25; Mt 26:28; He 10:29), of the paschal lamb (1 Co 5:7), of the suffering Servant (Is 53:12 in Rm 4:25; 8:32; Ga 2:20). But here for the first time the death is compared to "sacrifice for sin," the victim's blood having expiatory value (Lv 4-5; 6:17-22; 10:16-19; 16; cf. He 9:22). Hence the frequency of the terms blood and sin in the Pauline passages on reconciliation. It is not so much a matter of seeing the work of Christ in terms of blood, but a manner of affirming its ritual significance. Reconciliation is accomplished in a liturgical act which replaces once for all the temple ritual.

In the Eucharist all aspects of reconciliation are fulfilled: embassy in the liturgy of the Word, in the commemoration of the cross the reconciliation of the world to God, and finally, in the acceptance signified by the act of communion, each person makes his own the reconcilation that was accomplished for all.

VII. John 9:1-41 Here we have a description of the cure of a
  Gospel man born blind, and portion of the discussion
  1st cycle which ensued. John's hand is easily recognized, and the narrative resembles rather remarkably that of the cure of the paralytic.

In both instances the miracle is wrought on the sabbath day (Jn 5:9; Jn 9:14), for a person incurably ill (Jn 5:5; Jn 9:19-20) not far from a well (Jn 5:2; Jn 9:7). The persons cured react in the same way, with the common man's good sense (Jn 5:11; Jn 9:25-27, 30-33); they do not however recognize Jesus (Jn

5:12-13; Jn 9:11). In rather a curious fashion Jesus meets them again and leads them to reflect about him (Jn 5:14; Jn 9:35). Finally, in both instances the Pharisees are confronted with the problem of Jesus (Jn 5:15; Jn 9:11, 15). Such a structure is obviously more theological than historical, and invites an attempt to determine what John has principally in mind.

a) The problem of *knowledge* is fundamental in the fourth gospel. In the incident of the blind man John sets in sharp relief the progress of the blind man's knowledge, and contrasts the faith he achieves with the "knowledge" of those with him (his parents, neighbors and above all the Pharisees).

The blind man begins with insufficient motives. He doesn't know who Jesus is (v. 12), and simply shows allegiance to someone who has cured him (like people nowadays who join the Church because of its social or cultural achievement). Immediately afterwards, while still in this transition stage, his allegiance is put to the test. It is challenged by the bookish attitude, moral and theological, of synagogue authorities. So incorrigibly bookish are they that they can arrive at no explanation of the manifest facts of his cure. New converts likewise often find their enthusiasm waning. when scandalized by theological and moral systems that have little to do with the person of Jesus.

A third stage in the road of faith is reached when the blind man meets Jesus in person and experiences conversion to the Father (vv. 35-38). This is the moment when the convert experiences the personal encounter of religion, the communion with God. He has passed beyond the books of the theologians and can see the institution in proper perspective.

The blind man chose the uphill road of faith. Others with him, among them the very people whose learning could have served to deepen faith, deliberately rejected this sort of knowledge.

His parents, to begin with (vv. 18-23). Membership of the people of God for them was merely sociological. They did not want to face questions lest they should have to choose, or lest they be expelled by the authorities. This kind of obtuseness, a false concept of obedience, a fear of possible consequences, blocks the faith of many Christians.

But above all we have those Pharisee theologians, immersed in over subtle discussions and endless investigations, where the blind man's three words, repeated like a refrain (vv. 7, 11, 15), are sufficient to cover the facts. Infallible in their dogmatism, they go on challenging the facts to the point of becoming ridiculous. And when their backs are finally to the wall they have to resort to abuse (v. 28) and excommunication (v. 34).

Thus is God's judgment made manifest (v. 39). Those who think they see actually do not, but remain in darkness. The blind on the other hand come to the light, which, for Saint John, is life in communion with the risen Jesus, the light of the world.*

b) There are many auxiliary themes in the passage. John stresses the fact that the man was born blind (vv. 19-20 and 32-34). This detail focuses attention on the theme of *new birth* (3:3-7).

New birth is all the more significant because it challenges what seemed in previous birth unchangeable, the inevitable inequities of the human condition. So the acceptance of "new birth" means refusal to accept the conditions that go with natural birth. It means that love is pitted against all the uglinesses of the human predicament, and faith made to mould a better world.

c) Another theme is that of being *sent*. Christ is "sent" (vv. 4, 7) to accomplish the works of salvation (vv. 3, 17). Among these is the illumination of mankind; illumination not so much in the Western sense of intellectual "light," but "light" in the biblical sense of salvation.

When Jesus proclaims himself the light of the world (v. 5), he means to convey that his rescuing of men from darkness is a fulfillment of the scriptures (Is 9:1-6; 42:6-9; 55:1-9). But

*See the doctrinal theme: *light,* p. 210.

there is more than this purely messianic aspect. When John speaks of "works of the Father" and of being sent he is indicating that this light is the actual life of God. It is because he is Son of God that Jesus is the light and demands faith in himself (vv. 33-36).

d) The metaphor of "light" is a very natural one. Light signifies life just as darkness signifies death and sleep (Gn 1:3-18; Ps 103/104:19-24; Is 8:21-9:2). The symbol is all the more compelling in that there were then no means such as we have of dispelling the darkness of night.

We can easily understand how the prophets would tend to see any interference with the day-night rhythm, any encroachment of darkness as a punishment (Ex 11:4-8; Wis 17-18, 4; Am 8:9; 5, 18-20; Is 13:9-10). Darkness would be likened to sin, light to life according to the law (Pr 4:18-19; Ps 17/18:29; 106/107:10-16; Is 59:9-10). Salvation history would however transcend even this moral concept. Light becomes the Christ-event, which is destined to pass judgment on the darkness and end its reign (1 P 2:8-10; Rm 13:12-14; Jn 3:17-21).

From now on being in the light will mean communion with the risen Christ (Jn 12:46-47; 26:22-23; 2 Co 4:4-6). Faith is the expression of our connection with the light (Lk 18:39-43; Jn 9). As a bearer of the light it is the Christian's duty to bring it to others (Ep 5:8-14; Mt 5:15-16; Rm 13:11-14). The light of Christ and that of Christians is destined to have final triumph over darkness in the eschatological victory (1 Th 5:2-7; Rv 21:22-27; 22:16).

Jesus took upon himself the human state, with all that means—in particular the ambivalent quality of human communication. Rarely does one person reach the stage of penetrating another's mystery and communing with him. Conjugal love and friendship are exceptions; most people know you only from the outside. They accept the general estimate of you, know you only by your books and articles. Likewise with Jesus; few established a personal communion with him (the blind man, the sinful woman). Most knew him only by the Book (scribes, Pharisees, Nicodemus), or with a general, sociological sort of acceptance (his "brothers," the Samaritan woman). The awareness of some became explicit; in the case of others it remained implicit. Some took him for a healer or a prophet, others for the Messiah or the son of man . . . a few penetrated to the mystery of the man-God. But it all added up to a general human search; and it is clear from Matthew 25:31-46 that men who do not fully know the Lord can nevertheless be part of the Kingdom. But they must never absolutize their feeble versions of the truth; that was the mistake of the scribes in our reading.

VIII. John Here we have an extract from John's com-
3:14-21 mentary on the conversation between Nico-
Gospel demus and Jesus. The conversation was in
2nd cycle fact an initiation into faith (cf. Jn 3:1-15).
Jesus had made the observation that recognizing signs was not enough: one had to "see" the person, especially in his role as mediator, raised upon the cross, and in glory. Such a vision of Christ however could only be obtained by a new birth.

John goes on beyond these considerations to reveal, behind the person of Christ, the person of his Father, and the Father's plan for salvation.

a) As yet John does not use the word "Father" to designate the first person of the Trinity, only the word "God." But even if *God's fatherhood* is only faintly suggested, the phrase "only-begotten Son" (vv. 16, 18), indicates very clearly his relationship of love with the son. Furthermore, God's fatherhood where the world is concerned is indicated in the gift of that which he holds most dear (v. 16), and in the fact that eternal life is shared with men.

b) The fatherly gesture of God in sending his Son among men

becomes also a *judgment*. The one who believes is born into life, the one who does not believe is condemned (v. 18). The theme of judgment is the one with which John concludes his analysis of the conversation (vv. 19-21), while referring to the first exchanges between Nicodemus and Jesus.

John 3:2:	Nicodemus *comes* to Jesus	John 3:21:	he who does the truth *comes* to the light
John 3:2:	You have *come* as a master	John 3:19:	the light has *come*
John 3:2:	if God be not *with* him	John 3:21:	his works *in* God
John 3:2:	he comes by *night*	John 3:19:	have loved *the darkness*

This table illustrates the procedure as Nicodemus is initiated into faith. He thought he was in the presence of a teacher, but was actually encountering the light of the world. He came secretly, by night, and found himself obliged to choose between the light and darkness. On the evidence of the miracles wrought, he believed that God was *with* Jesus: he discovers that God is *in* him.

c) The beginning of verse 21 should be translated "does the truth," not merely "acts in truth." The phrase is without doubt a difficult one. Truth can be known, as the object of intellect, and can spur to action as a shaper of attitude. But as yet there is question only of truth-in-theory, as opposed to, or as distinct from, practice.

In Johannine language (Jn 1:17; 14:6; 18:37) truth really means the manifestation of what is hidden, rather like the term mystery in Saint Paul. Truth then is the depth of our being, the point of encounter between the event and eternity, the point where anguish merges into the courage-to-be. For Saint John it is something that "comes," or "is done," because it is linked with the person of Jesus and can consequently change our behavior.

Thus we can understand why he associates truth with judgment. A decision for or against truth is a matter of life and death. We either discover the real meaning of life and the whole structure, or remain content with superficiality and the banal.

Not even a perfect knowledge of the scriptures, and the signs wrought by Jesus, will suffice in order to understand the mystery of the Lord's personality, much less that of the Father and his love. That is why John indicates the development with precision: passage from external knowledge to faith, from a merely favorable attitude towards Jesus to an attachment to the Father and the gift he bestows of his life.

It is the duty of the Church too, whenever someone presents himself, to indicate the way that leads from mere benevolence or religiosity to true faith. And yet how many people has she not repelled for lack of faith, instead of leading them to Christ? How many others, admitted by her, remain in a state of mere religiosity, without a true education in the faith?

IX. Luke   Luke devotes a complete chapter to the para-
15:1-3, 11-32 bles of mercy: the lost sheep (15:4-7), the
Gospel   lost drachma (15:8-10), the lost son (15:11-
3rd cycle   32). The chapter could very well be designed
                   as a midrash on Jeremiah 31. In Jeremiah we
have the following figures: the gathering of the sheep (Jr 31:10-12), the woman finding her lost children (Jr 31:15-16) God pardoning his chosen son Ephraim (Jr 31:18-20). It is noteworthy that Matthew, in his parallel passage, 18:8-14, adds a further midrash on Jeremiah: that of the lame and blind entering the Kingdom (Mt 18:8-10), as prophesied in Jeremiah 31:8.

It is conceivable that there is actual allusion to Jeremiah 31 in the parable of the prodigal son. That text must have been familiar to the first Christians, because it is the Old Testament passage which best describes the new covenant (Jr 31:31-34). Thus there was good reason for making the parables of mercy a commentary on Jeremiah 31. It would deepen people's understanding of the new covenant, the basis of which is a love of God that is stronger than sin.

The younger son's motives are not particularly pure: it is the pressure of material need which brings about the conversion. This has at least the merit of throwing into sharp relief the gratuitousness and generosity of the father's *pardon*.

At the very moment when this love reaches its peak point of expression the elder son appears. Jeremiah 31 concludes with a description of the reconciliation between Ephraim and Judah, both tribes associated in the same covenant and the same abundance (Jr 31:23-31). In the parable however the father will not have the joy of reconciling the two sons by his love in the banquet of abundance. Like the scribes and Pharisees (Lk 15:1-3) the jealous elder son will refuse to be associated with the sinner. He justifies himself in the same terms as the Pharisee in the temple (Lk 18:10-12), showing the same pride, and the same disdain for the other (compare "this son of yours . . ." and "this publican here"). The younger son's prayer resembles that of the publican (cf. Lk 18:13). The whole parable then, like that of the Pharisee and the publican, aims to justify the benevolent welcome offered by Christ to all men, even sinners.

The elder brother too is made to realize that he will not be loved by his Father, unless he welcomes the sinner in his turn. The loving father expects that his mercy will be imitated. It is not he who shuts out his first-born: he shuts himself out because he will not love his brother (cf. 1 Jn 4:20-21).

So, out of the gratuitous love of God, a new covenant is born. It leads to conversion and is sealed in the eucharistic meal. In the covenant the ancient right of the first-born yields place, because God's love is open to all men.

This parable is a splendid illustration of the progress of repentance. It is noteworthy in the first place that both sons are sinners; that is the human condition. But one knows that

and shapes his attitude accordingly; the other refuses to acknowledge the fact and will not alter his life in any way. For both
God comes forward. He goes to welcome the younger son, but
he also welcomes the elder. God is there for all men, for the
sinners who realize they are sinners, and for those who do not.
There is no exclusiveness.

In the younger son's repentance we have, to begin with, the
human element. We mentioned earlier the lack of purity in
motive. He is converted because he is miserable, because, all
considered, his father's house is still better than his present
lodging with swine. With such imperfect sorrow he begins his
examination of conscience ("entering into himself": v. 17), and
even prepares the terms of his declaration to his father (vv.
17-19). However the essential realization for any penitent about
to turn again towards God is that of a God who comes forward
to welcome him. The welcome is of such warmth that the
penitent loses the thread of his prepared declaration (vv. 21-23).
The roles are reversed. It is no longer the quality of the penitent's sorrow that counts; the heart and center of the movement
towards repentance is God's love and his pardon. Unfortunately,
very often the sacrament of penance is treated as if pardon were
merely the response to confession, as if the initiative were
human merely, and not, as it is, God's coming forward, the
celebration of his recreating love. How very rarely does the
administration of the sacrament give a real impression of introducing someone to the joy of the Father.

B. DOCTRINE

1. The Theme of Light (and of Life)

The associated themes, light-darkness, life-death, are very pervasive in biblical literature. From Genesis to the Apocalypse we find them, and at each turning point in salvation history we find them readapted to the turning of the time. It is thus by no means surprising that they had a special place in the catechesis leading to baptism: nothing could be more suited for marking the various stages in the pilgrimage from unbelief to faith in Jesus Christ.

Any failure however to take account of the very palpable realities to which they are linked would mean inadequate understanding of the symbolic depth of these themes. Light and life are very concrete things. Throughout all salvation history they retain that value when seen with the eyes of faith, just as darkness and death were all along seen as obstacles to human happiness. And when it was realized that true light and true life were gifts to be received from God, in Jesus Christ, in the bosom of the Kingdom, people went on anticipating their triumph also in the visible world. It was unthinkable that the visible world too was not destined for transformation. Darkness and death would be no more. The kind of interiorization required under the regime of faith was never such as to indicate any modification in the harmony of God's creative plan.

This fundamental truth is brought home to us in the gospels of the fourth and fifth Sundays of Lent. They present a common teaching about light and darkness in two miracle-narratives: the cure of the man born blind, and the raising of Lazarus.

Light and life, the blessing of Israel

It was natural that man should tend to regard light and life as essentials of which he stood in need. Light is seen by religious man as a special gift of the gods, and life of course is the gift *par excellence.* Their opposites, darkness and death, are the enemies of human happiness, the evidence of being cursed from on high. Man must do all in his power to preserve these sacred gifts of light and life.

Israel saw them as the absolutely gratuitous gifts of Yahweh, the creator. The first act of creation is the separation of light from darkness; and in the final stages, to crown the great creative task, comes life. The very last stage is the creation, in Yahweh's own image and likeness, of the highest form of life, man.

These gifts were seen in their true significance in the historical context of the covenant. Yahweh had bestowed them on his people because he loved them, but in return he expected loyalty to faith. Man however from the very outset had sinned and, as a consequence of sin, was consigned here below to the kingdom of darkness and death. All that Yahweh required before introducing him to a kingdom which knew only light and life was a return to fidelity. Was not his own visage that of light (witness the theophanies), and was he not the living God?

Little by little Israel came to realize that the life and light needed by man to accomplish his destiny was more than just material light or bodily life. The notion of temporal retribution was inadequate because it was too brief. The man born blind is not necessarily a sinner, much less the sick man. Some sort of inward level had to be investigated. It was man's heart that had to be opened to God's light and life if he was to display the required fidelity. The heart must turn away from sin, from the works of darkness and death.

As interiorization grew more deep, the themes of light and life revealed the full dimensions of sin and infidelity. In consequence the prophets began to look to the future. When the day of Yahweh comes, a wonderful dawn of endless light and life will begin for the "little remnant" who remain faithful; but the impious will be utterly overwhelmed by darkness and death.

The living God will illuminate his own: his Servant will be the light for those nations admitted to eternal life.

Christ, light of the world and prince of light

The coming of the messianic era is a sign that from now on light has definitively triumphed over darkness and life over death. The decisive turning came with Jesus of Nazareth; because he is the light of the world. He is resurrection and life. Without sin, fully obedient to the will of the Father, the man-God in his humanity is the true light enlightening every man who comes into the world. In that light is the fullness of eternal life. In obedience he met the challenge of darkness and death, passing through darkness to the blinding light of Transfiguration and the perfect life of Resurrection. To achieve eternal life earthly life has to be laid down, made a gift of love. The high point of interiorization is reached in Jesus: life and light are found to have their real center in the very bosom of the Family of the Father which can never be approached by darkness or death.

Throughout his earthly sojourn Jesus made it clear by word and act that he was the light of the world and the prince of life. The Kingdom he was destined to inaugurate was already present in his person. Wherever he went darkness and death were forced to recoil. He cured the blind and raised Lazarus to life. All creation was touched by this incarnation of Light and Life.

To those who had faith in him, who agreed to follow him, he offered a share in the blessings he possessed. "He who follows me does not walk in darkness; he will have the light of life" (Jn 8:12). "He who lives and believes in me will never die" (Jn 11:25). On the one who believes he will bestow that living water which becomes "a spring welling up to life eternal" (Jn 4:14).

The Christian, a son of light, living in Christ

The time of the Church, the interval between the resurrection and the parousia, is still subject to the works of darkness and to death. Nevertheless the victory over these is already assured. In the Head of the Body it is accomplished; each of the members has yet to feel its full impact.

The Christian, once initiated into the Body by baptism, becomes a son of light and can say with Saint Paul "Life is Christ" (Ph 1:2). He gets the power to make light spread throughout the world of darkness, to kindle life where death held sway. He has part with the saints in light, lives for God in Christ-Jesus, and is summoned here below to the eschatological combat. It is a constant theme with Saint Paul. He should put on the armour of light and repulse the works of darkness. Always it is as if he were involved in the death of Christ, so that life may become manifest. All that is mortal must gradually be absorbed by life.

This light-life theme reminds the Christian that his own pilgrimage through earthly existence is an essential part of the salvation plan. The coming of Jesus did not mean there-and-then accomplishment of salvation-history; it received the all-important impetus then. The initial victory was won; but throughout all time the history continues until the Body attains perfect stature.

Furthermore unexpected insights into the nature of the human vocation itself begin to dawn. The light which awaits man is the blinding light of transfiguration; the life is direct intuition of God for all eternity. But here and now the glow of these colors the whole texture of earthly life. Wherever the Christian passes, darkness and death should recoil, and as they recoil the Christian realizes that he is contributing to the advancement of the whole human race. He is introducing man to universal love, the secret of the gospel. Light and life are gifts of God which ought to bear concrete fruit in works of faith.

The role of light and life in mission

Any human community that is not yet Christianized is still in the domain of darkness; death retains his power. Preaching the Good News of salvation, making the mystery of Christ take root there, means liberating this community from the sway of darkness and death and bringing it into the Kingdom of the Father. This continues to be true even when we acknowledge the fact, as every missionary should, that the human values of this community are the work of the Spirit, and stages on the road to evangelization. In the whole arduous process of the spiritual pilgrimage only life and light itself, that is Christ, can succeed in crushing the strength of Satan.

In a very special way the missionary is the light of the world and the witness of the Risen Lord. Nor is this any merely external role; it means continuous, daily, involvement. It demands struggle, sometimes harsh struggle, which may in perverse fashion take shape in the very conscience of the missionary. Just as in the time of Christ, the wisdom of the world is apt to reject the path of light and life, because it requires total self-renunciation.

The test for knowing whether mission is being conducted under the aegis of light and life is fraternal love. How often one has to repeat that the task which actually confronts the Church is altogether immense. In that all Christians are involved in the witness that must be borne, the missionary's work is jeopardized if he is not backed by the totality of Christendom. Modern man will only recognize the sign of light and life when he encounters it at those very junctures where he is aware of having to shape his own destiny. And Christians will give evidence that life and light are actually at work here below by the intensity of their search for solutions to those agonizing human problems which demand the concerted effort of all men.

The Eucharist, source of light and life

To have energy for their great task Christians must constantly be refreshed at the sources. Without Christ they can do nothing. It is in the eucharistic celebration that they are given light and life. When they receive the Word, share in the sacrifice, they become renewed by the one who, throughout all the time of the

Church, is at once Light and the Bread of Life.

This is not to make the eucharistic celebration a withdrawal from the world. The light and life that it provides for Christians makes them witnesses among other men of God's plan of love, which is brought to fulfillment by Christ's victory over darkness and death.

2. Auxiliary Theme for Lent: Prayer

Christian prayer is the integration, in Christ, of the life of the individual. It follows then that the Christian does not have the right of regulating prayer according to whim, making it a matter of personal choice or temperament.

Among all peoples prayer has always been regarded as an essential act; and in some cultural environments, India for instance, prayer, in general public estimation, is *the* important thing. The values of Western man seem to be different. What are we to say of prayer in the Christian framework? That the Christian simply pray is not sufficient; he must pray as he *ought*. Does the average performance give evidence that Jesus' teaching about prayer has actually informed the behavior of Christians? Nowadays there are many Christians who fail to perceive the link between prayer and actual living; their casual prayer has no real connection with their lives; it is a matter of empty formulas. But for others prayer *is* a deep spiritual experience, closely informing their daily lives.

Prayer and the event, in Israel

Israel, under the regime of faith, was always conscious of the salvific dimension in history, both collective and individual. The chosen people would look into the meaning of events, because the event for them was the point *par excellence* of intervention by the Totally-Other God.

Thus, for them prayer became above all thanksgiving, in connection with the event. Yahweh would be "blessed" for treating his people with generosity, mercy and fidelity — above all fidelity, never-failing, day after day, throughout the course of history.

But their prayer was far from being invariably serene; every page of the psalter has its quota of frantic supplications. Yet, what confidence in God underlies these supplications! Sometimes before the request is granted, he is thanked. Even when the request is not granted in the terms in which it is made, dialogue is never interrupted. It is always possible that Yahweh is leading his own by the unexpected paths of trial. God's purpose may indeed be foiled, at least apparently foiled. But the man of prayer never abandons himself to despair. He tries to penetrate the will of God and places his hopes in the future. Yahweh will certainly intervene to restore his rights wherever they have been infringed.

It is true that when compared with the prayer of Jesus that of Israel reveals inadequacies. But it contains essential elements which it will not be necessary to analyze later. It is a prayer of thangsgiving addressed to the absolute master of human destiny, the God who manifests his providential love in the unexpected, unforeseeable, events of history. God is good and faithful. That is the basic affirmation, against which as a backcloth the whole drama of Jewish history is unfolded, while thanksgiving and petition become gradually more correctly proportioned.

The prayer of Jesus, mediator of salvation

In the life of Jesus of Nazareth the gospels provide abundant evidence of the place of prayer. Sometimes, rarely indeed, they let us know the content of his prayer. It is always brief, and except for the sacerdotal prayer recorded by Saint John, presents certain constant features. Side by side with the traditional Jewish elements we find new dimensions. Indeed we may say that, with him, Jewish prayer undergoes a complete transformation. When he prays the prayer is elicited because of some event concerning the coming of the Kingdom: he wants to put the event in its proper setting in the whole salvation mystery.

So, in John 17, his prayer is altogether concerned with his death on the cross, the major event of salvation history. "The hour is come." When he prays he gives thanks. Whatever he has he attributes to God, because his purpose is to emphasize the absolute gratuity of God's generosity, its nature at once definite and unlimited.

All this might not seem to differ from Old Testament patterns. But in reality thanksgiving for him has an integral dimension that is altogether new. Thanks is all-embracing. Nothing stands outside God's salvific intervention: everything, even death, has meaning. His thanksgiving forges his life into a perfect unity; obedience even unto death on the cross to the will of the Father through love for all mankind. The encounter with death was for him, as for all men, a tragic encounter; but his obedience made of it the great moment of salvific intervention, that which saved the world.

If we analyze it further still, his thanksgiving is the perfect counterpart to the Father's salvific initiative, just because it is that of the man-God. When someone can see the mark of grace in every single event it is evident that he is God's own partner in the realization of the salvific plan. Being a partner, in the matter of prayer, has an important consequence. When petition accompanies the thanksgiving, it is the petition of one who realizes he will be heard. Jesus' prayer before the tomb of Lazarus is thus: "Father, I thank you for hearing my prayer. I knew indeed that you always hear me" (Jn 11:41b-42).

The ecclesial structure of Christian prayer

The Christian's prayer should reproduce the prayer of Christ. "Pray constantly, and for all things give thanks to God, because this is what God expects you to do in Christ Jesus" (I Th 5: 17-18).

His prayer is necessarily that of a member of Christ's Body, thanksgiving in all situations. It declares his identity and his power of intercession, associated as he is with the chorus of praise that emanates from the Church, the priestly people. Christ alone, the only begotten of the Father; is capable of rendering perfect thanks to God. But there is a sense in which the Christian's thanksgiving reproduces the qualities of Christ's prayer: he is assumed by baptism into the priestly assembly of adopted sons. That sonship is not anonymous; each member has his particular role in building up the Kingdom. The most personal prayer of the Christian always has an ecclesial dimension.

Grace invests all things for the Christian, as for Christ. Baptism enables him to discern the salvific power of God in the most ordinary details of everyday life. He will discern it above all in the place where one would least expect it, in death, in every vicissitude that demonstrates the tragic frailty and finitude of men. In prayer, in the most mundane circumstances, he will find himself sharing the Pasch of Christ. Always his thanksgiving will proclaim the death of Christ.

And, because he is associated with Christ in building up the Kingdom, his prayer can and should move from thanksgiving to petition. He will thus become more receptive to God's action, and will fulfill his role as adoptive son, one that can be fulfilled by no other person. When his petition is truly that of an adoptive son, he has the certainty of being heard. But in fact long effort is necessary, and steady stripping of the self, before the prayer of petition is purified and begins to reapproach the prayer of thanksgiving. "Father thy will be done, not mine." Such is the prayer that is always heard.

The missionary's prayer of intercession

All that has been said of the Christian's prayer is more true still of that of the missionary. And there is yet another consideration. The missionary's prayer of petition is first and foremost a prayer of universal intercession. His particular intentions accordingly become part of ecclesial prayer for universal salvation.

Christ's perfect act of thanksgiving on the cross makes him forever intercessor before the Father. He intercedes for all men, but he does not take their place in prayer. He places the act, of which the Church is here below the sign, that gives meaning, content and direction to the urge for prayer that the Spirit places in the heart of every man. Following him, it is the business of all Christians, as members of his Body, to do their part in making real to peoples and individuals his universal intercession. It is not that they pray in place of people who do not know Christ; but their prayer does have real salvific effect for each and every person.

So the Christian prayer of petition, being as it is an expression of universal intercession, has a specific character. And it is in harmony with the prayer of thanksgiving for universal salvation. God calls all men, in Jesus Christ, to build the Kingdom, which fulfills beyond all expectation the hopes of humanity.

The Eucharist, a thanksgiving always acceptable

In the eucharistic celebration we find in high relief all the essential elements of prayer. It is the ecclesial prayer *par excellence*, where Christ for love gives his life for the salvation of all men. As a thanksgiving it is always acceptable, not only because it is that of Christ but because it is that of the ecclesial priestly people. They have been rendered fit to offer to the Father an agreeable sacrifice. Each celebration then becomes an essential stage in building the Kingdom.

This is so because each celebration is part of salvation history, linked as it is with the death and resurrection of Christ, the central event of that history. It is the prayer *par excellence* of redemption (a commemoration that actualizes: cf. second theme of Holy Week). The proclaimed Word unveils for us, in all magnificence, the divine economy of salvation, as realized in Jesus Christ. In the homily it is developed further, so that the whole thanksgiving prayer becomes part of God's timeless Today.

Here we have, in order, thanksgiving, petition and universal intercession, the various aspects of that one perfect prayer which saved the world, Christ's prayer on the cross.

FOURTH WEEK OF LENT

I. Isaiah
65:17-21
1st reading
Monday

Chapters 65-66 of Isaiah are doubtless postexilic, and form a sort of apocalypse. Today's reading envisages the eschatological future of Jerusalem as a return to the original paradise of Genesis.

The passage indicates the renewal of Jewish religious thought on the occasion of the exile. Important themes like creation and *paradise*, the blessing and cursing of Adam, which had previously been relegated to the golden age of the beginnings of time, now are transposed to the future and become portents of the last times.

The author's only purpose for reflecting on the past is to perceive better the nature of the future. Ancient Yahwist tradition had read primal history as a steady human declension from fall to fall, to the very point of extermination (Gn 1-11). He takes the opposite view, seeing the course of history as a progressive ascent by the people, and he even questions the primordial curse and death itself (v. 20). The human story is not one of decline; it is the product of free and open collaboration between God and man.

This insight has a profound lesson as we survey the religious crisis in the actual world today. Two views are possible. We might analyze the situation from the standpoint of tradition and the past. This would be the conservative, not to say aristocratic, outlook; the past becomes a golden age, which we try to recapture by exalting the traditions and standards that used to be. Or we could view the present in the light of eschatological hope. We could try to shape it into what the kingdom of God will one day be, opening ourselves to the creativity and mutation so characteristic of the new nations. Maybe what is required of the Church now, at the cost of much sacrifice and renunciation, is some such change of viewpoint. In any case all individual Christians are confronted by the challenge. The dynamism of the secular city, however ambivalent, must not be judged by the standards of a pre-technological age, even though that age seemed more religious. We should try to see there, if we have the eyes to see, the outlines of the future city, the city of God, where freedom and human fulfillment will be finally realized.

II. John 4:43-54
Gospel
Monday

Matthew (8:5-13), Luke (7:1-10) and John all describe for us the cure of the centurion's son. Matthew and Luke see the incident as an early indication of the mission to the Gentiles. John does not do this; but he is at one with them in stressing the detail that the miracle is worked at a distance.

a) Though he does not take up the theme of Gentile mission, John does insert three verses (43-45) about the lack of understanding among Jesus' compatriots. The verses however cause difficulty. If the *fatherland* of Jesus is Galilee (cf. Jn 1:46; 7:41), how can two verses so mutually contradictory as 44 and 45 be juxtaposed (cf. Lk 4:24)?

The truth is that John, by "fatherland," means something other than the province where Jesus was born. As Jesus is "at home" in the temple (Jn 1:11; 2:16) because it is the house of his Father, so is Jerusalem his true spiritual fatherland. This is clear from John's anxiety to have Jesus go to Jerusalem for each festival, and to provide some sort of explanation whenever he lingers outside Judaea (Jn 4:1-3; 7:1-9; 10:39-40). Living as he did among Jews turned Christian, and forced by persecution to live away from Jerusalem, he likes to point out that Jesus had to encounter a similar "deracination." But this did not prevent him from accomplishing his mission; his experience of his fatherland was to meet there with his death, just as the prophets had (cf. Lk 13:33-34; Jn 1:11).

With his usual penchant for terms with a double significance, John makes Jerusalem Jesus' fatherland; because the "fatherland" is the place where the "father" lives (Gn 31:3; 12:1; 24:7, 40). Jesus' Father is the God who dwells in Jerusalem (Jn 5:13).

b) In order to maintain the prohibition for Jews against entering Gentile dwellings, Jesus must work a miracle at a distance, by his *word* alone. Throughout his career as thaumaturge there were only two such miracles (Lk 7:1-10 and Mt 15:22-18). Usually he heals silently by physical touch, as if his body possessed some sort of vital energy, uncontrollable by times (Mk 5:31; 6:5). Control is generally exercised by "touching" the sufferers (Mt 8:3; 8:15; 9:25; 9:29; Lk 14:4), or "imposing hands" (Mk 6:5; 7:32; 8:23-25; Lk 4:40; 13:13). But the gesture is not quite sufficient to show that responsibility for the act is being assumed. Thus in some miracle-narratives a point is made of showing how the healing gesture was accompanied by a remark (Mt 8:3; Mk 5:41). This clearly indicates the intention of Christ, of which of course the gesture is the full expression.

In healing the centurion's son Jesus contents himself with the Word, with an allusion probably to Psalm 106/107:20, where God "sends his word and heals." On the centurion's part there is an implicit recognition that Jesus comes from God, because he controls the actual word, powerful and efficacious (Ps 32/33: 6-9), of God himself.

Is is worth remembering that during the distribution of communion the faithful affirm their faith in the words of the centurion "Say but the word . . ." There is no magic in Christian liturgy; there is absolute dependence on the "Word alone," which was in Jesus' heart throughout his Pasch, which envelops us in some way throughout our Christian life, which is the essence of the affirmation made in faith by the Christian in the rite that places him in a special relationship with Christ.

III. Ezechiel   Ezechiel has completed his description of the
47:1-9, 12   new chosen people, gathered from the ends
1st reading   of the earth (Ez 34), in whom the ancients
Tuesday   are once more resuscitated (Ez 37). They are
                         renewed in holiness of heart. He has just
depicted the temple which will be the source of holiness (Ez
40-44), and the new Holy Land destined to be the province of
the holy ones. In the center of that land is the rock of the temple
of Sion from which flows a stream of living, sanctifying water.

a) The *living water* which in the last days will flow from the
rock of Sion (vv. 1-3) is the same as that which flowed in the
desert (Nb 20:1-8). Jewish tradition indeed had it that Mount
Sion was in fact the original rock of the desert which accompanied the people in the Exodus (cf. 1 Co 10:1-6). What
Ezechiel is proclaiming then is the marvelous age when this
rock will again refresh the faithful of Yahweh (cf. Is 33:16;
Za 14:8). Doubtless he is referring to the ablution ceremonies
of the Feast of Tabernacles which were a prophetic symbol of
the flow of water promised for the last days.

b) This living water makes of the desert of Judah a *paradise*
of trees of life (vv. 7-9, 12; cf. Ez 36:35; Is 43:30). Here
Ezechiel's thought has an original dimension. The themes of
paradise and planting are linked with those of rock and building
(cf. Rev 21-22; Ps 91/92:14). The stream of water issuing from
the temple becomes the new river of paradise (Gn 2:10). So
the key for man's return to Paradise is the liturgy of the temple
and the holiness it brings. Paradisal happiness, lost since the
fall of Adam, will be restored.

c) Nor is paradisal happiness the only fruit of this living
water. Even among the dead waters it raises up the living
(v. 9b). It has the power of *raising to life*. As the dead waters
are the symbol of hell, the living water has the power to snatch
the dead from their miserable fate (cf. Ez 37). In the miraculous draught of fishes (Jn 21:8-11) the evangelists perhaps

discerned the fulfillment of this prophecy. It was a sign of God's vivifying power at work among the creatures of his kingdom.

In the gospel of Saint John the passage is of great importance. It is clearly the inspiration of pieces like John 7:37; 21:8-11; 19:34 and Revelation 21:22-32. For the new humanity the Risen Lord is the center of cult. His holiness is such that it sanctifies all who share in it. His victory over death is so definitive that any man can as a result be raised up once more and be justified of his sin.

IV. John   Beginning with chapter 5, as a new phase of
5:1-3, 5-16   Christ's life is embarked upon, the fourth
Gospel   gospel gives us a new Christological dimen-
Tuesday   sion. No longer have we question of the
                      Messiah, but of the Son of Man, the envoy of
the Father. Instead of messianic "signs" we get mention of the "works" accomplished by the Father's envoy.

The Jews in their messianic expectation were prone to look for divine signs. Jesus offers them human works and claims no title but Son of Man. Indeed his miracles are not easily read signs: they provide insights into his personality, but for those who fail to recognize him and plan his murder they harden opposition.

Our passage today is the beginning of this new section. It exemplifies John's systematic manner of recounting a miracle; the occasion and the milieu (vv. 1-4), the desperate condition of the victim (v. 5), Jesus' efficacious word (vv. 6-8), reaction of believers and unbelievers (vv. 9-15), and finally the explanation (vv. 16-18), meant to deepen insight into Jesus' personality.

a) The fountain at which Jesus performed his first "work" as God's envoy was doubtless erected over a well of curative nature in the northern part of the city. The condition of the sick man was quite desperate; he had been seeking a cure for thirty-eight years. Jesus chose to undertake such hopeless cases, as Lazarus, buried for four days, or, again, the man blind from birth, in order to demonstrate the power of God by transcending as far as possible human possibilities. Henceforth the water from the well is deprived of curative value, the only source now of living water in this revitalizing sense will be the person of the man-God.

b) But the work was accomplished on a *sabbath* day. This observance had an absolute value for the Jews (Jr 17:21; Ne 13:15-22; Ex 31:12-17; Nb 15:32-36): they watched for every transgression. Jesus does not criticize the sabbath legislation; but he does affirm his own authority (v. 17; cf. Mt 12:8), thus naturally directing the attention of his audience to the mystery of his own personality (v. 18).

For a believer of course the logic was clear: God alone is above the sabbath; Jesus does that which only God is capable of doing. It was the Jewish belief that God rested from the work of creation on the sabbath (cf. Gn 2:2), but his function as judge was not interrupted. So when he presents the cure of the paralytic as an act of judgment (v. 14), Jesus is associating himself with the process of divine justice in the world, continuous on the sabbath as on other days. It is something not excluded by sabbath legislation.

The work then is a miracle in a double sense, transcending the law of nature, but also the law of Moses. It is perhaps possible to query the miraculous nature of some of Jesus' actions; it is never possible though to query the intention he manifests when doing them.

His desire is to reach out to the most miserable of his brothers and bring them health and salvation. Such communion with the poor however cannot be successful unless it be received as the gift of God, an exercise of his power.

For Jesus almighty power is not a metaphysical principle

designed to explain the world and natural phenomena. Thus he gives no demonstrations of might. On the contrary he chooses to perform miracles that reveal almighty power in the concrete, linked with some definite action, linked to a real human being whose faith has to be elicited. The God behind his miracles is not the God of the philosophers who controls the forces of nature. He is a God that "I," the moment I am ready to believe, can see. His miraculous power is not a sort of general bulwark on which I can always rely; it is the free act of someone who touches at a given moment my life.

Nor is this God the God of law, with everything organized and meticulously regulated. The obedience he requires from me is not obedience to some prefabricated system, but an obedience to the free personal will of God, a desire to do what pleases him. When Jesus works miracles he wants to demonstrate that our lives are not governed by a natural causality or legislative ordinance. The causality is something deeper than this, something that escapes philosophers and jurists, and becomes meaningful only in moments of free decision and faith.

Belief in miracle lifts us above both the law of necessity and the necessity of law; it fixes our gaze on the free encounter that takes place between two persons, God and the believer. When one is a believer, it means that behind nature a person is discerned. It means that in the very midst of the seeming determinism of secular things we are living in communion with God.

V. Isaiah 49:8-15   The prophet describes the return from exile
   1st reading   in terms of the original exodus from Egypt.
   Wednesday

   a) God summons the prisoners forth from darkness (v. 9). The *road of return* spreads out before them, flanked by pasturage, where rugged mountains and desert places are transformed into wells and meadows; it is the miracle of the Exodus all over again (vv. 10-11). The mountains which acclaimed the people then (Ps 113/114) acclaim them now too (v. 13): the return is the fruit of God's unchangeable love for his people (Ho 11:8; Is 54:8).

b) This future depicted by Second-Isaiah is in symbolic terms that can be understood by the people without attracting the enemies' attention. Mention of a return to the desert, of a child recovering its *mother's love*, could not conceivably be construed by a pagan ignorant of scripture as a proclamation of a new covenant. But the Jew who had read for instance God's letters of repudiation of his spouse and children in Hosea (Ho 2:4-15), or the announcement that chastisement would be temporary only (Ho 2:16-25), could not read this and many other passages (Is 47:1-3, 8; 49:17-22; 50:1; 51:17-52, 2; 54:1-5) without rejoicing in the fidelity of God's love, and plumbing the mysterious secret of its extension to his ever undeserving creature, man.

VI. John **5:17-30** *Gospel* *Wednesday*	This reading is taken from a discourse (Jn 5:14-47), the general purport of which is to demonstrate that the Father has really given Jesus the power of transmitting divine life to men.

Moses' message had been regarded as a *Word of life;* but the life in question was terrestrial life, limited to the years of earthly existence (Dt 4:1; 8:1; 30:15-20; 32:46-47). Some Jews nevertheless were already teaching that the life promised by the law would be everlasting (Lk 10:28; Jn 5:39-40).

Christ claims this for his own word, the power to give divine life (Jn 5:24; cf. Jn 12:47-50). The man who puts his message of fraternal love into practice can only do so by accepting that love as a gift of God. When he preaches love he gives divine life. There are two moments in this process; but they coalesce into one and the same hour (v. 25). The present moment, when those who are imprisoned by the death that is sin hear his message, are converted and enter into life (v. 25): and the future moment of resurrection from the dead (v. 28; cf. Mt 22:29-32), when everything will become clear. The latter moment is shaped by the former (v. 29).

Thus, as he grants life to sinners by the proclamation of his Word, Jesus is preparing the final resurrection of the dead. For this reason John calls him Son of man (Dn 7:13), a title reserved for the one whose judgment would open a path to definitive life. The destiny of the Son of Man was to judge and condemn sinners. Christ however has the power to give them life. Henceforward, accordingly, belief in the resurrection of the dead will require faith and conversion.

Christ's word then comes from God and brings with it divine life. God is revealed in that word, as any person reveals himself through the medium of language. All language is the product of free personal initiative; even the simplest human utterance is always a grace and gift. Once any person however, divine or human, decides to reveal himself in words, the words must be comprehensible for the hearer too. His language must draw upon terms within the hearer's experience. God thus speaks of "Father," "happiness," "kingdom" because these words have very precise connotation for the hearers. The language he uses is the language of human experience.

There is another, more profound, consideration. It is not as if human experience were a mere language reservoir from which God could draw terms and illustrations, while standing so to speak outside that experience. When he communicates he borrows more than language: he takes on the experience itself, its ups and downs, in the person of Jesus Christ. His Word then becomes a Word of life insofar as it succeeds in unveiling deep inside us the real meaning of our attitudes and our lives.

Just as the Word of God becomes meaningless if light is not thrown on the meaning of human experience, so does the Word of the Church become hollow if the spread of the gospel is not associated with secular and earthly objectives. The eucharistic celebration itself is only an empty ritual if man's secular life is not embraced in the thanksgiving.

VII. Exodus   This is an account of Moses before God after
32:7-14   the incident of the golden calf. He sees God
1st reading   denouncing the obstinacy of the stiff-necked
Thursday   people and deciding to be done with them,
                     while making Moses himself the patriarch of
another people (v. 10).

Despite the honor done to himself by such a proposal, Moses demurs. A promise by God, given once for all, cannot be rescinded, whatever the transgressions of the people. Beyond all doubt Moses emerges from this episode a nobler figure. He might have made a fresh start, but he chose to suppress personal ambition and become an intercessor with God for the people. With absolute confidence he subordinated everything to the fulfillment of this divine promise for the chosen people (Gn 15:5; 22:16-17; 35:11-12).

His selfless prayer won him particular recognition from the people, who would always see in him the perfect mediator and *intercessor* (Jr 15:1; Ps 98/99:6; 105/106:23; Si 45:3). It was the role he played initially after the plagues in Egypt (Ex 5:22-23; 8:4; 9:28; 10:17) and would continue to play throughout the sojourn in the desert (Ex 5:22-23; 32:11-32; Nb 14:13-19; 16:22; Dt 9:25-29).

In the situation where the people found themselves weak and fatally prone to sin before a powerful and severe God, the idea of a mediator was a very natural development. They gladly chose as their spokesman with God the one who seemed most worthy and one who seemed endowed with divine powers. Throughout this narrative one original characteristic of the mediator is noteworthy. God will only recognize as such one who espouses the cause of humanity, is totally involved with it, despite its sinfulness. He must not be some rarefied denizen of the heavenly spheres, but someone absolutely representative of mankind.

Consequently he is not the "just one" in the legalistic sense of the term, but the one who is ready to serve the people absolutely at the risk of being involved if necessary in their downfall. God is better represented among men by the mediator who strips himself to the level of his flock, not the one who is always vindicating God's power and holiness.

VIII. John   The cure of the paralytic (Jn 5:1-15) leads
  5:31-47   to a sharp cleavage between Jesus and the
  Gospel   doctors of the law, which John chooses to
  Thursday   describe as a judicial process. In verses 16-18
          the case is stated. Jesus makes his defense
in verses 19-30. He discusses the evidence of witnesses (vv. 31-40) and makes his indictment (vv. 41-47).

a) Jesus is alone in defending himself. Jewish jurisprudence required "two or three" *witnesses* before recognizing a deposition in tribunal (v. 31). He must then present his witnesses. The first is the Father (v. 32; cf. Jn 5:37; 8:18). But only Jesus can say whether that testimony be true (here, imperceptibly, we have the accused slipping into the role of judge). The second witness is John the Baptist (vv. 33-36); but even by Jesus' own admission (cf. Jn 1:19-28) his testimony is weak. He is the lamp only, not the light, and his testimony is not firsthand. Finally, as the third required witness, there is scripture (v. 39; cf. Rm 7:10). It speaks indeed of Jesus but its testimony is likewise weak because it does not give what it promises.

We are left then with the only truly decisive testimony, that of the Father (vv. 36-38). It is verified by the "works" and miracles that Jesus accomplishes, receiving them from the Father.

b) In taking to himself the task of evaluating the various testimonies he adduces, Jesus slips imperceptibly into the role of *judge*. We see him perfectly at home in the seat of judgment delivering sentence against his accusers (vv. 41-47). He is not seeking personal vindication; he does not act in a civil capacity. But he means to vindicate the glory of the Father, which is being impugned by Jewish refusal to accept his works.

The sentence is delivered according to the deposition made by Moses himself (vv. 45-47), the very source where his accusers hoped to find their best arguments (cf. Dt 31:19-27). If he has transgressed the law, the law in fact transpires to condemn, not him, but his accusers.

The human society into which Jesus came was completely demoralized, individual instances of alienation for this or that reason being multiplied. A poor man is crushed by a profit economy, a blind one deprived of the comfort he needs, a paralytic denied the means of fulfillment, all sorts of persons frustrated and despised for lack of the love that would recognize their dignity.

These were the unfortunates Jesus knew, and he himself · tasted the alienation which persecution and contempt induces. Revolt against such a state of affairs surged up in his heart; he wanted a society in which love would bring recognition of human dignity. And so a number of the miracles he wrought were meant to make his brothers happier and the world a more tolerable place.

But miracles were necessary. The means toward that ideal of personal intercommunion which he had, had to be experienced as gifts of God. It is only through "works" that are accomplished indeed, but yet bestowed, that men will reach a new order. Man does the works, but the Father gives them.

IX. **Wisdom**
2:1a, 12-22
1st reading
Friday

Second century Jews were still dreaming about a political restoration under a Messiah. A Son of man would come on the clouds (from upper regions, that is) to release them from the sway of Gentile nations. Daniel's apocalyptic glimpses into the future encouraged them and kept hope alive. By the following century, however, at the time *Wisdom* was written, conditions were considerably altered. There seemed to be no prospect at all of political independence, and even religious independence had become precarious.

Indeed, amongst contemporary communities of the diaspora, the just man who maintained election by God, and claimed *knowledge* of him (v. 13) to the extent of calling himself son of God (vv. 13, 16, 18), was generally challenged and ridiculed by others (vv. 12, 14-15).

The reaction was fairly scornful. How could Greek philosophers and scholars accept the pretensions of Jews, uneducated for the most part, to wisdom, or their knowledge of an ineffable God? Their dietary or liturgical customs rendered the Jews "eccentric" (v. 15). But the principal source of offense was their belief. In the Gentile world doctrines about reward for the just by God (v. 16), and above all about choice of one people in a covenant, with a special spiritual filiation and a special knowledge, seemed ridiculous.

Our passage today, mainly concerned with the situation of Jews in Alexandria, parallels, in a rather extraordinary way, the life of Jesus. He too claimed to be son of God (Jn 5:16-18; Mt 27:43), and to have a knowledge better than the most learned of the scribes (Jn 8:55). He encountered challenge and ridicule (Mt 27: 29-44), was a living reproach in the eyes of his compatriots (Mt 26:3-4, 23), and was condemned to death to vindicate the promise of help given him by God.

X. John	John, in his usual fashion, is reproducing here
7:1-2, 25-30	a scene that must have been often repeated
Gospel	in Jesus' career, every time his teaching
Friday	by "authority" was challenged by the book-

learning of scribes and doctors of the law (Mk 1:22; 6:2; Mt 22:22; Lk 4:22).

But John's analysis is deeper than that of the synoptics. If in fact Jesus had a knowledge that penetrated men's hearts better than that of the scribes, it was because he replaced technical knowledge of scripture with a *direct knowledge of the Father* (Jn 3:12; 5:24; 6:45). The Word of God for him was not principally that stated in scripture, but that elicited directly from living. As the Pharisees saw it, he was of the common people, unskilled in the law (Jn 7:49): in actual fact he was on a plane where they could not join him. He was the envoy of the Father, in close communion with him. The scribes were so dominated by the idea of exegesis that they could no longer see God in the event, in Jesus above all.

The phrase "cried out" in verse 28, as applied to the teaching of Jesus, is highly important. One did not "cry out" in giving exegesis of a text: the phrase obviously designates proclamation of a prophetic nature (cf. Jn 7:28, 37; 12:44), meant to indicate the authority Jesus possessed because of his communion with the Father.

XI. Jeremiah 11:18-20
1st reading
Saturday

It seems that the prophet Jeremiah was of profoundly depressive temperament. At the beginning of Joachim's reign, a violent indictment by him against a temple cult had resulted in a prosecution for sacrilege. He was exonerated (Jr 26:24) but was deeply wounded. Realizing his fate he then turned to composition of his "confessions," a literary genre new to Israel. They reflect the tension set up in his sensitive soul by the call of God (Jr 16:1-13, etc.). Our reading today is but a brief extract from that section, where he laments the day he was born and likens God's call to a seductive enterprise.

It would be wrong however to regard these confessions altogether as the outpourings of depression. The fact that they are (like many psalms indeed) in the first person singular is not sufficient reason for singularity in interpretation. In fact the "I" is normal in collective community prayers, above all when the liturgical assembly is aware of its mediating role between God and the people. Jeremiah is assuming a liturgical role. Having proclaimed God's will to the people, he moves from his personal situation to formulate a prayer to God of general intercession, and he describes, in lamentation form, the plight of Israel.

a) There were in fact several persecutions of the prophet (v. 18; cf. 12:3-6, etc.). In the view of contemporary sages one prophet's death would not be calamitous. Always, because of the presence of priests and sages, there would be sufficient "Words of God" without having recourse to those of Jeremiah.

b) This reflection leads Jeremiah to formulate a prayer. Its dominant note is the desire for *vengeance* (v. 19; cf. Jr 20:12), a normal sentiment in Jewish prayers of the period (Ps 5:11; 10:15; 30/31:18; 53/54: 7, etc.). In a religion based on temporal retribution this is understandable (cf. Ws 2:10-3:12). Only in the New Testament was such an idea transcended (Mt 5:43-48).

c) Preoccupation with his fate leads him likewise to certain imagery, which is destined to characterize the portrait of the *suffering Servant*. Here we have the theme of conspiracy (vv. 18-19; cf. Is 53:8-10; Ac 4:25-28; Jn 11:47-54) and that of the lamb led to the slaughter (Jr 11:18-19; cf. Is 53:7; Ac 8:32-35).

d) However, the most original theme in his thinking is that of his *seduction* by God. Most narratives of a calling indeed emphasize the manner in which those called are received. For Moses we have the urge to give up (Ex 32); for Elias discouragement (1 K 19); for Jonah deception (Jon 4); for Jeremiah depression (Jr 20) etc. It is particularly painful to feel excluded from a community because one has pointed out certain needs or borne witness to the spiritual. And the prophet's quailing before his mission (Jr 20:10-11) and its demands becomes that of the people too (Jr 20:9). All this is valid insofar as it underlines the gulf between personal wishes and the will of God. It is valid also, even to the point of psychological disturbance or crisis of faith, insofar as it points up the immense distance separating man from the true God.

All in all, then, the tension endured by the prophet is simply the natural disturbance inevitable wherever the mystery of God strikes the life of a man. Doubtless the man to whom God is but an idea or a definition will never experience the drama of such encounter, or have to be emptied of self in order to be aligned with the will of God. How was it that Jesus, that supreme example of total encounter between God and man, managed to evade the law, not to lose himself totally?

Human liberty I suppose, even in this blinding moment of mystery, is not crushed by God. Man lets himself be "seduced": he gives himself only to the person who has a right to take. Here we have the *raison d'être* of Christ's obedience on the cross, and the Eucharist summons us to follow that.

XII. John	Jesus is attending the feast of Tabernacles
7:40-53	(Jn 7:1-13), during which he reveals himself
Gospel	as the only source of living water (Jn 7:37-
Saturday	39). The reading describes the reaction and
	division caused by this announcement.

a) The people were unaware that Jesus was born at Bethlehem and regarded him simply as a stranger from Galilee, which they disdained because everyone was welcome there (Ac 2:7; Mt 26:69-73). The book of Ruth which advocated *collaboration between Israel and the Gentiles* had little impact in Judaea. They continued to look upon the mixed population of Galilee as people unfitted to share in the messianic restoration (Jn 7:52; Jn 1:45-46).

b) Christ's pronouncement about himself (vv. 37-39) had made an impression on the crowd. Many took him to be the messianic prophet (Dt 18:15; Jn 1:21). But at once the fanatics in exegesis took issue with that; he did not fulfill the conditions, as far as their knowledge went (davidic origin, birth in Bethlehem and so on: 2 S 7:12; Ps 88/89:4; Mi 5:2). Others went further still and wanted to have him arrested for imposture (v. 44). He should be brought before the Sanhedrin, the highest authority in this matter, where the greatest specialists in exegesis were to be found. However, Nicodemus apart (v. 51), there was no member of the Sanhedrin capable of pronouncing with accuracy about Jesus' human origins (v. 52). How then could they pronounce about his divine origin? *Learning* is incapable of reaching to knowledge of Jesus. So, *a fortiori*, is public opinion. How could they?

The whole discussion brings into focus a theme that is a very favorite one with John. He was convinced that no amount of poring over scripture or analyzing the facts and doings of Jesus could lead one to his person, at once divine and human. There was only one way, faith. Today there are procedures which obscure that person, just as surely as did the quibblings of his contemporaries. Being self-satisfied about our good conscience while failing to be engaged at the deepest recesses of our being, substituting apologetic for theology or casuistry for moral teaching: these are *our* mistakes.

FIFTH SUNDAY OF LENT

A. THE WORD

I. Ezechiel
37:12-14
1st reading
1st cycle

The prophet is in exile on the banks of the Kebar confronted by a vast plain, and it is against this background that he has a vision of his people's future. For the beginning of his account of this vision we should probably turn to Ezechiel 3:16a, 22-24a. Verses 12-13 were added subsequently, after the exile, by a disciple of the prophet.

a) As he surveys the plain before him, Ezechiel thinks of the numerous places where the skeletons of his compatriots have dried in the sun after their flesh and entrails were consumed by birds of prey. Biblical metaphors about *bones* indicate that they were regarded as the most profound part of the person, the most resistant to events. Hence here the *bones* (v. 11; cf. Jr 8:1-3) signify the better element of the people, the essential core.

He tells the people that all is not lost, that under God there will be a national restoration comparable to a new creation. This time God will not himself bring it about, but will entrust the responsibility to the prophetic ministry. The new man henceforward will have life breathed into him, just as in Genesis 2:7, by the breath of Yahweh; but this time the new spirit will be in the guise of prophecy (vv. 5-10).

The restoration will be a veritable re-creation: the prophet will breathe into new creatures the breath of a new covenant and the strength to cleave to it (cf. Ez 11:14-20).

b) A disciple of Ezechiel, influenced by Isaiah 26:19, added two verses (12-13) which altered the prophecy into one of the *resurrection of the body*. His purpose was to hint that perhaps the restoration would be postponed to the last days; but, in that event, Jews dying in the meantime would rise again to share the happiness of their descendants. The gloss colored not only future interpretation of Ezechiel 37, but also the thrust of many New Testament passages: Revelation 11:11; Matthew 27:51-54; John 5:28, and perhaps other texts as well.

Christians believe in the resurrection of the body; but have abandoned naive versions of that doctrine, like re-galvanization of the corpse or some mysterious regrouping of cellular complexes. Ezechiel's image is of course absolutely symbolic, and when his disciple speaks of resurrection, there is no material suggestion.

Nevertheless the whole passage does have relevance to the Christian doctrine, insofar as we find here an affirmation that corporeity is directly involved in eternal happiness. There is a sharp cleavage from Greek thought, where the concept of immortality concerns only the disembodied soul.

Has the classical exposition in this matter, the Christian doctrine, that is, and Ezechiel, been altogether satisfactory? Our usual teaching is that after death the soul exists apart from the body until the general resurrection. One sees the fairly misleading influence here of Greek thought. Because, while fully allowing that the individual destiny is linked to the collective, does not the question arise whether total separation of soul from body would not mean destruction of the person? Can a man be altogether divorced from the "center" where his person was expressed, where he communicated with others? However that be, some deepening of theological thought seems to be called for. What really does happen to man at the moment of death? How can he achieve a true liberation unless some sort of spiritual corporeity, valid for universal communication, continues to make his humanity integral?

II. Jeremiah
31:31-34
1st reading
2nd cycle

If this passage is really by Jeremiah it surely constitutes the peak point of his thinking. Nowhere else, and never again, in the Old Testament do we find so rich a text. It was used extensively by Jesus, Paul, and the author of the letter to the Hebrews either to explain the Eucharist, or to determine with exactitude the relation of Christianty to historic Israel.

In the old covenant, ratified on Sinai (v. 32) God's law seemed essentially exterior to men. Already in the deuteronomic reform there was awareness of the necessity of an *interior law* (Dt 6:6, 11, 18; 30:14) but the interiorization was the result of human effort. It meant a gradual alignment with the exterior law. Jeremiah's text goes much further. It affirms that the interior law is the gift of God. There is no evidence of a desire to abolish all external law. Jeremiah's close association with the deuteronomic reform is evidence to the contrary. What we do have is an emphasis on the necessity of an ethic which is not solely based either on the sanction of an external law or on human effort, but on communion with God at the deepest level of the self.

How did Jeremiah arrive at this concept of a law of God written in the heart? God is an examiner of the heart and the loins according to him, in the sense that he is present at the very core of our thoughts (heart) and passions (loins) (Jr 11:20; 12:3; 17:10; 20:12). It is only when the heart and the loins have been tested that God admits men to his presence.

The beneficial result of this sort of divine presence will be a softening of the hardened heart (Jr 3:17; 7:24; 9:13; 11:8; 18:12; 23:17) and that intimate union between Yahweh and his people (v. 33) which he describes in conjugal terms. "They shall be my people and I shall be their God" (Jr 7:23; 11:4; 24:7; 30:22; 31:1; 32:28).

The covenant was the very last area in Jewish thinking to be considered in terms of renewal. The notions of a new Jerusalem, a new temple, a new king, were fairly acceptable; but the covenant seemed so definitive as to transcend renewal. In the New Testament the notion of this new covenant is pervasive. In celebrating the Supper, Jesus confronted men with it (1 Co

11:25: cf. also 2 Co 3:1-2; Ga 4:21; He 8:6-10). There was no question though of condemnation, by this expression, of the Old Testament. It was always the same single act of divine mercy that was being described. What was promised in the old covenant was accomplished in the new.

III. Isaiah   This little poem of Second-Isaiah fits well
   43:16-21   into the general framework of the Book of
   1st reading   Consolation. The broken people are encour-
   3rd cycle   aged by the vision of a new future.

There was no way for Second-Isaiah, believing as he did in the unicity of God and consequently in the unity of history, to foretell the future except by reference to the past. It was not a matter of regarding history as a constant re-beginning (cf. v. 19). The view was that all events, of whatever kind past or future, carry the stamp of one and the same God, pointing always towards the single purpose of liberation.

Accordingly, the prophet depicts the future of the people, and above all the return from exile, as a *new Exodus* (vv. 16-19). This takes place in a paradisal atmosphere where universal peace and harmony combine to make the journey back quite marvellous (v. 20).

Such a presentation springs from the very innermost recesses of the human spirit. Any particular phenomenon, isolated, and taken singly, may seem without significance. To understand it, the thing itself, in this case the return from exile, is related to the phenomenon in myth or history which seems to crystalize the meaning of individual and collective destiny, here the Exodus from Egypt.

In Christian terms the intervention by Jesus in history is one of those events of primordial nature, and it is by reference to it that the people of God get insight into their own history.

Jesus is the Man. The life and death of each of us is overhung by his, and gets meaning from that fact (Jn 11:1-45). Our sufferings fill out the pattern of his (Ph 3:8-14).

IV. Romans
8:8-11
2nd reading
1st cycle

The verses just preceding our passage (Rm 8:4) had introduced into the description of Christian life the famous contrast between "flesh" and "Spirit" that was destined to be one of the cardinal themes of Pauline thought (Ga 5:16-24, etc.). Our reading is meant to be an explanation of the contrast.

Flesh is used to characterize the path chosen by the self-sufficient man, where there is no turning toward that divine help which is the *Spirit*. The law, even though of divine origin, can belong to the order of flesh whenever man so misuses it that he makes it a pretext for confronting God on a basis of title and merit. "Living according to the flesh" then means resorting to that very self-sufficiency that brought downfall for Adam and for mere observers of the law. It means capitulating to death (to isolation, that is, from God and his eschatological life). "Living according to the Spirit" means accepting the fact that the Spirit "dwells" in us; it means being open to communion with God, so that he can lead us towards life and peace. When the Spirit dwells in us, it is as master (verses 7-9 have the theme of authority), even though he seems to dwell in a dead body (v. 10) as he did in the body of the buried Christ.

V. Hebrews
5:7-10
2nd reading
2nd cycle

The author of the letter addresses Christians who are upset by the course of events in their time, and wonder what priest to trust. He puts forward Christ as the one high priest they seek and makes them witnesses, so to speak, of the inauguration of the new and definitive priesthood.

The *new high priest* fulfills all the conditions required. If he cannot claim heredity like the descendants of Aaron, that is because his priesthood is according to the order of Melchisadech (vv. 5-6).

The first condition is that the high-priest should come from among men because he represents man before God. Jesus fulfills this perfectly "throughout all the days of his flesh," by obedience and by the prayer of the suffering Servant (vv. 7-8, cf. Mt 27:46, 50; Ph 2:6-8). In fact he has achieved the ideal of sacrifice and obedience combined, just as the prophets had described it (1 S 15:22-25; Am 5:21-25; Ps 39/40:7-9).

The second condition is choice by God. That one's charism be derived from God is absolutely essential. Otherwise the priest would not be a mediator (cf. v. 4). Jesus fulfilled this condition, as the author sees it, at that moment when the Risen Lord became the source, for all, of salvation. God's choice was thus (vv. 9-10) according to the prophecies of the suffering Servant (Is 52:14). So the priesthood of Christ is associated with his entry into glory (vv. 5-6). The priesthood is an eternal one, in heaven, and it promises entry to divine life for all who accept it.

VI. Philippians 3:8-14
2nd reading
3rd cycle

Chapter 3 of the letter to the Philippians fits badly into its context. Consequently exegetes who regard the letter as a combination of passages from various letters to Philippi find their principal arguments here.

The chapter deals with heretics of Judaeo-Christian provenance (vv. 1-6), who are influenced by gnostic "perfectionism" (vv. 12-15). Once more Paul makes an apologia for his ministry and vocation. While canvassing certain topics already familiar (compare verses 4-6 with 2 Co 11:21-22; verse 9 with Rm 10:3;

1:17; Ga 2:16), he brings up a few new insights of high importance.

a) One of these is *sharing in the sufferings of Christ* (v. 10), something that can only be understood in the light of those doctrinal discoveries that Paul never ceased to make throughout his life. His early letters and discourses consider suffering from the eschatological standpoint: it is the trial which precedes the advent of the last days and entry into the Kingdom (Ac 14:22; 1 Th 1:6; 3:3-7; 2 Th 1:4-7; 2:7). It proclaims the return of Christ and enables disciples to imitate their master (1 Th 1:6; 2 Th 2:14-15). The Messiah had to endure suffering as a preliminary to his kingship; so too the messianic people before entering the Kingdom must in turn endure (cf. Rm 8:17-18).

Previously, in 1 Corinthians 1-2, suffering, above all the death of Christ, and in consequence all Christian mortification, seemed an occasion for God to display his power over evil. But then Paul felt the need to justify the association between Christ's death and Christian mortification. In Romans 6:3-11, among other things, he points out that baptism makes of Christ and the Christian one single body in passage from death to life. The Christian is united with Christ by his very body (1 Co 6:15; 10:17; 12:12-27; Ga 2:20); and so his sufferings, especially when they arise from his mission and his witness (2 Co 1:4-7; 4:7-12; 5:14-21; 13:3-4) become in a mysterious fashion those of Christ.

Thus mention of sharing in the sufferings of Christ (v. 10) presupposes the whole theology of communion *(koinônia);* because in the letter to the Philippians union between Christ and the faithful is seen in a context of love, that is foreign to the early Pauline writings.

b) Thanks to this *knowledge* (v. 8) of suffering, Paul is able to assert that all the advantages of Judaism no longer matter to him at all (v. 7). When he denies any value to the intellectual systems offered to their initiates by gnostics, he is reviving an ancient sapiental motif (Ws 7:7-14). Jewish sages had previously countered the pseudoknowledge of the world with their own understanding of the things of God. Paul's knowledge is not intellectual merely; it is a personal relation, a "communion" in the vital power of Christ, who passed from death to resurrection (v. 10), and who enables us in turn to pass from the death of sin to the life of God (v. 11). There were precedents in the Old Testament for regarding knowledge of God as a life rather than a theory (Nb 16:28; Jr 23:16; Is 21:10; Dt 18:15-16), and Paul is now affirming that such knowledge is a share in the life of the Risen Lord and a renewal of our own life (verses 11-12; Col 3, 5-11).*

c) As distinct from Christians who are proud and perfectionist, Paul portrays himself as a *pilgrim searching,*** unsatisfied, hungering for divine justice. He has not yet "reached the term" (the phrase is borrowed from the vocabulary of the mystery religions, verse 12), meaning that he has not yet achieved his full initiation into the mystery of Jesus. What he is aiming at is no ideal intellectual or moral perfection but "the prize in the race", which is none other than the resurrection of the dead (cf. v. 11). The arena-metaphor here differs from that in 1 Corinthians 9:25. Here the runner already sees the goal. He is no longer daunted by the thought of the course that must be run, but by the final leap that will give him the prize. That is all that counts now, to the extent that he forgets all previous joys and miseries.

The race then is not without a goal. Paul knows what he is making for, because he knows he has been called (v. 14), just as any sinful man is called to the faith and reconciliation (Rm 11:29; 1 Co 1:26; 7:20; 2 Th 1-11) won by Jesus Christ.

In the Church just now the idea of being in pilgrimage is particularly fertile. We are just emerging from a period in

---

*See doctrinal theme: *victory over death*, p. 220.
**See doctrinal theme: *maturity in faith*, p. 226.

which missionary success, stable institutions, unalterable truths and absolute power could create the impression that the Kingdom of God was already a reality. But now, with so much in question, with dechristianization on a massive scale, with collapse of, and challenge to, institution, it is evident that the Church is "not yet" the Kingdom. Instead of being a people in possession, it becomes again a people in pilgrimage. The biblical nature of this experience is a good reminder and can serve to restore serenity to those disquieted by change.

Because the Christian adventure of our time is not without meaning, the runner has his eyes fixed on the goal, the fullness of Christ for all men. Yet taste for adventure is not witness to Christ, nor does pure humanism suffice for such witness. The Christian knows where he is going, and though he may not know the snares that beset his path, or the kind of dialogue the world needs, he keeps his eyes on the goal. He is prepared in advance to encounter anything, make any sort of experiment, provided only the goal be reached.

VII. John 11:1-45 Jesus is approaching that journey to Jerusalem
    Gospel   which, his disciples well know, is a journey
    1st cycle   to his death (cf. Jn 7:1, 8). The disciples
            agree to follow him, not without hesitancy
and depression (vv. 8, 12, 16). From the outset though he wants them, all dubious as they are, to understand that this journey will issue in the victory of life over death, the gift of life by means of death.

a) The narrative of Lazarus' resuscitation is altogether designed as the best illustration of the *life-death* paradox. It is as if, for John, Jesus actually waits until his sick friend is really dead (vv. 5, 17, 39); he wants to reveal his power over death at the very moment when death is to have power over him. It is also paradoxical that his own death is hastened by his resuscitation of a corpse (v. 47).*

b) Invariably for John the work accomplished by Jesus is designed to reveal his divine personality (v. 40, the theme of glory). It is so with this narrative of *resurrection*. Martha believes only in a resurrection at the end of time (v. 24). Jesus reveals that he is this resurrection (I am: v. 25), not just now, but above all later on, after he has won his victory over death, for which, as John sees it, his godhead now prepares him.

c) It is obvious that John's version of the Lazarus incident is designed to prefigure the *paschal drama*. In Lazarus, Jesus is confronted by death and is already "troubled" as he will be in Gethsemane (v. 33). But the episode carries too the hints of Jesus' own resurrection: Mary's tears at the tomb (v. 33, cf. Jn 20:11), the tomb itself and the heavy stone (vv. 38-40; cf. Jn 20:1), the winding sheet (v. 43; cf. Jn 20:5), and above all the fact that Lazarus is "let" go free (v. 44; cf. Jn 20:17). John, a believer before the empty tomb of Easter, finds Jesus' Pasch already in the death and raising of Lazarus.

About the impressions of the risen Lazarus, what he could have seen while dead, how it felt to be restored (provisionally of course) to life, John does not give the slightest information. That has no interest for him. He does not see Christian life as a sort of advance taste of paradise arbitrarily conceded by an all-powerful Lord, divorced from all decision on the part of the person concerned.

For him these "returns to life" brought about by Jesus are above all "signs" of God's own activity, which is life, at work in the whole texture of the human experience, including death. It is only when illumined by faith that the lesson of the resurrection miracle is really understood.

Thus it is more important to know who Jesus is than what happened to Lazarus. We should realize that through Jesus Lazarus found a way, even in the grip of death, of sharing in

*See the doctrinal theme: *victory over death*, p. 220.

life. This is what faith means; and this sort of knowledge is very different from that manifested by Martha and Mary, when they affirm their belief in a final resurrection.

VIII. John   This is John's account of Christ's entry to
12:20-33   Jerusalem (vv. 12-19) and his glorification
Gospel   before the Gentiles (vv. 20-36). The inci-
2nd cycle   dents take place on the second day of the
                   last week of the public life. Just as John had
given a day by day account of the first week of the Messiah
(1:29, 35, 39; 2:1), so is he anxious to do the same for Christ's
last days (12:1-12; 13:1; 18:28; 19:31). And just as Phillip and
Andrew were prominent in the first week, so too, as the end
begins, they find themselves featured (Jn 13:21-22).

The structure of the passage is fairly clear. There are two
successive revelations of Jesus' personality (vv. 23-28 and 31-32)
which meet with incomprehension on the part of the crowd
(vv. 29 and 34). Then Jesus reveals the true meaning of the
manifestations (vv. 35-36) and reacts to the incomprehension
by hiding himself from the crowd (verse 36).

a) In the synoptic accounts of the entry to Jerusalem a source
was used which stressed, with reference to Psalm 118/119, the
glory of Christ. Care was taken to indicate that the glory was
the fruit of rejection (the rejected stone becomes the cornerstone). John's version has the same bias: to the account of the
manifestation of glory (v. 23) he hastens to add the parable
of the grain which only bears fruit by dying (vv. 24-25).
However, while being faithful to the primitive interpretation
he adds an original nuance. His understanding of glory gives
him a deeper insight than the synoptics into the facts. Once
Christ's glory is manifested, the disciples are enabled to "understand" (v. 16, in the same sense as previously, Jn 2:22). Then
the fact that the Gentiles can now approach salvation has im-

portance. The glory is no longer that of a national messiah; it is that of God, who sheds his light over the whole world (vv. 20-23). It is such that Christ, though troubled by his imminent death, displays no misgiving or doubt. Where the synoptics have him in anguish, for Saint John he remains detached and lucid (Jn 12:27-30; Mt 26:36-45). And, once again, John introduces the equivocal theme of "elevation," which can denote elevation on the cross as well as elevation in glory (v. 34; Jn 2:19; 3:13-14; 8:28; 12:32-34; cf. Is 52:13; Ph 2:9-10). The royal elevation is, at one and the same time, a salvific one.

b) So it is that the whole passage carries a series of hints meant to indicate that there will be a sequel to the death of Christ. When Jesus confronts the crowd for the last time the Jews refuse to see. The Gentiles on the other hand open themselves to the Savior. This allows John to stress a particular aspect of the forthcoming glorification: the *regathering* of the nations (v. 32; cf. Is 53:12). Jesus is aware of the universal fruitfulness of his approaching death.

Indeed the opposition between Christ and the Jews stems from two different notions of fruitfulness and glorification. In their view only the means of power could lead to glory; for him the only possible means was the paschal mystery of his Passion. This polarity between humiliation and glorification is reflected also in the equivocal character of the term "elevate."

c) Considerable reference to time throughout the passage (the hour; now; has come . . .) is meant to show how closely this revelation of glory is linked with salvation-history, and with the great turning in the course of time that marks the *hour* of Christ's death and resurrection (cf. Jn 4:23; 5:25; 12:27, 31; 13:31; 16:5; 17:13).

d) The finale of the discourse, as John has it, with its focus on the idea of *light,* is an admirable summation. Elevated on the cross, the tacit appeal of Jesus draws all men, so that all may walk in the light, that is — believe in him. Faith will definitively reassemble all humanity round the cross, and this will be the messianic community of the final times. The throne of the new king and lord will be the cross.

God's glory, in scriptural terms, does not mean, as in our idiom, renown. It means that genuine idea of value, importance, respect imposed by God. The bible is often pessimistic about man in isolation, and ridicules the "glory" of the man "who does not properly weigh" (in Hebrew the word glory actually suggests weight): Psalm 48/49:17-18. Only God can have genuine glory, proper value (Ps 61/62: 6-8; Is 6:1-6).

The New Testament proclaims that in Jesus God's glory is manifested (He 1:3; 2 Co 4:6; 1 Co 2:8; Jn 1:14-18). His works reveal that glory; he is truly the first man to have weight, to have value. And he derives that from his communion with God, above all at the time of his passion and resurrection (Jn 10:30; Jn 17:19; 12:28).

That glory overflows to men (Jn 17:10) through sacramental communion (1 Jn 5:7; Jn 19:34-36) and through the sharing of the Father's life which Jesus has (2 Co 1:22; Col 1:10-11).

B. DOCTRINE

1. The Theme of Victory over Death

In addition to the ordinary reflections prompted by the gospels of the fourth and fifth Sundays, the narrative of the raising of Lazarus suggests analysis of the idea of victory over death.

Throughout the whole pattern of earthly existence, throughout all social relationships, runs the thread of death. It is not just the final event of our pilgrimage: it is the culminating point, the crystalization, of a challenge which never ceases to confront the human being. Every event, of whatever kind, is stamped by death, and always has the nature of challenge, because man's fundamental aspiration is life. And if the Christian is the only genuine realist it follows that he must meet death face to face, that is, in faith, the most demanding of disciplines. But it is also the most necessary of disciplines, because the paschal mystery is the core of Christianity. And that means victory over death, accomplished once for all in Jesus Christ.

The discipline is more than ever necessary now because we are concerned with the evangelization of modern man. It is modern man who with his mastery over nature has the dream of relieving earthly existence of death, the weight which crushes it. Just because of this, because of concrete hopes raised in some quarters, it becomes imperative for the Christian to be as exact as he can about what he means by passing from death to life. The belief is at once a recognition of death and a victory over it.

Yahweh, the living God of Israel in search of life

Life is the most precious gift to which man can aspire. But it is a fragile gift because it is always threatened by death. Man is always trying to escape death, by whatever means, mostly by plumbing the unpredictable, the chances of history. Life belongs to the gods. If we would have it in any stable sort of way, we must establish communication with the domain of the gods and share possession of life by conciliating them. So there were liturgies for inducting pagan man, in his search for life, into the mysterious world of sacral space and time. Then came the philosophers and mystics, who took as their point of departure the very same basic myths the liturgies had used, and provided a metaphysic for the few. They promised ways of union with God, by exaltation of the "soul" and rejection of the "body." There was little point in worrying about suffering and death. These affected the body only, and only mattered because the view taken of reality was wrong!

Israel, using the way of faith, left the pagan ways aside. The God of Israel, Yahweh, was absolute master of life. He was a living God, but was also the All-Powerful God, and no one could climb the ladder which led to him. The chasm dividing the Creator from his work was unbridgeable. He manifested himself, transcendent as he was, by intervening in the event. Throughout a very concrete history he governed the vicissitudes of his people. Everything, good or bad, success or failure, was a divine epiphany. Life then was a totally gratuitous gift: man received it, but was not master of it. Yahweh however in giving life to man, saves him also, because on earth man is the prisoner of death, the consequence of sin. His duty was to be faithful to Yahweh's covenant. The time would come when death would disappear, when the terrestrial condition would yield place to a new land, a land of the living that would last throughout a blessed eternity. While bearing witness to the permanence of sin, messianic hope was also witness to the passionate quest of a people in search of life.

The victorious challenge of death by Christ

From all this Jewish thinking one step still remained to be taken. For the Jew death was the consequence of sin; the advent of salvation must necessarily mean the abolition of death. This indeed was an attitude of faith; but it was still that of a sinful man, who wanted life under ideal conditions in terms of the terrestrial existence that he understood. When Jesus came he inaugurated the Kingdom of life on this earth. It was not of this earth, but it took its roots from here. He also confronted death victoriously. In other words to this man who was sinless death finally delivered its meaning. It was not what it seemed to sinful man to be, the impregnable barrier to life. Death was in fact the way which led to veritable life.

In both his life and his teaching Jesus was constantly challenging death. His message is summed in one single principle: brotherly love that is limitless. If a man loves like this he is always encountering death, and he only succeeds in overcoming the obstacle by being free from sin while faithful to his creatural condition. Loving all men means accepting a sort of life that death cannot touch. It means indeed acceptance of a life to which the acceptance of death, in obedience to God, is the gateway. Jesus' own earthly career was a complete testimony to this doctrine. He was obedient to his creatural, terrestrial, condition, even to death on the cross. When the hate of his enemies made them turn to death as their weapon, the challenge of death reached its greatest intensity, but obedient acceptance of death on the cross became the gateway to life. It marked the moment of total surrender of self to love.

But of course Jesus was the only one to open this way. According to God's plan man is created to be a member of the divine family and the life to which he aspires is a divine life. But man's sin lay in the fact that he disputed with God's control over a life that was not creatural. What Jesus showed was that only the man-God was capable of pointing the way to divine life. Every man can possess eternal life and become a child of God if he is linked to Christ. He honors his vocation to "sonship" by being faithful to his condition as "creature"; by agreeing to confront death victoriously as Jesus did, in obedience to the living God.

The relation of the Church to the cross of Christ.

The Church is the Body of Christ. Each man's salvation depends upon his link with the Body, because Christ is the only mediator. When we consider the cross of Christ, and the great moment of salvific mediation, what can we learn about the mission of the Church and the meaning of membership in the Church?

As a salvific institution, it is the Church's mission to bring men into the Kingdom by introducing them to the paschal mystery. This kind of initiation into a spiritual sacrifice is really sacramental. It produces grace, even as it builds up in charity the multitude assembled from the four winds. However it is only fruitful when centered on the sacrifice of the cross. The Word is of quite paramount importance in Christian initiation. Through it the believer, in common with his brothers, becomes aware of the great weight of death which presses down upon all the vicissitudes of human existence, upon all human relations individual and collective. And death must be confronted, lucidly and obediently, wherever it presents itself. It is thus that the evangelic law of universal love takes real shape; it is thus that we come to know the efficacy of genuine life. To pass death by, to ignore it when it presents itself is to remain in sin. It is to deceive ourselves with some illusory brand of efficacy; to accept in fact the victory of death, because the kind of life for which we opt is still vitiated by death. In all, the Church's mission is to make men live here on earth as children of God. As such they know the life that animates them for all eternity; they have in Jesus Christ the power to look on death as he did, the indispensable gateway towards true life.

The Church's mission makes her the permanent sign of the living God among men. By means of her members scattered throughout the world she offers all men the key to the only life that can satisfy them. In the midst of events she points the way to that life. It is the way of obedience, obedience even to the death on the cross, the great way of universal love.

The good news of the paschal mystery

Modern man differs from his predecessors in his attitude towards death. He finds death inherent in the human condition, a biological happening that affects all life. He deplores it of course as a stumbling block to all his aspirations, but his reaction is not the same. In the past, feeling himself completely helpless before death, man would seek refuge in those numinous liturgies which offered contact with the divine. Or, if he were Jewish, he would see death as a consequence of sin, to be abolished with sin, with the advent of the Kingdom. For all, death was the state of fallen man.

But modern man is not passive before death — he meets it head-on. Thanks to his ever-increasing mastery over nature, he tries by every means to roll back the frontiers of death, confining its dominion merely to the aging of the organism, forcing it into the domain of the predictable. If it succeeds in evading him still, all that leads up to it from birth onwards is being gradually shown of unforeseeable elements. Earthly life becomes less and less hazardous; there is much more security; fears common in the past are being surmounted.

It would be a grave distortion of witness, if the Christian concentrated on stressing the inevitability, in spite of everything, of death, hinting at a future filled with wars, famines, earthquakes, unforeseeable disasters, and so on. Christianity is not a matter of prophesying doom. Furthermore, men nowadays tend to have grave misgivings about any religion which concentrates solely on the consolations after death. That seems an evasion of earthly responsibilities. The Good News of the paschal mystery is not just the hope of blessed immortality, to follow a death in pious resignation.

The truth is that, so far from robbing the proclamation of the gospel of its persuasive weapons, modern efforts to make the world more habitable really clarify its essentials. The death that confronts man at every moment of existence is not basically biological death, or the hazardous nature of earthly happenings. It lies in the great frustration which bedevils his spiritual liberty: the inability to assuage by possession of created goods his thirst for the absolute. The death which oppresses us is a spiritual event. We feel it particularly in moments of great insecurity, above all when confronting physical death. On the other hand security of any kind can make us forget that spiritual death is a constant reality, which must be contemplated realistically and obediently if we are to promote that life which does not end. When man has succeeded in constructing a secular city that is more habitable, and surrounds himself more and more with the securities he needs, it is true that he runs the risk of shrivelling, of resorting to pride and forgetting the true nature of his liberty. But if he keeps his eyes open, it is also possible for him to set in really clear perspective the authentic human adventure to which he is summoned.

The proclamation of the death of Christ in the eucharistic celebration

The Eucharist is the memorial of the Cross. Day after day we commemorate there Christ's death, and the gate that was opened to life in the Risen Lord. What do we really mean by it all? A remembrance merely of this great decisive moment?

By no means. When Christ's death is proclaimed and commemorated in this assembly, we are first of all affirming that he alone victoriously confronted death, in perfect fidelity to his condition as creature. And secondly we declare our resolution, following him and by his help, to take the same way of obedience. The occasion then should be one that sharpens our insight about death in all its ramifications. We realize very well that the increased security of modern life can bring about in sinners such as us a great blindness. Everything goes on as if death were not there at all, as if there were no obstacles any more to spiritual liberty. For that reason it is more than ever imperative that the Mass should become our realistic moment. The Word should enable us to touch death sensibly, the death we are called to vanquish through our living link with Christ. This is not morbid. The Christian looks at death to triumph over it. Confronted in obedience it yields up its meaning and becomes the gateway to life.

2. Auxiliary Theme for Lent: Maturity in Faith

In the old Christian countries it might very easily be taken for granted that Christians are natural believers. A long Christian history does mold a culture and influence gradually the general scale of values. But a Christian might accept this scale of values and yet fail to be a believer. Full exercise of faith always means continual discovery of the living God and encounter with him. Such encounter will inevitably lead to the desire for new conversion and deeper emptying of the self. The cradle-Christian should, in other words, make his personal pilgrimage along the road that leads from Adam to Jesus Christ through Abraham. Time is necessary for this, a long process of maturation.

When, every year, the Church enjoins a Lenten period of preparation for the feast of Easter, she is really helping the Christian community towards maturity of this kind. And Lent, unless faith is at work, could sink to a level where moral effort and ascetic practices take precedence over deepening of theological insight.

The desert, a time of maturing for faith

Our spontaneous reactions always belong to the pagan element in us: they have nothing to do with faith. This was just as true of the Jewish people as of others, and we have Jewish history to prove it. There was a constant need for prophets to recall the people to the regime of faith. Living as believer meant mobilizing all one's energies, all one's person, in obedience to Yahweh's plan, however disconcerting the turns taken in the salvific process. God wanted a religion of the heart. This kind of total concentration could not be achieved in a single day; it required time, gradual interiorization, conversion that was ever more lucid in insight.

There is nothing surprising here. Regularly in the lives of prophets high turning points would be preceded by a time of preparation. Forty days became the symbolic period. Before the revelation of Sinai Moses spends forty days in solitude on the mountain. Before meeting the living God on Horeb Elias journeys for forty days in the desert. Any real, authentic experience of the living God, it seems, requires a preliminary process of interior adjustment.

In Jewish history itself there was that unusual period, forty years in duration, which stood as exemplar for such experiences: the desert sojourn which led to the promised land. Successive generations would ponder its lessons and gradually deepen the insights of belief.

It was of course a time of preparation, leading to the Promise, to salvation. And the preparation was accomplished in the desert, where insecurity was a daily diet and men had to depend on faith. In all a time of trial, where God made trial and man was tried, where one discovered what one was worth, and the measure of one's sin. If it was a time of grace, it was also a time of defiance and revolt.

Just because of men's sin, the desert sojourn failed to produce all the fruits of God's grace. It had its dimension of failure because the land of promise was not the land of salvation: the Kingdom had still to be awaited. Yet, in a very special way this experience never ceased to touch the nerve center of Jewish sentiment. It would always be preeminently the blessed time of genuine encounter between God and his people. In future conjectures about the eschatological Kingdom, the vision of a desert where everything springs into bloom would be standard.

The forty days of Jesus in the desert

Before his public proclamation of the Kingdom, Jesus of Nazareth personally relived for forty days the spiritual experience of the desert. For him, as for the people previously, it was a time of trial; but, unlike the people, he overcame the temptation, and in obedience fully cooperated with God's plan.

It should be very carefully noted that this was not a mere symbolic reenaction of the people's experience. Jesus retired to the desert before his public ministry because he too personally felt the need of a high moment of proof and preparation. He too had to become adjusted interiorly to the business of his Father. There was no question of automatic acceptance. Prayer, solitude and fast were a necessary preparation for the Good News of salvation.

The real meaning of his sojourn lies in its success, his victory. He could now say, in very truth, that the Kingdom he was proclaiming had already come: "it is among you." The salvific will of God had at last, in him, encountered the full fidelity of obedience. The whole three years of public life, down to the death on the cross, were already present in germ the first time he made the momentous announcement. The desert sojourn prepared the paschal act. His victory there will be his victory later when condemned to death. But the glory of the victory is not of this world. The Kingdom he proclaimed, the true Land of Promise, transcends earthly horizons.

The time of the Church and the time of Lent

A constant tension characterizes the time of the Church. Ever since Pentecost, until the Lord returns, she has to go on building herself on the basis of what was accomplished once for all by Christ's Resurrection. Little by little the totality must be permeated so that the mystery of Christ have full stature. Such a task requires time in enormous dimension. But, because the First-Born of humanity is already risen from the dead, we know the task is gradually being accomplished. Between what is done and what remains to be done lies the tension, an inevitable tension, in that our hope about the future is based altogether on what Jesus did two thousand years ago.

Within the fold of the Church the tension is properly controlled. Each member, by reason of his living relationship with Christ, is enabled to travel the long road of faith along a trail already blazed. Grace leads him to encounter the God of Jesus Christ. The Spirit is at work in his heart, so that he can in very truth say "Father." But he should actively cooperate in the task of the Church; all life and all domains of living, must be clothed untimately in the mystery of Christ.

There is no steady uniformity about all this. Man being what he is, emphasis must be laid at one time on this aspect of our pilgrimage in faith, at another, on that. Lent is the precise period when the Church asks the faithful to emphasize one of the two essential aspects: they should now prepare themselves as a community in a special way for the great Paschal moment. They are asked to give evidence of a faith that is lived in interior poverty in the service of God and men. This time of preparation will be succeeded by paschal time when the emphasis will be on the eschatological aspect of our faith.

The time of mission and the time of Lent

The times of the Church and of mission are identical. The building up of the Church to its required stature requires that the Good News of salvation be proclaimed to add nations. Then only shall the end come. In the hearts of all men and at the roots of all cultures the Spirit of Christ is at work. However it is only when the mystery of Christ takes firm root, that men and races can bring this work of the Spirit to proper fruition. Two millennia of history have only succeeded in broaching this gigantic task.

The role of the individual Christian fits into the structure of universal mission. As a member of the Body, he has the means of achieving successfully his own pilgrimage of faith, but he must pour all his personal energies into it too. This is not easy;

above all for the missionary it is difficult. He leaves the known land, the christianized one, and carries the Good News to a new people. He shares their life and confronts paganism at its very roots. It is the example of his personal fidelity which will provide the model for them.

Thus Lent only acquires its full meaning when we live it in a spirit of universal mission. All Christians do not have to quit their country, but all have the responsibility of seeing to it that the Church be among men the great sign of salvation. Lent can never be a purely interior thing, or an individual thing. It is essentially collective, a time when all are made to feel their involvement in the communal missionary thrust.

Today, as always, the missionary realizes that the Word he preaches is a call to conversion and penance. The unbeliever too has his long Lent, a tortuous journey through darkness towards the God of Jesus Christ. How can the missionary fully appreciate this unless he is schooled himself, many times, by the disciples of the Church's Lent?

The Eucharist and mature faith

In the eucharistic celebration the presence of Christ among us is that of one who sums up in his person the marvels of the desert long ago. He is living water, bread from heaven, the way, the guide, the light by night. The sharing of his flesh and blood enables the believer to encounter the living God.

And, because it is a sign of the transfiguration that has already been accomplished of humanity and the cosmos, the Eucharist makes Lent a uniquely Christian observance. We all traverse the time of trial in awareness of victory. Each day as we break the bread the tenor of our lives follows the great pattern, from desert-trial to resurrection-victory. This is the rhythm which matures faith.

And yet, the sign given us of the already transfigured world is but a sign, evanescent like all signs. What *is* proclaimed each time, with transparent clarity, is the death of the Lord until the day of the return.

FIFTH WEEK OF LENT

I. Daniel 13:1-9;
15-17; 19-30;
33-62
1st reading
Monday

It is possible that this passage was compiled scarcely one hundred years before Christ. Originally the name Daniel did not appear. Very probably it was added because its etymology (God my judge) describes so well the young man in question. Then, because of the similarity in name, the passage was inserted in the book of Daniel, but at a stage too late for recognition in the Jewish scriptural canon.

It is a *haggada,* obviously of polemical character. Doubtless it was a tale put together by the Pharisees in their controversy with the Sadducees and aimed particularly against the dissolute old men of the high priest Jason's entourage.

Susanna stands for the spirit of Israel, which remains faithful to God as spouse. She refuses to commit *adultery* under the garden trees, which represent the sites of ancient "adulteries" against God by the people (Ho 2:15; Jr 2:20-25; Ez 16:15-20; 1 K 14:21-25).

The story then is that of the just who remain faithful to God, despite solicitation by Gentiles and Sadducees. When persecuted they sing of their certainty of proximate deliverance by God. It is impossible that he will forget them.

IIa. John 8:1-11
Gospel
Monday

This passage is not Johannine. It does not appear in the most primitive manuscripts of the fourth gospel, and its style resembles much more that of Luke, who could very well have been the author. Luke displays an anxiety to chronicle all evidences of attention by Jesus to women, and of his determination to transcend the contemporary juridical practice with regard to pardon and mercy. The narrative fits perfectly the

231

context of Luke 21:37-38. Indeed that whole chapter of Luke has many allusions to Daniel (cf. vv. 7, 9, 12); and, if we add to it this passage, the combined texts could be regarded as a *midrash* of Daniel.

In any case it would seem that the author had the Susanna narrative in mind. We have in both passages the accusation of adultery, the reversal of the situation, an allusion to old men (v. 9), the anxiety of the accusers to have their victim "in full view" (v. 3), an appeal to the law of Moses about stoning (Dt 22:22-24). Thus Christ is presented as the new Daniel. Not only does he vindicate the innocent, as the young man in the Susanna passage, but even the guilty (v. 11), thus making it clear that God's judgment is grace and pardon.

Susanna of course represents Israel, and if we are to find a parallel between the passages in this detail it would be by taking the adulterous woman as an image of Christ's humanity. Susanna is saved from Jason's old men by the observers of the law; humanity is saved by Christ from the scribes and Pharisees, old men too — even if they are the very ones who saved Susanna.

How was it that the saviors of Susanna became the accusers of the adulterous woman? Because Christ had come in the interval and laid the foundations of a new ecclesiology. Daniel had been, before God and man, the witness of a "just" people, perfectly obedient that is to the law. The law however judges acts, not persons. Now, in Christ, God is judging persons. He knows that, deeper laid than sins or legal justice, there is a zone in each person where a dialogue with God in sincere faith is possible. That is why Susanna is not an image of the Church; the impression would be too legalistic. Members of the Church have a better symbol in the adulterous woman. They can transcend their sin, and accept the chance of encounter and dialogue offered them by Christ. Thus they will be led one day to sin no more, not just to obey a law but to obey a conscience that has known Love.

IIb. John 8:12-20 Jesus is taking part in the feast of tabernacles,
Alternative which was characterized by a profusion of
Gospel lights. John chooses this moment to describe
Monday the revelation of his "luminous" personality
(v. 12), which made him the target of the
Pharisees who resented such pretensions (v. 13-20).

a) When the feast opened in the evening, it was customary
to light golden lamps in the temple precincts and in each home;
and subsequently, for several evenings, there were torchlight
processions. There was multiple religious symbolism in this
feast of lights. It recalled the luminous cloud of the desert
(Ex 13:21-22), but above all it proclaimed the messianic era
when God would save his people (Is 60:1-3; Ml 4:2; Is 42:6;
cf. Rev 21:23).

Jesus asserts that he is the *light*, the definitive light (note the
"I am"). He is that not alone for Israel (which will in fact
reject its glow: Jn 12:46-48), but for all nations because he
can snatch from death (Jn 1:4-5; 1 Jn 2:9-11) every man, even
the Gentile, who listens to his message (Jn 12, 23).

b) The Jews criticize the *witness* to himself which he gives
in claiming to be light of the world (vv. 13-19). And from
the strictly juridical point of view they have good reason. The
Jewish law was that testimony was only acceptable when supported by "two or three witnesses" (Dt 19:15; cf. v. 17). Jesus
is not thus supported, hence the testimony is invalid.

On this question of procedure the Pharisees consider themselves dispensed from study of his declaration. But Jesus reacts
by turning the procedural question to his own advantage, thus
focusing attention on the assertion itself. A sort of judicial
process against him takes shape in which men wish to judge
him "according to the flesh" (v. 15, cf. Jn 7:24), that is to say
in a human fashion, on his exterior actions. He calls his witness,
his own Father. But this witness is invisible, one whom only
those who "know" the Son (v. 19) can see. And that sort of

knowledge will only be possible when the Son has returned to his Father. Consequently the issue of the process cannot be in doubt: the Son's testimony will not be accepted, he will die. But at that moment another witness, the Paraclete, will make his appearance. The verdict will be appealed and Christ's memory will be vindicated (Jn 16:8-11).

c) Jesus asserts furthermore that he himself will pass judgment on the actors in this scene (vv. 15-16). The *judgment-sentence* will be countersigned by the Father and will certainly pronounce condemnation on the Jews. The reference here of course is not to the last judgment. What is stressed is Jesus' certainty that, in one way or another, the Father will confound those who plot against his life.

The advent of the messianic era means that from now on light has won the definitive victory over darkness. Because he himself was light of the world, resurrection and life, Jesus of Nazareth brought that about. The man-God, sinless, altogether obedient to the will of the Father, is in his human nature the light that enlightens every man who comes into the world, and possesses eternal life in its fullness. He accepted his human condition, challenged the hour of darkness and death, so that he might emerge in the blinding light of Transfiguration, the perfect life of Resurrection. To live eternally where death and darkness have no more sway one must have the power to renounce this present life, to deliver it up in love.

For John the whole life of Jesus, his actions and his words, contributed to reveal him as light of the world and prince of life. The Kingdom that he inaugurated by giving up his life is present here and now. Darkness and death recoiled from his path wherever he went; he cured the blind and raised up Lazarus. All creation is touched by this incarnation of light and life.

To those who recognize him in faith and agree to follow him, Jesus offers a share of these blessings. "Anyone who follows me will not be walking in the dark; he will have the light of life" (Jn 8:12). "Whoever lives and believes in me will never die" (Jn 11:25). The believer shall have living water which becomes for him "a spring welling up to life eternal" (Jn 4:14).

III. Numbers
21:4-9
1st reading
Tuesday

The brazen serpent, or more accurately the "fiery serpent" (*saraph,* whence the word seraphin) was probably a relic of the old idolatrous fertility cults that was preserved in the temple until the reform of Ezechias (2 K 18:4). The fact that legislators and prophets made no attempt to remove it earlier from Yahweh's sanctuary suggests that it was quite popular.

Inability to remove the symbol made it necessary to adopt another course, exorcism of its associations by incorporating it into Exodus history. Our passage today is probably concerned with that precise end. One of the numerous crises in the desert is depicted and the object is related to the spread of a serious malady, which was probably due to an epidemic of poisonous serpents (vv. 5-7). The author tells how Moses interceded and put an end to the scourge, not so much by fashioning a bronze serpent as by an appeal to the people's faith (v. 9; cf. Ws 16:5). This is a testimony, fairly weak as yet, to the salvation God will provide for man if only he has sufficient faith to turn to God and has a mediator who can bring that solution and determine its conditions.

Were it not for the popularity of this symbol in primitive Christian communities, we might well be dubious about something so naive and suggestive of magic. Doubtless the popularity was due to the Wisdom passage (Ws 16:1-7). Here a contrast is drawn between the behavior of the Egyptians and the Jews when a like scourge afflicted both. The former were overwhelmed because they had not faith and lacked a mediator who could ask God to end the scourge. The Jews on the other hand found in their faith sufficient strength for conversion, and, above all, they could rely on their mediator.

Doubtless early Christians here saw a parallel with the circumstances of their own salvation. For them the images of Moses and the brazen serpent were fused into that of Christ elevated on the cross (Jn 3:13-16; 12:32). But it was necessary, just as in the case of the Jews, for those to whom salvation came from Christ to have enough faith to turn their gaze to him (1 Co 10:9-10).

IV. John 8:21-30   Each day the exchange between Jesus and
      Gospel   the Pharisees grows sharper. Always he mani-
      Tuesday   fests himself in enigmas; but this time he is
                     driven to declare who he is, and to speak, but
still in vague terms, of his divinity ("I am," vv. 24, 28).

a) The first part of his rejoinder stresses the paradoxical *opposition* that divides him from the Pharisees. They want to kill him, but he will die when he pleases (v. 21); they accuse him of sin, but it is they who are destined to die in their sin (v. 24); they want to consign him to the depths of hell, but he is destined to go up "on high" (v. 23); they want to "elevate" him on the cross, in fact he will be "elevated" in glory (v. 28). They "seek" the face of God (Ps 26/27; Am 5:4-6; Ps 104/105: 1-4), and now they "seek" to kill God's envoy (v. 21). They think that he will kill himself (v. 22), but in fact he is the great "I am" (vv. 24, 28), the attribute of the one who is beyond all the vicissitudes of history (Ex 3:14-15; 33:19; Is 43:10-13).

b) The contrast between the two *worlds* (v. 23) has nothing to do with philosophical dualism. In fact there is only one world, a good world, the one that God has created (Gn 1; Jn 1:9-10). But its structure has been impaired by man's sin, and his sin is refusal to recognize the great "I am." Long ago they refused to recognize its manifestation (Ez 7:27), and they are refusing to recognize its manifestation now in him.

In fact the precise accomplishment of Jesus was to make one world again of two apparently distinct ones. And in that task he constantly invoked the will of his Father (vv. 28-29). It was his obedience to the one that sent him that nullified any effort on the part of man to build a world distinct from God.

That very tension of opposition between two apparently distinct worlds that Jesus experienced is like the tension we encounter today. So many of us seem to be torn between the Christian world, and what appears to be the secular one that obtrudes itself more and more. Attempts on our part to reconcile them are hazardous. The world that Jesus opposes is one where God is excluded. We find that sort of world just as much within the confines of the Church as without. Just as indeed we find the world of God without the Church as well as within. In other words the dividing line between the two entities does not coincide with the boundaries of Christianity.

V. Daniel 3:14-20, The story of Nebuchadnezzar's statue is a
91-92, 95 *haggada* with very many fictional elements
1st reading (Dn 3:1-30). The purpose was to encourage
Wednesday 2nd century Jews in their resistance to pagan
authority. The song of the three young men which follows the *haggada* (Dn 3:46-90) is a text apparently of the Maccabaean period, and was inserted in the book of Daniel before that book was translated into Greek.

The scene is an immense plain where a very large crowd is gathered. In the center is the emperor's statue, just as formerly, on a similar plain stood the tower of Babel. The statue doubtless was like an immense stele or obelisk, with a huge brasier before it for sacrifices. Such a setting was ideal for staging a *confrontation* between partisans of Yahweh and their opponents. The dramatic challenge occurs just before the opening of the ceremony (vv. 14-17); and immediately the author's hagiographic bias becomes evident. The persecutor is converted, just as in histories of martyrdom, and Yahwism emerges victorious. It only remains to chant the triumphal hymn of Yahweh (vv. 46-95).

Behind this legendary tale we can discern a concept of the mission of the chosen people, and of the Church, when confronted by any sort of tyranny. Authority can sometimes seem so powerful, and coercive instruments so overwhelming, that all the world becomes silent and subservient. Only people who believe in an absolute stronger than the instinct for self-preservation can resist it. Christians have discovered that sort of absolute and they call it Life and Love. How many Christians really do challenge tyranny of this nature?

VI. John 8:31-42   Here we have a continuation of the conflict
  Gospel   between Jesus and the Jews. There are
  Wednesday   two themes in John's account: freedom, and
                    paternity.

a) At the outset Jesus affirms that becoming his disciple, "hearing" his Word that is, but more especially "keeping" it and "living" in it (Jn 8:51; 12:47; 14:23-24) is a decision for *freedom* (v. 31).

The listeners immediately see equivocation. The term suggests that freedom which was acquired once for all at the Exodus, and promised previously to Abraham (v. 32; cf. Gn 17:16; 22:17-18). No Jew can be a slave (Lv 25:42). If an enemy seems now to hold the people in servitude, that is merely a transitory stage, to be ended very soon by the Messiah.

Jesus' rejoinder takes things to the deepest level. If they are children of Abraham, as indeed they are, they are so as slaves not as sons (v. 35); because they are sinners (v. 37). This point about double descent from Abraham, free and servile, must have had very great impact on early Christians. We find it again in Galatians 3:6-29; 4:21-5:1; Romans 4-8; Hebrews 3:6. It was a way for Christians to see themselves as seed of Abraham, like the Jews, but as sons really, not bastards or slaves.

If the Jews belonged to the free line from Abraham, they would welcome Jesus' word of truth, because it was a fulfillment of the promise to Abraham (vv. 39-40). As it was, they failed to see that his message was in direct continuity with that addressed to the patriarch. There was only one way for them to belong to Abraham's free line, to be free (v. 36) and no more slaves.

b) Reference to sonship makes the Jews retort that they are true sons, not slaves. They regard themselves even as sons of God (v. 41), because they are not born of "prostitution" (cf. Ho 2:4). The meaning is that they are not idolatrous infidels, but faithful to God's law.

Jesus' answer is similar to his point about Abraham's *paternity*. As in the case of Abraham, there are those who really have God for father, and those who have Satan (v. 44). He himself belongs to the first group; he comes from the Father (v. 42; Jn 5:42-43). People who claim to be sons of God should surely recognize the Son *par excellence*. If he is a stranger to them, is not that proof they have another father (v. 44)?

An exponent of the contemporary disciplines of psychology or psychosociology would find this text of profound interest. He could recognize a well-known theme: "Father-rejection," and also the polarities of the great crisis that now besets the world, in particular the academic world.

After millennia of matriarchy (nature, fruitfulness, fatality, autocratism) the human species gradually passed to patriarchy (foresight, history, law, creativity, freedom). It was during the patriarchal period that Jesus revealed the Father; but prior to that the Jews put themselves in a patriarchal context by recognizing Abraham as their father, and setting up socio-cultural structures to suit that choice and perpetuate it (law, circumcision, wisdom).

There are three possible attitudes to the Father, all of which appear in our text. He can be conceived of as so powerful that he wields a sort of possessive, autocratic, enveloping control like the primal Mother. Of such a kind was Abraham's fatherhood of the people, something all-embracing that devoured freedom and dulled creativity. It was a "maternalized" fatherhood that produces in children the sort of retardation well known to psychologists. Such were Jesus' Jewish contemporaries. The phenomenon is not unique. Paternalism of social authority today is so efficient, so possessive, so all-embracing that sometimes subjects become suicidal.

The second attitude is that of Satan. Oedipus-like he revolts against the Father, dooming himself to an emulation that can never succeed. Such is the state of many nihilist thinkers. They are right in challenging the excessive claims of social authority; but their wish is to destroy that authority, to assail rationality itself. They cannot deal with their Oedipus-complex, and turn to drugs, become hippies or suicides.

The third attitude is that of Christ. Unlike Satan, he creates in himself the image of his Father. He is of course another person. He rebels against his Father, Abraham, and against the symbols of that paternity (law, justice, circumcision), but he does so "in the name of the Father." Unlike Satan's his rebellion is not nihilist but innovative; whatever of the paternal heritage can be preserved he accepts.

Among Christians nowadays there is a "father-revolt." Social authority, in the Church as well as elsewhere, has become both paternal and maternal. Paternalism manifests itself in socio-cultural techniques (like the school) which are really alienating because sometimes they condition the person, or because they

deal in irrelevant controversies that belong to previous generations. In his revolt the Christian is perhaps helping to restore
to modern man the self-respect and freedom that will lead him
to find the image of the Father in himself, and conform to it.
We should always remember who the Father is whose image
we bear. Jesus Christ alone can tell us that.

VII. Genesis   This account of the covenant of Yahweh with
17:3-9   Abraham is a priestly document, and rela-
1st reading   tively late. The authors have in mind either
Thursday   the exiles of Babylon, reminding them that
God has not forgotten them, because he made
a fixed covenant with their forebears; or perhaps the small
remnant of the faithful in Jerusalem after the return, to allay
their fears. Throughout the passage then the Abraham we find
is doubtless the post-exilic image of Abraham rather than the
historical person.

a) In the eyes of the priestly authors a first essential in the
covenant of Abraham is the *promise of the land* (v. 8). The
detail was not part of the ancient Yahwist and Elohist traditions
about the patriarch's life. Yahwist traditions were mainly concerned with foundations of sanctuaries, etymological data, one
or another folk-tale. The indications of more edifying objectives
are already evident in the Elohist (the theme of mediating
prophet or father whose affections have been wounded). True,
there is a brief allusion to the promise of the land (Gn 12:7;
13:14-15); but it is clearly a later addition. It does not appear
to have been inserted before the 9th century, probably during
some such period as the reign of Asa, when a desire to restore
the full kingdom of David was manifest. In any case the detail
is recent. In Yahweh's discourse with Moses (Ex 3:7-8; 16-17)
or the old patriarchal blessings (Gn 27:27-29; 49:8-12; Nb
24:5-9) there is no mention of a promise of land. Not even in

the prophets do we find any allusion before Jeremiah and the deuteronomic reform (Dt 6:10, 23; 7:13; 8:1; 10:11, etc.; Jr 16:14-15; 23:7-8; 11:3-5). The theme was reserved for the prophets of the exile above all. The people would one day recover their land because of the initiative God would take to bring them salvation (Is 49:8; 54:2-3). Indeed, in Isaiah 49: 22-23 and 45:14-15, the very words used in proclaiming the promise of "possessing the land" to the exiles are those of the promise to Abraham. Nor is the promise in Isaiah made to all the people, only to those who seek Yahweh. It is a select group, known for their fidelity, who will inherit the land (Is 14:20).

In view of all this, it is easy to comprehend how at this particular time a promise of land to Abraham could assume such significance. In proclaiming that it had been made originally to the patriarch himself the prophets of the exile were stressing the fact that execution of the promise depended not on human resources, so feeble at this time, but on God's own initiative. Furthermore, being as it was addressed to the father of believers, the necessity of faith in the whole matter becomes evident. The land will be given only to the select group who are distinguished by faith. This is the essential doctrine, with all its implications, to which verse 8 alludes.

b) The second note of the covenant-narrative in Genesis 17 is the *change of name* from Abram to Abraham. In fact the two words seem to be merely different versions of the same name, which means: "He is sprung from a noble father." Priestly editors however associated the name Abraham with *ab hamon,* meaning "He is father of a multitude," thus illustrating one of the important details of the covenant (cf. vv. 4 and 5). They seem here to have been influenced by Second-Isaiah. The change of name was a frequent theme for him; and very often Jerusalem herself, she that was widowed and abandoned, becomes with him not alone the spouse and beloved of God, but is promised to a marvellous posterity (Is 62:1-4; 56:5; 62:12; 44:2-4; 51:2; 49:20-21). His handling of the topic of change of

name is meant to encourage the exiles to believe in a change
of destiny. If this were already discernible in the life of the
patriarch, the people would realize that there really was a God
controlling history. Whatever the vicissitudes of that history,
he directs it firmly and faithfully according to a design that was
there before time began.

VIII. **John**	The trend of discussion in this passage might
8:51-59	seem on the surface nonsensical. The Jews
Gospel	insult Jesus: "You are a Samaritan and have
Thursday	a devil" (v. 48), that is to say: "You are
	mad." He takes the remark seriously and

replies to it. Later on the Jews introduce the name of Abraham.
Jesus takes this opportunity of formulating a new statement on
this theme. The Jews do not really belong to Abraham's line
because they lack the faith that leads to recognition of who
God is. The line is a race of free men and how could people
who are slaves to unbelief belong to it. He himself on the other
hand, who is of God, cannot be convicted of sin (v. 46).

His argument is thus. Because he is without sin he can claim
to be of the line of Abraham, and thus of the people "of God."
The Jews on the other hand are wrong in their claim to be "of
God," because they are in sin (v. 47). From the whole discussion John elicits some important themes.

a) In the first place: the *incomprehension* of the Jewish
authorities when Christ accomplishes signs that reveal the
mystery of his relations with the Father. Throughout his whole
gospel indeed John gives various instances of incomprehension.
We have that of the multitude who saw only their own immediate profit in his miracles (after the multiplication of the
loaves: "They follow because I give them bread," Jn 6); or
those who saw only signs of the beginning of terrestrial messianism. But the incomprehension of the authorities is more striking.

Though their office fits them to recognize the Messiah, they cannot discern the personality of Christ. His miracles, they allege, are performed "for his own glory." That is why Jesus is anxious to show that he seeks not his own glory but that of the Father (v. 54).

b) Secondly, with Jewish incomprehension John contrasts the *knowledge* that Jesus has of his Father and the means of attaining a similar knowledge. The Jews do not "listen": he does (v. 47). They "dishonor" Jesus: he "honors" the Father (v. 49). They do not "know": he does (v. 55). They do not "keep his Word" (vv. 51-52): he "keeps the Word of the Father" (v. 55).

All these are familiar phrases in Jewish theology. They were thoroughly convinced that they knew God, kept his Word, listened to him, paid him honor. What Jesus is doing then is demonstrating the inadequacy of their knowledge, and contrasting it with his own. His knowledge is derived from the communion he has with the Father (v. 58; cf. Ex 3:14; Is 43:10-13; see also v. 47), and requires total abnegation where human resources are concerned (vv. 50, 54).

c) Finally there is the theme so favored by John: the *hour*. Jesus' enemies will not have the initiative in the matter of his death. However it seems to be the result of human machination, there is a deeper, more mysterious, will involved, that of the Father, who determines the hour (last verse).

In all, the complete passage is concerned with the problem of discovering Christ's personality, penetrating to it underneath the signs he accomplishes.

IX. Jeremiah   This passage was commented on with Jere-
20:10-13   miah 11:13-20 on Saturday of the fourth
1st reading   week of Lent, p. 203.
Friday

X. John 10:31-42 Jesus had just been claiming communion with
Gospel   the Father to the point of what the Jews
Friday   considered to be blasphemy (Jn 10:30). They
                  immediately, in conformity with the law,
gathered stones to assail the one who dared compare himself
to God (v. 31; Lv 24:16; 8:59).

Jesus, not without anger, demands the reason for the stoning;
and his replies are all couched in stern terms. He speaks of
"your law," indicating that he himself is detached from Jewish
legalism (v. 34: a point which shows that John wrote at a time
when Christians felt the distance between themselves and Jews).
He makes a play on words. Psalm 81/82:6 gave to human
judges the title of "God" or "Son of God": who had the right
to deny him, entrusted as he was with the task of a more
decisive judgment, a similar liberty (v. 42; Jn 8:59)?

Jesus displays anger because he is convinced that the proper ·
method of discovering his *divinity* is not by discussion and
dialectic. The only valid evidence is that of his works (Jn 14:11;
5:17, 21). Perhaps indeed his very adroitness in evading the
subterfuges of his enemies is one of those works of power (v.
42; cf. Jn 8:59).

XI. Ezechiel   Ezechiel wrote during the decade 590-580,
   37:21-28   just twenty years after a final attempt by King
   1st reading   Josias had succeeded in bringing about a brief
   Saturday   reunion of North and South (2 K 23:16-20),
                    and ten years after the fall of Jerusalem.
He is the prophet of restoration, not alone for the city, but for
the whole country, North and South, just as the founding
patriarchs had traversed it.

a) Today's reading is composed of images of *restoration* that
were already very familiar at the time of writing. Mentions of
the davidic shepherd (v. 24), possession of the land (v. 25),

the new covenant (v. 26), the restored sanctuary (v. 28), above all, a purified people (v. 23) recur and recur in Ezechiel (cf. Ez 34:23; 28:26; 40-44).

b) If this passage be different it is certainly so because of the opening verses (20-22). Nowhere else in the Old Testament is *reunification* of the chosen people described in such precise terms. They are furthermore a commentary on the symbolic gesture which the prophet had just enacted, when he took two batons of wood, symbols of the two kingdoms, and rejoined them.

The restoration then, for Ezechiel, is a reunification of the tribes. His point of view is understandable when we remember that the tribes in fact remained independent for a considerable time, at least during the era of the judges, having no concept of unity except a religious one (Jos 22-24). The common bond then is the unanimous acceptance of dependence on Yahweh. When a political unity is achieved for a time under David and Solomon, it is successful in so far as the idea of theocracy is kept to the fore. The particular mission of David and Solomon indeed is to make the people aware that the basis for unity is the link with God.

Never again however were the chosen people to regain this purely religious unity. Not even in the Church has Ezechiel's prophecy been fulfilled. The Church assembles her members without any particular political or social links, other than those already there on the secular plane; and she would fail in her mission were she to impose the like. When religion gets confused with political or cultural structures the very *raison d'être* of unity is jeopardized. Schism will very soon present itself and unity can only be restored by a process of purifying faith.

XII. John
11:45-57
Gospel
Saturday

This is an account of the Sanhedrin session which decreed Christ's death. The passage is colored by the biblical theme of conspiracy against the persecuted Just one. A variant of

verse 53, adopted by the Vulgate reads:
cogitaverunt ut interficerent (Ps 2:2; 21/22:17; 70/71:10; 40/41:
8; 82/83:4; 139/140:5-9).

Caiphas' proposed solution is the opportunist one. He wants
to avoid complications or entanglements with the occupying
power. What after all does a man's life matter when weighed
against such possibilities (the phrase "for the people" in verse
50 is probably not original)? John manipulates this sentiment
into a prophecy of the redemptive effect of Christ's sacrifice
(Jn 6:51; 10:11-15; 15:13; Mk 14:14). The effect will be so
far-reaching as to transcend the Jewish nation itself and bring
about the *reunion* of all peoples.

Accordingly, following his usual procedure, he once more
contrasts two kinds of "knowledge" of Christ: that of the Jews
which leads them to decide his death for opportunist reasons,
and that of the believer who can discern the propitiatory value
of this death. To the nationalism of Caiphas he opposes the
universalism of the cross which is inspired by the doctrine of
the suffering Servant (Is 53:10-11). As an aspect of this universalism he revives the theme of "reunion" (Jn 10:16; He
12:22-23; Mt 25:32; Rev 7:1-9), a very traditional one which was
limited formerly to the tribes of Israel (Ez 37:20-28; 48:31-35;
Dt 4:9-13; 23:1-9), but which the gospel now extends to the
whole universe.

The price of a people's unity is a man's death. It is a price
perhaps that plenipotentiaries in international parleys refuse to
pay. We have plenty of commissions and confrontations; but
every one who sits down at a round table knows before he sits
how much he is prepared to yield (that which least concerns
his profit and touches only the peripheries of himself) and what
he must hold on to at any price. Yet he joins the session as a
defender of the truth, forgetting that Christ who was truth
itself was ready to die, involving in his death that very truth.

In return he received, all gratuitously, new life, the fullness of truth and the people's unity.

It is only the attitude of Jesus, shaped by communion with his Father to the point of failure and death, that will enable Christians today to bring about reunion. Any prayer for unity that has not a paschal dimension is hypocritical.

PASSION SUNDAY

(or Palm Sunday)

A. THE WORD

I. Matthew
21:1-11
Gospel for
the blessing

Today's first biblical passage is the gospel of Christ's entry to Jerusalem, the final episode of the journey to Jerusalem (Lk 18:31-43).

a) Zechariah 9:9 is the key to interpretation. A king will come as Messiah; but contrary to the traditional dress for great monarchs he will be clothed in poor apparel. Matthew speaks of a she-ass and her mate; but that is due to his anxiety to render faithfully the rather faulty text available to him.

When Jesus thus manifests himself in poverty his disciples and the crowd greet him with messianic acclamations (vv. 8-9). The eulogy is inspired above all by Ps 117/118, the canticle of the new Jerusalem, very characteristic of the feast of Tabernacles (v. 9). Matthew's introduction though of the title "son of David" strengthens the royal and messianic emphasis of the psalm.

b) In Matthew's description of the procession the crowd wave branches (Luke gives a less oriental impression by speaking of mantles only). Perhaps the entry account is influenced by the traditional ritual of the Tabernacles feast where it was customary to wave branches (Lv 23:33-34; Ne 8:13-18). The episode of the sterile figtree (in the following verses) cannot have taken place just before Pasch but must belong to some festival of fruitfulness. Figtrees are not in fruit so early. Then the episode of the sellers in the temple is a fulfillment of Zechariah's (14:21) vision of the Feast of Tabernacles.

In Jewish liturgy the feast of Tabernacles coincided with the harvest. By celebrating fruitfulness it closed the year and asked for divine blessing on the new year. It was this concern with the new year that gave the feast a nuance of prophetic spiritualization and made it somewhat eschatological. There were particular ceremonies, to the accompaniment of Psalm 117/118, which celebrated the fruitfulness of the last days (Jn 7:38-39) and the enthronement of the future Messiah.

In all, what the evangelists have done is assemble the traditions concerning the entry to Jerusalem, and present them in a context of enthronement like that of the feast of Tabernacles. The Messiah anticipated in that ritual has in very truth arrived.

Lest however the messianism should seem too material, there were some corrective touches. The poor apparel (Ze 9:9) is not that of a powerful Messiah. Furthermore, care was taken to couple with Psalm 117/118, so very suitable in this context, the parable of the murderous vineyard workers as well as some other verses from the same psalm which show that Christ will not be full Messiah until after his death (Mt 21:42). Finally the whole entry was placed during the days preceding Pasch rather than during the feast of Tabernacles, at the cost of making the figtree episode somewhat incomprehensible. They were concerned to emphasize the close link between the paschal death of Jesus and his kingship.

The enthronement of the Messiah is accomplished by the cross. There is no other way that leads to glory, and herein lies the paschal mystery.

II. Isaiah 50, 4-7 *1st reading* *Mass*	Commentary on this passage will be found with that on Isaiah 50: 4-9, Wednesday of Holy Week, p. 275.
III. Philippians **2:6-11** *2nd reading* *Mass*	This hymn to the Kenosis and glorification of the Lord is probably pre-Pauline in origin. It is made up of three strophes, sometimes given as two:

Verses
6 and 7a:

two mentions of God: contrast between God's state and that of a slave, with the theme "he has emptied himself."

verses
7bc and 8:

two mentions of man, with the theme "he lowered himself."

verses 9-11:

contrast between slave and Lord, the obedient and exalted one. In verse 9 the exaltation and the giving of the Name are parallels, like the bending of the knees and the acclaim in verses 10-11.

The whole hymn parallels the customary Pauline elaborations about Christian charity. It lies in self-emptying, after the example of Jesus (2 Co 8:9; Rm 15:1-3).

a) In contrasting Jesus' divine state with his *servile* one Paul does not mean to say he abandoned his divinity or that he became man only in appearance. The problem of natures does not arise, nor is the context incarnational. In the first strophe for instance it is not said that Jesus was God, but only that he possessed a rank of equality with God. Likewise, in the second, the humanity of Jesus is not denied; but it is stressed that the Lord allowed himself to be confused with men (v. 7; cf. Rm 8:3). He could have appeared on earth as Lord demanding divine honors, but he did not. Saint Paul frequently requires that our charity should display that renouncement of self of which Christ gives us a living example (2 Co 8:9; Ga 4:1-5; He 11:24-26).

There is some allusion in the hymn to the suffering Servant (compare verse 8 with Is 53:7; 53:10; 53:12), but it sharpens that image by its use of the typically biblical contrasts "Lord-slave" and "lower-elevate" (Lk 1:52; Mt 23:12; Lk 18:14; 2 Co 11:7).

b) The gradual descent in humiliation is paralleled by a *triumphal ascent* in glory. Again the imagery here transcends that of the suffering Servant, who is "elevated" only (Is 52:13).

Christ goes further because he gets the title of Lord (Ps 109/ 110), one that entitles to the honor of "genuflection" and "proclamation." These rites were reserved for God alone. Kings had already prostrated themselves before the suffering Servant (Is 49:7), but "because of Yahweh." Before Christ, on the other hand, men prostrate themselves as before God, all the time glorifying the Father.

  c) Possibly too Christ is presented here as a replica of Adam. The word *morphê*, which is generally rendered in English "state" or "condition," may be itself a translation of the Hebrew word for image (cf. Gn 1:26). Christ would be the image of God as Adam was, but, unlike Adam, he did not use the title to make himself equal to God (v. 6; cf. Gn 3:5). Such a view would reinforce the interpretation which refuses to see in the hymn a definition of Christ's divinity. We should have instead a parallel between *Adam and Christ,* the pride and disobedience of the former countered by the humility and obedience of the latter. The eulogy of Christ would be centered on his fidelity to the end to his human condition, even unto death, whereas Adam sinned by trying to avoid fidelity and thus escape death. The one to become actually God's equal is he who shows himself loyal to the human state.

In our different cultural context, this hymn and its message could easily be misunderstood. It might seem that the thirty years spent in the human condition were parenthetical really, an accident, as if God the all-powerful, the judge, had for a brief moment forgotten himself, for love indeed, but hastened then to recover his proper lordship. That would make our God always the all-powerful and only in parenthesis the God of Christ. The godlike state would be something anterior, unrelated really to what was manifested in the humility and obedience of Jesus. He would be just abdicating his privileges for a time to serve the poor; some sort of facade, instead of the plenitude of divinity, would be the image presented during the public life. Indeed his gesture in sharing human proverty might seem a patronizing one, a sort of luxury, open to resentment by humanity.

The hymn in fact says nothing of a preexisting divinity. The major affirmation indeed is that the God manifested in the incarnate Jesus is the veritable God, because Godhead is service. Christ's obedience is not alone obedience to his terrestrial condition. Nor is it submission to the decree of a God exterior to him; it is fidelity to all that divinity implies. So it is that forever Jesus is the victim of what he accomplished, in his own person first of all and then in those who want to imitate him.

IV. Matthew **26:14-27:66** *Gospel* *1st cycle*	The versions of the Passion according to the three synoptics form the gospels of this day. The best procedure seems to be to provide an analysis of the characteristics of each individual account. Thus we shall approach

the great mystery of the passion and death by three very well-defined paths.*

Straightway, in Matthew, one becomes conscious of the importance of a single theme: fulfillment of the scriptures. For Jewish Christians, who expected a triumphant, glorious Messiah, he is demonstrating that the prophecies foretold a suffering Messiah, that the whole development of the Passion, down to the smallest detail, was contemplated in scripture.

The agony in Gethsemane was foreseen in Psalm 41/42:6 (26:38). When Christ is arrested he is careful to state that this was a *fulfillment of scripture* (26:54, 56), thus rebutting the view of those who thought there should have been armed resistance. Jesus actually alludes to being treated like a brigand (26:55), the reference being to the situation of the suffering

---

*See too the doctrinal themes: *cross,* p. 259 and *redemption,* p. 264.

Servant according to the Septuagint version of Isaiah 53:9, 12: "placed in the company of the accursed."

During the exchange with the high-priest, Matthew again stresses the temple theme (26:61), which is "accomplished" in Christ's person, and he quotes (more fully than Luke) the text in Daniel 7:13 about the Son of man (26:64). He is the only one to describe the death of Judas (27:3-10) because he sees it as a fulfillment of scripture (citing Ze 11:12-13).

Unlike Luke and John, both Mark and Matthew insist that Jesus made no reply to Pilate. They are thinking of the silence of the suffering Servant before insult (Is 53:7). Likewise Matthew's allusion to the washing of hands by Pilate (26:24-25) is doubtless due to the fact that he sees it as a rite fulfilling the law (Dt 21:6-9; Ps 72/73:13). The response of the crowd to Pilate is a traditional expression "may his blood be . . ." (27:25; cf. 2 S 1:16). Perhaps Matthew saw here a prophecy of the rejection of the Jewish people.

Although the other evangelists do not show the same precision, he tells us the drink offered Christ on the cross was gall, a fulfillment of Psalm 68/69:22 (Mt 27:34). Similarly, the drawing of lots for Christ's garments and the cry on the cross he sees as fulfillments of Psalm 21/22 (Mt 27:35). He is the only one to add the insults by the Jews, "He has saved others . . .," one taken from the mockery of the Just one by the impious (cf. 27:43; Ws 2:18-20).

Again he is the only one to describe the events after Jesus' death: the rending of the temple veil, the dead arising, the earth trembling are all signs of the day of Yahweh as foretold by the prophets (Am 8:9). He is alone in mentioning the wealth of Joseph of Aramithea (Mark mentions his notoriety, Luke his piety), because he is so anxious to verify the prophecy of Isaiah 53:9: he shall have his tomb with the rich. It is worth noting that in Isaiah the real meaning of this text is that the servant will be confused with the impious.

It is beyond question then that Matthew is concerned to

explain facts by the Word, the word of the fulfilled scriptures, the words of Jesus himself (so much fuller than in the other versions). We are not dealing with a simple account, but with the beginnings of an elaborate theology of fulfillment. The events of the Passion do not contain anything accidental, but form part of God's plan for the world.

So true is this that he is able to make of the Passion the end of the ancient era and the beginning of the era of the *Church*. His gospel, more than the others, stresses the eschatological and ecclesial import of these events. The collapse of the old economy is heralded by the rent veil of the temple, the advent of the new introduced by earthquake. The conversion of the centurion is the first fruits of the conversion of the nations. The priests, when they relinquish to the "disciples" the body of Christ, are abdicating prerogatives and leaving the Church to be the sign of Christ in the world.

One rather difficult feature of Matthew's account is the mention of *guards* by the cross (Mt 27:36 and 54), and especially at the tomb (Mt 27:62-66), not paralleled in the other evangelists. The key to the problem is provided by Matthew in 28:11-15.

His purpose, or that of the tradition he represents, in this detail would seem to be apologetic. He wants to counter the Jewish story of the removal of the corpse. His faith in Christ is so intense that he is prepared to compose a history which will refute this Jewish lie definitively. If that be deceptive by our historical standards, it could be fidelity to a truer sort of history, that of faith. Matthew is well aware that faith does not depend on verification of the manner of Jesus' exit from the tomb.

V. Mark	Considerably shorter than the parallel ver-
14:1-15:47	sions, Mark's account of the Passion is con-
Gospel	fined to the essential structure of events. It is
2nd cycle	nevertheless composite. A nonsemitic source
	has been identified (14:1-2, 10-11, 17-21,

26-31; 43-46:53; 15:1, 3-5, 15a, 21-24, 26, 29-30, 34-37, 39, 42-46), and a semitic, probably Petrine in origin (14:3-9, 12-16, 22-25, 32-42, 45-52; 15:2, 6-14, 15b-20, 25, 27-28, 31-33, 38, 40-41). Often the doctrinal influence of one or other source manifests itself. The semitic source for instance, is concerned to show the isolation of Jesus, to stress the mockery and insults that Jesus meets with silence.

a) Thus the isolation of Jesus becomes gradually more and more emphasized. Having already lost the support of the crowds and his relatives, the Passion brings desertion by his own disciples. Whenever Matthew speaks of him being "with" his own (Mt 26:36; 26:40; 26:51) we can be sure Mark will not use the formula. Those who should have watched with him in Gethsemane fall asleep (Mt 14:37-40). At his arrest the disciples flee (Mk 14:50), and, to make the flight more sorry, Mark shows a special interest in the detail of the boy who fled naked (Mk 14:51-52). His isolation is evident throughout the Sanhedrin session. Then when false witnesses are produced against him (Mk 14:56-60) and when Peter makes his denials (Mk 14:62-71), there is only one witness found to testify "twice" (Mk 14:72, the detail is peculiar to him) in his favor as the law required: the unfortunate cock. The isolation is absolute. Even his own Father will abandon him (Mk 15:34-35), and his disciples will remain "at a distance" (Mk 15:40).

b) Likewise he emphasizes the *silence* of Jesus throughout the trial (Mk 14:61; 15:3-4). Unlike Luke and John he gives only one word from the cross, because he wishes to be faithful to his design of stressing the "messianic secret" (Mk 5:43; 7:24; 9:30). The silence was always Jesus' way of showing the great difference between his real mission and what people expected, between the mystery of his real person and the titles people gave him.

The mockery and insults directed at Christ get full attention (Mk 15:16-20, 29-32; cf. also 5:40; 6:2). The opposition of the leaders of the people is a dominant note in the whole gospel

(Mk 3:6, 22), and here he shows how it leads to Christ's death (14:53-64).

The silent isolation stresses Mark's style of vindicating Jesus' messianic dignity in the midst of the most outrageous obloquy. We have the equation of the king of the Jews with a homicidal rabble-rouser, the macabre royal enthronement in the guard-room, the derision around the cross, all of which put the isolation of Jesus in his messianic pretensions in high relief. Scarcely however has the end come when he is recognized as "Son of God" (15:39) in a profession of faith that in itself obliterates all the mockery of the crowd. And a small group of disciples begins to form (15:40-43) who are to be, not distant from Christ, but the nucleus of his Church.*

VI. Luke   Luke's main anxiety is to set the events of
22:39-23:56   the Passion in a context of mercy and love.
Gospel
3rd cycle

a) The whole narrative becomes a revelation of the *love* of the Father for his Son and for mankind, the cross being the great sacrament of divine mercy.

Accordingly he does not generally dwell on the culpability either of the Jews or the disciples: where the blood of Christ washes out all stains there is little point in determining respon-sibility. He does not give us the detail that Jesus found the disciples sleeping three times (Mt 26:40-47), nor does he, like the others, tell us that the disciples fled at Gethsemane (Mt 26:56). He has no mention of Peter's swearing before the servants of the high priest (Mt 26:74). Even Christ's enemies are depicted in less hostile terms. We are not told they spat upon Jesus (Lk 22:63; cf. Mt 26; Lk 67 and 27: 27-31), or that they bound him to bring him to Pilate (Lk 23:1; cf. Mt 27:2).

*See the doctrinal themes: *cross* and *redemption*, p. 259 and p. 264.

Then, Judas' betrayal is glossed over very lightly (there is no mention of the agreement in Mt 26:48), and his suicide (cf. Mt 27:3-10). Finally he differs from all the other evangelists in not wanting to stress the isolation on Calvary. He does not quote Zechariah 13:7 (about the dispersal of the flock), and, contrary to Mt 27:55-56 and Mk 15:40-41, mentions the presence there of friends and acquaintances (Lk 23:49).

b) Thus, in the glow of the great *pardon* of the cross, practically everyone is absolved. Pilate himself, on three different occasions, seems innocent (Lk 23:4, 13-15, 20-22, all details peculiar to Luke). One of Jesus' opponents is actually healed after an apostle has cut off his ear (Lk 22:51). During the moment of the betrayal by Peter, Jesus has time to look at him and lead him to repentance (Lk 22:61). Where Matthew and Mark have Christ give cries of despair on the cross (Mt 27:46), he gives us the exclamation of forgiveness for all Jews (Lk 23:34). In the same way he is the only one to mention the pardon for the thief (Lk 23:39-43) and the urge to repent which seized the centurion himself (Lk 23:47). That very caricature of reconciliation, the rapprochement between Herod and Pilate (Lk 23:6-12), is almost allowed to be a fruit of the pardon of the cross.

c) The secret of all this pardon and love rests in Jesus' particular communion with his Father. Luke alone allows us a glimpse of this intimacy. In the Lucan prayers of Jesus the tone is so much more personal than that of the other synoptics (Lk 22:42; cf. Mt 14:36; Lk 23:34; cf. Mt 27:46; Lk 23:46; cf. Mt 27:50). And we have the solicitude of God himself (peculiar to Luke) as he comforts Jesus in his agony (Lk 22:43). The intuition of divinity is always there. The title "Son of God" is lifted above the merely messianic context of Matthew 26:63 and Mark 11:61 to become something special (Lk 22:70), practically an attribute of godhead. The death itself is not, as in Matthew 26:61-62, caused by Christ's attack on the temple, but by his oral affirmation (Lk 22:71) of divinity.

B. DOCTRINE

1. The Theme of the Cross

In the christological hymn of Philippians 2 and the Passion narrative we meet the Savior as a condemned person. The cross brings Jesus' life to a close. Far from being an accident of history, the final event crowns all that went before; before he dies Jesus says "All is consummated." The death on the cross then is not just one element, with others, of our faith: it is the core of our faith, that which opens up to resurrection, to eternal life, to definitive salvation in the kingdom of the Father.

What Saint Paul called the "scandal of the cross" continues to be present in every generation. Why should the salvation of humanity hang upon this, a Savior who ends his life in this manner? Surely a Savior is one who lifts up humankind, liberates them, fulfills their destiny according to God's plan. Can such a plan as this be called a plan of love? If God is a loving Father how could he derive satisfaction from an act so apparently destructive, so completely alienating?

Suffering and death in the messianic search

Jewish man, like every man, sought security. Happiness naturally seemed a matter of wealth, abundance, fruitfulness, social unity. All these things indicated God's blessing. But, unfortunately, death awaited everyone at the end of life. And then, once the chosen people were installed in Palestine, social injustice became rampant and the numbers of poor multiplied. These were contrary to the happiness willed by Yahweh. Consequently death, suffering and social injustice must surely be the result of sin. But on the day of Yahweh an Israel that has remained faithful to the covenant will be saved: death will be no more; the poor will reap the abundance they have been deprived of by human wickedness.

As faith deepened these attitudes underwent a gradual transformation. The poor man destined to be admitted by Yahweh to his Kingdom could not be just one who was the victim, in body, of injustice and cried out to heaven for vengeance. It was the man who, in obedience to Yahweh, welcomed insecurity; the man who let himself be stripped because he sought true security not in himself but in Yahweh; the man who remained unrebellious before death and every kind of terrestrial insecurity because he trusted in the merciful goodness of Yahweh.

Such insights on the part of "the poor of Yahweh" were destined to issue later in the figure of the suffering Servant. Leaving aside questions about the individual or collective character of this messianic image, we can say that the Servant in whom Yahweh is pleased is of a special kind. Not only does death find him disposed to God's will; when death strikes him it has the assistance of human injustice:

"A thing despised and rejected by men,
a man of sorrows and familiar with suffering,
a man to make people screen their faces,
he was despised and we took no account of him" (Is 53:3).
He confronts death in all its awfulness because of human sin. He is rejected, condemned, deprived even in dying of the warmth of friendship.

This great image left nevertheless one major question unsolved. Is the Servant a mere instrument in the hands of Yahweh? Or, when he encounters death in these terms, does he emerge victorious? Jewish thought reached here a limit that only the coming of Christ could transcend. The Servant doctrine penetrates to a very deep understanding of suffering and death. But it does not tell us how, by obedience unto death, man cooperates actively in his own salvation.

The passion of Jesus and the realization of human destiny

Jesus intervened in history and presented himself as the Son of man who fulfilled the task of the suffering Servant. The combination of these two messianic images revealed at once the kind of man who realizes human destiny, and the true identity of the man-God.

He did the work of the Servant of Yahweh. He had a lucid understanding of the grim weight of death which oppressed all terrestrial existence. But above all he had to encounter death in the midst of human hate. The light of every man that comes into the world, he who preached in this world a brotherly love without limits, was rejected by his own people, the very people whom he wished to make witnesses of universal love before all the world. His death on the cross, the total isolation that it meant, can only be understood in reference to the basic human hostility that his mission encountered. The Jewish people condemned him because his ideal of universal love jeopardized the privileges of the covenant (not its responsibilities). He accepted death on the cross, the ultimate choice, that of laying down life for those one loves.

The point of consequence is that he did the work of the Servant as Son of man. There was nothing alienating about his death. He undertook it with a keen awareness that this was the way to realize human salvation, to show a fidelity to God that would be authentic, to cooperate freely and actively in the achievement of human destiny. "He emptied himself," says the christological hymn (Ph 2:7): he went the length of complete despoliation of the self which implies absolute acceptance of the creatural condition. The hymn goes on "He was humbler yet, went to accepting death, death on a cross" (Ph 2:8). All of this he did despite the extra burden added by humanity's great sin, refusal to love. When he gave his life in absolute love, he deprived death of all its power and, transfigured in soul and body, entered the deathless kingdom as first-born of the new creation. Death itself changed meaning as a result of what he did. Henceforth it denotes that state of self-despoliation that love demands, and leads all of man, body and soul, to an eternal destiny.

It was only because Jesus was man-God that this achievement

was possible. The "divine" destiny of the human being was brought about by his absolute acceptance of humanity. The response he made though to the Father's initiative was adequate because it was the response of a Son. He could present himself as Son of man, created "in the image and likeness of God," and fulfill the human being beyond the wildest dreams by providing entry to the Family of the Father, because his own nature really was divine. He was the Lord. The messianic image of the Son of man became in him the mystery of the man-God.

The Christian and laying down life for love of others

Admitted to adoptive sonship through his living link with Christ, the Christian is called to imitate Christ's fidelity to the human condition. In the tradition of the suffering Servant, he should challenge death wherever it presents itself, above all when it is the result of inability or refusal to love. There is no equivocation about the precept "Love one another as I have loved you," that is, to the point of laying down our lives. Loving with the love of Jesus means loving the other, in full recognition of his otherness, across all the barriers men never cease to build between themselves, as individuals and as groups. It means loving down to the very roots of hostility and sin that make an enemy of the other, creating unity at the precise point of alienation. It means embracing the suffering that rejection by the other will bring, the sentence to death for having loved, the actual dying.

But this love to the limit of death, because it sustains the example of the Son of Man, is a victorious love. Obedience in suffering and death is productive of life. It is active acceptance, leading to the fullest expression of the creature as "image and likeness of God"; and it also embraces in the passage from death to life the entire cosmos.

Thus love, suffering and death, in Christian terms, are intimately connected. Not that the Christian looks for suffering or death. If they come, above all if inflicted by the other (the case of martyrdom is exceptional), for love of God and men he will welcome them. Because he will want love to achieve its full expression in him and to complete his purification.

The Church's passion a sign of salvation in Jesus Christ

The Church will encounter suffering and death in proportion to the witness she gives to universal love. Worldly wisdom balks at universal charity, because of the price that must be paid in self-despoliation. It is the missionary members of the Church, clerical and lay, who bear the brunt of her Passion. She charges them to encounter the world and implant there the mystery of Christ. The deep-down motive for every missionary vocation has to be charity; and one day this love will meet rejection, sometimes in very subtle fashion, imperceptible even, in that the rejection festers deep within the man himself. Suffering and solitude will be the inevitable consequence: the cross will cast its shadow over the missionary's life. If he can blend all this with the universal love that animates him, he will find that the scandal of the cross becomes a sign of salvation. Love like this invariably touches those who are the object of it. You can embrace it, or reject it; what you cannot do is remain indifferent.

While the law of charity which is its essence is the source always of the Church's Passion, at different epochs this mysterious agony will assume different aspects. The reason is that the concrete requirements of charity may vary. In Saint Paul's time the great problem was the Jewish-Gentile encounter. Today the biggest challenge to Catholicity is what we euphemistically term "exchange between cultures," avoiding the more realistic word "clash." In the years that lie ahead Christians will have to determine precisely a policy that will loyally maintain the truth about man revealed in Jesus Christ. That has not been done. Christians can be sure of one thing however: they will inevitably encounter opposition. Modern man, engaged upon attempts to solve his problems on a planetary scale, leans more and more towards a view of man that excludes God. We can depend upon it that the new wisdom of the world will be, and is already, an atheist one.

Sharing the Passion of Christ

"Until the Lord comes, every time you eat this bread and drink this cup you are proclaiming his death" (1 Co 11:26). Every eucharistic celebration is linked to the cross of Christ. Sharing the bread and the Word conforms us to the death of Christ, to the great spiritual sacrifice which gave it meaning.

Only this living link with Christ, strengthened ceaselessly by the Eucharist, can give us the essential insight about the law of charity: how it is bound up with suffering and death. Here of course the role of the liturgy of the Word is capital. It can construct in the consciences of the faithful the proper sort of "channels" and thus enable sacramental grace to be really efficacious.

2. The Theme of Redemption

Some further reflection on the universal aspect of Christ's death seems suitable at this point. When he died on the cross, he did so for the salvation of all, "a victim of propitiation for our sins" (1 Jn 4:10). In passing from death to life, not alone did he fulfill the highest human possibilities, he was constituted the first-born of the new generation, the core of all creation which was embraced in the event.

To indicate this all-involving aspect of the Calvary-event, two formulations have become traditional: that Christ, by his death, ransomed humanity; and that he expiated for the sins of all. We should realize at the outset that these biblical expressions have a very positive meaning. "Expiating" essentially means "purifying," making "pleasing to God." Sin is wiped out in the process: the link between man and God is restored. "Ransoming" means freeing from the slavery of sin and joining with God.

The liberation consists in being possessed in a new way, that is, by God.

Jewish notions of redemption and expiation

Expiatory rites were a feature of all religions. The purpose was to purify individuals, or the group; and reestablish their relationship with heavenly powers by ritual practices. The role of the king and priest was essential. They represented the people, spoke in their name, and all members of the group considered themselves involved in what these did. Clearly enough, in anthropological terms the basis for such representative action was the social bond that unites groups.

The Jewish people had such rites as well; but the regime of faith, as it deepened, gradually modified them. They realized that salvation depended on a redemption, the initiative for which lay altogether in the hands of Yahweh. Yet it could not be brought about without man's fidelity. Yahweh in history had joined himself to his people by freeing them from Egyptian slavery and that of sin. Always the redemptive event *par excellence* remained the Exodus. But the Exodus led to the Covenant. In the desert Yahweh's redemptive initiative had been countered by the people's infidelity and unbelief. Time and again Moses and Aaron had to expiate their people's fault by intercession and only their intercessory prayer could arrest the divine anger.

The connection between the people's fault and the suffering of a just one becomes more evident in the personal drama of Jeremiah. The germ of an idea appeared that was to culminate in the image of the Servant of Yahweh.

"And yet ours were the sufferings he bore,
ours the sorrows he carried.
But we, we thought of him as someone punished,
struck by God, and brought low.
Yet he was pierced through for our faults,
crushed for our sins.

On him lies a punishment that brings us peace,
and through his wounds we are healed . . .
Yes, he was torn away from the land of the living;
for our faults struck down in death" (Is 53:4-5, 8).

Thus, for all the time traditional liturgies of expiation were being practiced, in certain circles of the poor the religious thought of Israel was being deepened in a remarkable way. The challenge of death, brought about by the people's infidelity, was oppressing spirits more and more. But, among the more perceptive, the idea was being stressed that the people's sins would be expiated by the suffering and death of an intercessor.

The great redemptive act of the cross

His life and death made Jesus the perfect fulfillment of the messianic image of the Servant of Yahweh. Calvary was the event which ransomed humanity, expiated the sins of all by reuniting humanity with God. Let us consider briefly, how.

The coming of the Son of God in the flesh had already of course affected all humanity. There is a sense in which those primary ties which make a man a member of the human race were by this redefined. All men formed a network radiating from the man who was the Son of God.

Furthermore every man, anterior to his action as an individual, is involved in the totality. Here in this domain of spiritual solidarity Jesus' life, and above all his death on the cross, affects humankind in a completely new way. For the first time in history someone goes to the very limit in love of God and love of man. He gives up his life, and the death he encounters was the direct result of human sin. His acceptance makes love victorious over hate and sin. The solidarity of sin is broken and yields to that of love; the very hate that brought about his death gives him the opportunity to display a love that somehow changes the very nature of death. It now takes on a redemptive and expiatory dimension; the sin of the world is pardoned; his death becomes the Exodus of humanity, and the definitive

Covenant. God, in Jesus, wrests man from the hellish prison of sin, and draws man forever to himself.

The redemptive nature of the Christian's suffering and death

Mere inclusion in the new solidarity set up by Jesus Christ is not sufficient. A man must exercise his freedom and respond to the offer of salvation by entering, through baptism, the Body of Christ. Once he is a member of that Body the Christian has a function to fulfill in the task of human salvation. It is through his members that Jesus continues his redemptive work in every age and in every environment.

The suffering and death of the Christian then, because it is bound up with the suffering and death of Christ, can have redemptive and expiatory value. And the sharper the Christian's realization of how his own sin and that of men generally works against his ideal of universal love, the more inescapable will be his suffering. Yet, because he realizes that, since the death of Christ, love is victorious, he knows he ought to weave his suffering into the pattern of his charity. This is how he is summoned by love to lay down his life.

And all the time he knows too that on this earth he is a sinner. While laboring as a member of the Body for the redemption of humanity, his own need to be "ransomed" never ceases, to be set free from slavery and joined with God. Day after day, week after week, the Word performs in him its liberating work, leading him to us.

Intercession by suffering and death in mission

The Church must have witnesses if she is to carry out her task among non-Christian peoples. And any missionary worthy of the name has to bear witness to universal love, be an artisan of Catholicity and peace, a reassembler of what has been dispersed. He must be involved in his environment, will inevitably encounter sin in others and in himself, and consequently will face suffering and even death. The secular way, even when the objective is human brotherhood, is not that of Catholicity: there is an endeavor to avoid that facing of death required by genuine love. And so the witness of the builder of Catholicity will always be distasteful; in one way or another men will endeavor to ward it off or suppress it.

The missionary is summoned to follow his master, to be touched somehow by persecution. He will not have to seek it: it will manifest itself in challenges of greater or less dimension. Saint Paul is always talking about the missionary's conflicts, and the ones that pained him most were those with brothers in the faith. It all means suffering, sometimes death, invariably solitude. The redemptive value will be measured by the growth in love that it all brings. One should emerge larger, more purified, rejuvenated, capable of new beginnings, a new future. When such a missionary makes his thanksgiving, his spiritual sacrifice, it is a veritable intercession, reckoned in favor of those who caused the suffering.

On the cross Jesus said, "Father, forgive them for they know not what they do." This is the highest expression of intercession, in suffering and death. It is natural that we should find it echoed throughout the long history of mission, among apostles and martyrs.

The extension of Christ's intercession in the Eucharist

Now that Christ has come, it is no longer necessary for the High Priest to pass beyond the veil and carry out there the expiatory rite *par excellence*, by sprinkling the blood on the propitiatory stone. This has been accomplished once for all by the one and only Priest of the new covenant. He used blood that was efficacious in a different way, his own. He gave his life, and is today always living to make intercession for all mankind.

The intercession is made sacramentally in the Eucharist, where unending the death of Christ is proclaimed. By sharing the bread and the Word we benefit from that intercession, and, as members of the Body, we are also interceding in a manner pleasing to God. Every Eucharist is in very truth a major event in salvation history. All creation is involved, and the paschal rhythm becomes more and more pronounced.

HOLY WEEK

A. THE WORD

I. Isaiah 42:1-7
1st reading
Monday

The four "Servant of Yahweh" poems (Is 42:1-4; 49:1-6; 50:4-9; 52:13-53, 12) are nowadays regarded as a collection put together by a disciple of Second-Isaiah. At a later stage, for some undetermined reason, they were inserted at different points in the Second-Isaiah corpus. Taken together they form perhaps a scenic presentation of the Servant's enthronement.

The first four verses of chapter 42 certainly belong to the first poem: about verses 5-7 there is some uncertainty. The first poem however is very closely linked with the second, particularly by the identification of the Servant with the whole people of Israel.

Light of the nations (Is 49:6), the Servant-Israel should spread his radiance to the ends of the earth (v. 4) by manifesting the salvation of Yahweh (Is 49:6) and bringing law and instruction to the nations (vv. 1, 3, 4). Doubtless there is no question of a specifically missionary role. God gives salvation to Israel only, thus confounding the nations who will have to recognize the one true God (cf. Is 52:10) and Israel's privilege. Indeed the Servant-Israel refuses to preach to the nations (v. 2; cf. Ac 11:19): he acts only by his presence and the witness of his life. The prophet's image is probably that of an Israel dispersed among the nations, but enjoying sufficient freedom and respect to demonstrate in a dramatic fashion Yahweh's especial concern for them. He goes further still, Isaiah 49:6, in advising the servant-people that it is better to use the occasion of the diaspora for testifying to God's light throughout the world, than to be relocated in Palestine. Consequently, though it cannot be maintained that the poem is devoid of *universalism*, the notion as yet is extremely associated with the Jewish center.

II. John 12:1-11
Gospel
Monday

The narrative of the Bethany anointing raises many exegetical problems. Primitive tradition it appears has preserved an account of such an anointing at the house of a certain Simon (Mt 26:6-13; Mk 14:3-9) by a woman who remained anonymous.

John's version gives us further details. He names the woman; Mary, the sister of Martha and Lazarus. Then he goes on to emphasize that the anointing was one not of the head only, as in Matthew and Mark, but of the feet as well (v. 3), to the point of prodigality (a detail which reminds us of another episode, perhaps a distinct one, narrated by Lk 7:36-50). The prodigality doubtless is stressed by John as a contrast to Judas' avarice (which again he is alone in mentioning).

Straightway, by noting the proximity of the Pasch and the presence of the man Lazarus, John gives the *anointing* narrative a paschal coloring (vv. 1-2). Judas objects to the expenditure. Three hundred pence probably represented a worker's wage for a whole year (Mt 20:2 speaks of a penny per day). Jesus, in reply, gives a whole new meaning to Mary's unction: "Leave her alone, she had to keep this scent for the day of my burial." Judaism attached a more serious moral obligation to the care of corpses than to charity for the poor. While the reply silenced Judas, it is none the less difficult to interpret. He may mean that Mary here is anticipating the care that will be given his corpse (Jn 19:38-42): hence the anointing is a sign of death. But it could be also the sign of his resurrection. There will be no anointing of the tomb; consequently Mary is now using the unguent she has kept for that purpose (v. 7) to anoint his body which will not be possible after his death because his body will rise again.

The second interpretation seems preferable. The anointing described then would be more then the prelude to anointings to come: it would be the actual tomb-anointing. The risen Christ will not receive any subsequent one, and this becomes the veritable sign of resurrection. This would explain why, in contradistinction to Luke, John does not mention in chapter 20 an intention on the part of the women to anoint the corpse.

One has only to read explanatory commentaries on confirmation or the unction of the sick to realize how difficult it is to bring home to people nowadays the significance of anointing ceremonies. Is there not too much tendency to rely on awkward parallels, whether they are drawn from similar rites in other religions or from modern life (as for instance talk about oil and engines)? John has no such preoccupations. He is little concerned with the burial associations of such anointing; the essential symbolism for him is the association with resurrection. The recipient is charged with a new life, saturated, as a tissue is saturated with oil. Though they do have the association with the shadow of death and sin, anointing-rites nevertheless equip people for the living of a life that evades death. The anointed person is set free: he is lord.

III. Isaiah 49:1-6 Exegetes discern two distinct themes in this
 1st reading   extract. The first (vv. 1-3 and 5b-6) ex-
 Tuesday   presses a universalist sentiment: the second
                  (vv. 4-5a) describes a prophetic investiture.
Second-Isaiah, having seen in Cyrus an envoy of God now expresses his disillusion. While favoring the reconstitution of Israel the king is at the same time setting up again the temples of Mardouk and pagan new-year festivals. There is an oracle of his downfall: God will soon send his people a new messenger.

Concluding his meditation about the failure of Cyrus' mission, the prophet comes to regard himself as the envoy Cyrus ought to have been. He eulogizes his *prophetic function* in terms previously reserved for the king. His mission will even have a universal dimension and his name will be proclaimed by God (v. 1: cf. Is 41:25). The sword of Cyrus which ought to have annihilated the kings is entrusted to him (v. 2; cf. Is 41:2). Where Cyrus could have become the light of nations (v. 6: cf. Is 42:16) had he remained faithful, the prophet now steps in.

He finds himself called by God from the moment of his conception, like Jeremiah (vv. 1 and 5: cf. Jr 1:5). Like Ezechiel's, his mission is one of whetting the sword (v. 2; cf. Ez 21:14-22). Like a new Jacob, he must wrestle manfully throughout the night (v. 3; cf. Gn 32:23-33). Disillusioned though he be, he wants to continue the tradition of his predecessors, the prophets of Israel (v. 4; cf. Jr 15:10; 20:9 and Is 49:4).

In this picture of a prophet the primitive Church would subsequently discern the traits of Christ (compare verse 3 with Mt 3:17 and verse 6e with Luke 2:32). Yet the prophetic function that was fulfilled in Christ did not terminate with him.

The Old Testament prophet could see in the event (in this case, Cyrus' intervention in Jewish history) possibilities for communion and covenant between God and men. Christ was a prophet because he manifested the presence of God by his personal reaction to events.

The Church is prophetic because through faith she discerns in secular events the shape of the coming Kingdom. She applies her own standards of criticism to every social system, revolutionary or conservative, just as Second-Isaiah did with Cyrus. Does it contribute toward the ideal of human unity in Jesus Christ?

She does not know exactly the nature of the relation between this world and the Kingdom. But she does know, and proclaim, that whatever we make of this world, a hell of hate and suffering or a better place to live, it will be from this material that Jesus will build his Kingdom.

Consequently each Christian must determine his prophetic role in these terms, in the world, and in the Church. He must try to discern what furthers the advance of the Kingdom, and what impedes it. For all of us the Eucharist ought to be the greatest indicator of prophetic mission, because it is the center of prophetic proclamation of the Word. In this assembly the most active critics of certain ecclesial structures should find a home.

IV. John 13:21-   This is the preamble to Christ's discourse of
33, 36-38   farewell to the apostles. He foretells the
Gospel   betrayal by Judas (vv. 21-30) and makes it
Tuesday   a stage in his own glorification (vv. 31-32).
Then the terms of Peter's intervention give him an opportunity, as he replies, of embarking on the discourse (vv. 36-38).

a) A chill note is struck among the group by the mention of the *betrayal*. Jesus only reveals the identity of the betrayer in symbolic fashion. He offers him the dish in a last gesture of friendship. In refusing this friendship Judas pronounces judgment on himself, and becomes overwhelmed by sin (Jn 8:44).

b) The direction of events however remains in the hands of the Lord. He himself gives the dramatic signal by bidding Judas do what he has to do (vv. 27 and 30). The "night" begins, but it is Jesus himself who initiates the process.

It is a paschal night, under the light of a new moon, to be illuminated in a definitive fashion by the *glory* of Jesus (vv. 31-32). He has taken the initiative in deciding the hour of his death, but because that death means glorification by the Father. It is clear that, for John, the idea of glory is not restricted to resurrection but applies to the death as well. It too reveals the divine life (cf. Jn 3:13-14; 8:28; 12:32-34).

c) Peter, with a presentiment of something ominous about to happen, says that he is ready to die for Jesus (v. 37). The boast has all the more irony because Jesus is about to die for them. He is rebuked by the prediction of his own *betrayal* (v. 38). It is the supreme moment of crisis. Amid a heavy silence Jesus begins the farewell discourse (Jn 14:1-31).

In this last supper episode three persons are playing with death in three profoundly different ways. Judas sets no great value on life, especially another's life. His own life is lived with the emphasis on its superficial adjuncts, like money. The absolute value that life should have he gives to money (cf. Jn 12:4-6). How could he appreciate a level of living where he never moved? Life as such is cheap to him, his own as well. He never penetrated its meaning.

Peter has some good insights. He realizes that the meaning of life lies in relationship and giving; there is no other way of really living. But he shows shallowness. The man who offers his life in this way is not really self-aware. He is offering something exterior to himself, of greater weight and import than his superficial self. Just as lightly he could withdraw his offer, or be crushed by it. The mere velleity does not mean laying down one's life.

Jesus gives up his life, but with what a measure of awareness! He surrenders it to his friends as well as his opponents. He decides the hour and directs the course of events. The awareness extends to the deepest roots of life, the point at which it is created, quickened, and given. In his mysterious person the giver was not distinct from what was given. Everything was gift, and was given absolutely. Could it be that he knew, as God, that person and gift are mysteriously the same?

V. Isaiah 50:4-9a   Our reading is from the suffering Servant
   1st reading   poems. Four in number, they were inserted,
   Wednesday   fairly awkwardly, in the earliest portions of
                Second-Isaiah. Today we have the third poem.
The Servant speaks of himself. He contrasts his halting language (v. 4) with that of the great prophets of the people (Ex 4:10; Jr 1:6). He goes on to consider the insults he has suffered during his mission, and borrows his vocabulary from the ancient prophets to describe them. He "offers his back" (cf. Is 51:23);

he "presents his cheeks to those who pierce him" (cf. Ez 21:14); he "does not cover his face" (cf. Ez 16:52; Jb 14:20; 30:10). Convinced however that God will save him (v. 7), he does not resent the insults (Jr 1:18).

One aspect of the *suffering Servant* image has its origin probably in the figure of Jeremiah. His destiny was to act out in person the exile events (Jr 13:1-11; 16:1-13; 18): he carried on his shoulders both the sins of the people and their chastisement.

He is alone among Old Testament prophets in stressing so heavily his personal drama. Mild and loving, he is required to sustain insult, persecution and injustice. He stands out as a guiltless figure in a society of sinners (note the lamb comparison Jr 11:19; 15:10-21; 18:18-25; 20:7-18); and, confronted by shallowness, stands for interior sentiment in religion, is aware of personal crisis. His prophecy conjures up the shape of a new covenant, which will be based on interior sacrifice, on conversion of the heart, and on personal responsibility.*

Second-Isaiah develops his whole doctrine of the Servant (Is 42:1-4; 49:1-7; 50:4-11; 52:13-53, 12) by frequent reference to Jeremiah's career. The Servant, in his suffering, becomes a substitute for the great multitude who should have suffered for their sins; and, by so doing, is enabled to make a new covenant, of universal import, with God. But, while giving us this personal aspect (in terms of Jeremiah), Second-Isaiah is equally insistent on the collective aspect (Israel persecuted by the Gentiles).

It is impossible to say which aspect is the primary one; the preponderance of exegetical opinion leans perhaps towards the collective. Though Jesus himself has only one explicit reference to the theme (Lk 22:37; Is 53:12), primitive Christian tradition discerned numerous parallels. The messianic vocation after the baptism was seen as that of a "Servant-Son" (Mk 1:1; Is 52:1). His healing miracles were those of a servant expiator (Mt 8:16; Is 53:4). His humility is that of the Servant (Mt 12:18-21;

*See doctrinal theme: *spiritual sacrfice,* p. 300.

Is 42:1-3; Mk 9:31; Is 53:6, 12). The very failure of his preaching recalls Jeremiah and the Servant (Jn 12:38; Is 53:1). Nothing brought out so clearly as this theme the need for the savior to encounter suffering and death in accomplishing his design (Ac 3:13-26; 4:25-30; Is 53:5, 6, 9, 12; Mk 10:45; Is 53:5; 1 Co 11:24; Is 53:5).

Jewish thought penetrated to this insight about an expiatory death by a just man for sinners, precisely because of the keen Jewish feeling about earthly retribution. Some meaning had to be found for the suffering of the just. Indeed Jesus may have found in this very doctrine the strength necessary to accept passion and death. He would be the just one expiating for others. After that, death could no longer seem a meaningless end; it was an integral part of his mission. Moreover, in the Servant doctrine, humiliation as an experience was linked with exaltation. It is because he deliberately yields himself to death that the Servant sees posterity and can seal a new covenant. Jesus likewise becomes aware that his death will issue in a glorification. He embarks on this mysterious experience, confident that it contains the secret of exaltation.

In it all he displays the nature of his godhead. Not alone does the Servant image show us Jesus accepting the human condition in absolute fidelity. It shows us too his godhead, the God who was not content to be the absolute, all-powerful, of myth and metaphysics, but revealed himself as the "God for others." The humanity of Jesus as Servant is neither an accident nor an episode in the being of God. It is the most perfect manifestation of what he, as God, is. It indicates a new kind of transcendence: that of absolute universality in love for others to the utmost limit in death and self-despoliation.

This does not detract from essential divinity. Myth and metaphysics are not the sole means of affirming something. Remembering Jesus as Servant, we realize that God, in Christ, is not someone momentarily forgetting divinity while spending some years among poor humans. This is the truly transcendent God, whose transcendence takes the form of loving service to others.

Nor does the dimension of expiation in his service argue a vengeful God, whose anger must be appeased by the blood of his Son. It means that Jesus gave his service at once the character of a victory over basic egoism, and the stamp of divine transcendence, where sin is no more possible.

Indeed it is only too true that an authoritarian and vindictive God, accomplisher of prodigies, jealous of his power, had no point for Christ. With him certainly, that notion did die. But if divine transcendence is no longer spelled out in terms of omnipotence, it is none the less there, in terms of love and service. In serving men, in "expiating for them," he was not betraying godhead. On the contrary, he was revealing its true nature; his other-regarding achievement makes him the "Totally-Other."

There is a sense in which every Christian is also the servant of others, insofar as he promotes the human cause. He lives implicitly God's own transcendence, which is manifested in love for man and the stripping of man's sinful limits. But this is only implicit, on the humanist level. In Jesus, on the contrary, it all becomes objective and explicit. If we follow him, there is a decisive turning which leads to victory over sin and death.

So, if we would have it this way, not the humanist way, but his; we must be explicitly linked with Christ. Our altruism then becomes the altruism of God; and it is in the eucharist that the God who implicitly informs all our service becomes explicit.

VI. Matthew   This is the narrative of the betrayal by Judas
  26:14-25   and the preliminaries to the paschal supper.
  Gospel
  Wednesday   a) The first question that presents itself is
                     that of the *date of the Supper*. Matthew
speaks of the first day of the azymes (v. 17), the first day, that is, for eating unleavened bread (Ex 12:1; 23:14). Usually

it was on this day the paschal meal began (we should note that the new Jewish day began at 6 in the evening, about sunset: cf. v. 20). According to Matthew however the first day of the azymes precedes the paschal meal (compare verse 17 and verse 20). We encounter a further complication in John 19:14, 19, 31, 42. Following him, the immolation of Christ takes place at the moment when the paschal lamb is immolated in the temple as a prelude to the evening repast. That would mean that the paschal meal was eaten several hours after the death of Christ.

The various chronological data could be reconciled by assuming that Jesus and his followers were using the calendar of some special group (Qumran possibly), which was this year some hours in advance of the official temple calendar. This would explain the mysterious remark in verse 18. Possibly also Jesus was deliberately anticipating the paschal meal. Whatever way we view the matter, it seems certain that he was deviating from the official observance. He may have wished to show how removed from the Jewish world he already felt himself to be, and his emancipation from ancient Jewish rubrics.*

b) Verses 14-16 and 20-25 are altogether concerned with the *betrayal* by Judas. The ridiculous sum of money he received is that set by the law as the price of a slave (v. 15; cf. Ex 21:32; Ze 11:12). Like John 13:21-30, Matthew avoids giving the impression that Judas took the initiative. Jesus, as Lord of life and death, must be the one to determine his "hour." He himself foretells the betrayal (v. 21), makes a last gesture of friendship towards Judas (v. 23, derived from Ps 40/41:10), confronts him unequivocally with his responsibilities (v. 24) and lets the betrayer know that he is aware of the whole plan (v. 25). All the time Judas seems no more than some fantastic puppet; Jesus has chosen to die and nothing now can alter that.

To understand the significance of the whole Judas episode, and Christ's attitude, we should remember what a Jewish meal

*See the doctrinal theme: *eucharistic repast,* p. 306.

was like, on the purely natural level. Too much stress can be laid on what is indeed secondary, the bread and wine shared. The really important thing is what Jesus did with these. He "took" the bread and wine. That is to say: he used something, a created thing, which for a Jew was a gift of God's love, a beginning of salvation. What he meant to signify was his own communion with God. Then he shared the bread and passed the wine cup around, meaning to indicate his desire to share with others their communion.

Not only does he not condemn Judas; he offers him total communion. Questions about the sacrilege of Judas, whether or not the bread he ate was consecrated, are really not important. It is the gesture that matters, not the food: the gesture gives the food its significance. Jesus throughout his life was too accustomed to eating with sinners to be concerned with excluding Judas from this close intimacy. Judas, and he alone, judged himself by shutting himself out.

Thus the Eucharist, because it is essentially a communion offered to sinners by Jesus, is more than any other the sacrament of pardon. Sinners may be absorbed into the divine life, at least insofar as they refrain from condemning themselves by withdrawing.

VII. Isaiah
61:1-3a, 8b-9
1st reading
Mass of the
Chrism

Though chapters 60 and 62 are usually attributed to Second-Isaiah, exegetes are inclined to single out chapter 61 as the work of a later disciple. The author describes the prophet's vocation (v. 1-3), and then goes on to analyze his message (vv. 4-11).

The style of verse 7, of which the second half appears in the reading, is, anticipating that of the beatitudes, antinomic. Answering to a double share of opprobrium we have a double share of happiness; to ignominy, a lasting *joy,* the characteristic of the *"eternal" covenant* between God and his people. Moses' covenant was eternal: it was weighed down by the threat of punishment and exile (Dt 30:15-20). The new covenant is going to be universal. All the nations will marvel at the new people, the sign of benediction (vv. 9 and 11, which should probably be juxtaposed).

Verse 10 can be regarded as a conclusion. Having listened to the prophecy, the people rejoin and sing their *magnificat*. They don, like a festive garment, the salvation received from God.

The eternal covenant will mean more than an indefinite sojourn in the land of Promise. It will mean a sharing of God's own life and unending dependence on his limitless love. No one people will enjoy an exclusive privilege: all nations will be welcome.

The Eucharist is the memorial of the Lord's sacrifice, sealing the new alliance with God. The fact that the savior is thus open to all men *(novi et aeterni testamenti* pro multis)* gives our Christian life a double dimension: unremitting attachment to God, and openness to all humanity.

VIII. Revelation This is the epistolary dedication to the
1:5-8 Churches of the Roman province of Asia,
2nd reading which John prefixes to the Book of Revela-
Mass of the tion. It is such a tissue of biblical allusions
Chrism and reminiscences that an inventory of these
seems to be sufficient commentary.

a) The author begins with the hope that the *Trinity* will bring grace and salvation to his audience (vv. 4-5). Is it certain that the Trinity is in question? The periphrase "He is, he was,

---

*It is worth noting that the word *aeterni* does not appear in the gospel accounts of the Supper. Under the influence of Isaiah 61:8 and Hebrews 13:20, it was inserted in the primitive Roman canon.

he comes" (vv. 4 and 8) clearly refers to the Father. It is Jewish in inspiration, an expansion of an expression known since Exodus 3:14 ("I am"), and showing that God is not altogether of the present, but also of the past and future. "He is, he was, he will be" was the expression sometimes used to name God. In John however "he will be" is replaced by "he comes" to stress the fact that the Father is master of the course of history. He comes as judge.

The reference to the second person of the Trinity is sufficiently clear not to need demonstration here (cf. b below). Not all exegetes however are agreed about reference to the Holy Spirit in the figure of the seven Spirits (v. 4: cf. Rv 8:2; 3:1; 4:5; 5:6). Some see here a reference to the angels of creation. This dedication, they argue, like most of the epistolary dedications of Saint Paul, would be liable to mention only the Father and the Son. An epoch when pneumatology was groping as yet for vocabulary and expression found the figure of seven spirits quite attractive.

b) *Jesus Christ* is honored with three titles (v. 5). He is *first-born* amongst the dead, because he is the first to be exempted from the law of death (1 Co 15:20; Col 1:18; Rm 6:9), and the only means whereby other men can conquer death (1 Jn 5:1-5). He is the faithful *witness*, because he has until death borne testimony to the plan of his Father, because in him all prophecies are fulfilled and the divine promises realized (cf. Ps 88/89:28, 38). Finally he is *principal* among kings of the earth (Is 55:4), because he has received all power from the Father (Dn 7:13-14), and demonstrates this, as the Book of Revelation will go on to show (cf. Rv 11:15; 17:14; 19:16), by guiding the destiny of earthly kingdoms.

c) It seems likely that verses 4-5 are a thanksgiving after the manner of Jewish blessings, where several titles of glory are attributed to God. With verses 6-7 we come to the commemoration of the *work of salvation* realized in Christ. John recalls the love of Jesus for all, the fact that by his death he purified us of sin (Gal 3:13; Ep 1:7; 1 P 1:19), and constituted a people of royal priesthood (Ex 19:6; cf. 1 P 2:1-10; cf. also Rv 5:10; 20:6; 22:5). Verse 6 is interrupted to introduce a short doxology, after the New Testament fashion, of, Christ as Savior (Rv 4:8, 11; 5:9-13; 7:12; 19:1-7; Rm 11:36; 16:25-27; Ep 3:20-21, etc.). But John immediately returns to his commemoration by predicting the early return of the Lord. He shall come on the clouds like the Son of Man (Dn 7:13). He shall be "seen" (following Ze 12:10) and the nations will be converted (Ze 12:10-12). These are details from the Christian description of the last times (Mt 24:19-31). To see the Lord coming on the clouds, for a Jew, meant believing in his transcendental origin. For a Christian it meant belief in his resurrection and lordship (Mt 26:61-64; Ac 7:55) and being converted to the kingdom now inaugurated.

The reason the resurrection is so central to our faith is because it reveals the true identity of the Messiah. In cooperation with his Father Jesus overcame the obstacle of death and so becomes first-born among the dead. So loyal is he to the earthly condition that he verifies the prophecies. To all his brothers, to all the nations, as adoptive sons he offers a share in his resurrection, on one condition. They must give evidence of a faith that "sees," and a conversion that gives effect to the remission of sins brought about by the Lord's death.

The Eucharist is the expression in act of such faith and conversion, and for that reason anticipates the coming on the clouds of the Son of God.

IX. Luke 4:16-21   Matthew shows us Christ as an itinerant rabbi
Gospel   (Mt 4:12-17). Luke on the other hand is
Mass of the   somewhat of a liturgist. He begins and ends
Chrism   his gospel with accounts of incidents in the
temple (Lk 1:5-23; 24:50-53), and has the
ministry open during the sabbath liturgy in a synagogue.

This liturgy generally comprised two readings. The first, from the law (Pentateuch), was read and commented on by a "doctor of the law." The second, which was a more recent introduction, had to be an extract from the prophets and could be read and commented on by anyone who was at least thirty years of age. Jesus, being thirty, asserted his right to read and comment. His first public discourse then is actually a liturgical homily.

a) Luke has not preserved the actual discourse: he sums up its essential content in a single verse: "Today, it is accomplished" (v. 21). These few words are a perfect model of what the *homily* should be. The liturgy of the Word is no longer simple moral catechetic. Nor is it the affirmation of the eschatological hope of the prophets. It proclaims here and now, today, in the assembly, the fulfillment of the Father's plan. Instead of meditation on the past, whether that was a golden age or one of decay; instead of dreaming about a marvelous future, the here and now of life should be lived, as the focus of the Lord's coming.

Subsequently, the apostles were faithful to the homiletic style of Jesus (cf. Ac 13:14, 42; 16:13-17; 17:1-3; 18:4). The Christian liturgy of the Word was the offspring of the Jewish. Memory of the past and hope for the future were brought to accomplishment in "celebration of the now." Are the homilies delivered in our Christian assemblies after the model of Jesus' homily, or those by doctors of the law?

b) Apparently by design, Jesus (or Luke) has the reading finish just at the point where Isaiah 61 proclaims "a year of grace." There is no mention of the following verse about the judgment of the nations: "And a day of vengeance for our God" (Is 61:2). Doubtless the purpose was to stress, exclusively, the grace of God. What provokes the astonishment of the assembly (v. 22) are his words of *grace,* and they give rise to the incidents described in verses 25-30. Then, in the quotation of Isaiah 61:1-2, the addition by Jesus (or Luke) of a verse borrowed from Isaiah 58:6 is also significant. It is about the freedom offered to prisoners, and it reinforces the idea that Jesus' mission is one altogether of grace, not of condemnation.

Such a proclamation of God's grace and love extended to all men was inevitably distasteful to the Jewish audience. The intensity of their eschatological hope was in proportion to the intensity of their hate for the Gentiles.

c) Luke gives a good deal of prominence to the role of the *Spirit* in Christ's life. At the baptism the Spirit confirms his messianic vocation (Lk 4:1); for the accomplishment of the miracles he lends his power (Lk 5:17; 6:19; 9:1); he helps in choosing the disciples (Ac 1:2) and gives reassurance during Christ's mission (Lk 10:21). He is the gift of the Father (Lk 11:13) and the sign of the last times (Lk 24:49; Ac 1:4-8; 11:16; 2:14). Luke's recording of the homily at Nazareth has a deep significance. It shows Christ's own recognition of his spiritual vocation.

An understanding of Jewish mentality enables us to see how, for Jesus, a presentation of himself as the prophet sent by God meant also the obligation of realizing immediately what the Word proclaimed. Word, for the Jew, is efficacious. Proclaiming oneself the servant of God means demonstrating that. The Christian too should believe with the same conviction that the proclamation of God's redemptive love to the world is at once its realization. The liturgical proclamation of God's Word is efficacious because it transforms the hearers into witnesses.

X. Exodus This is a description of Jewish ritual for the
12:1-8, 11-14 paschal meal. It emanates from priestly
1st reading sources, that later legislative strata of scripture,
Holy Thursday that is, which are marked by an anxiety to
rekindle in the Jews of the Promised Land the open attitude displayed by their ancestors on the day of deliverance from Egypt.

a) By eating upright with loins girt during a vigil, the Jew was demonstrating that the Pasch concerned him personally and was bringing about his personal deliverance. Then the ancient observance of the immolation of the *lamb* and the sprinkling of the doorposts was highly important. Not only was the lamb immolated; it was eaten, thus further involving the participants in the mystery of the feast.

b) The priestly redactors had inserted the ritual in the perpetual calendar, which was in use among certain strata of the population. According to the new computation, the month of the Pasch (March-April) became the first month of the year, where previously the feast of the New Year had coincided with that of the Tabernacles (September). Such an arrangement anticipated the Christian era, when the feast of Tabernacles became totally absorbed in that of the Pasch.

c) The rite of *unleavened bread* had its origin in a custom of the barley harvest. It was forbidden to mix old leaven with new flour. Consequently one had to wait for the flour to generate its own leaven, and unleavened bread would be eaten over a certain period. However the Jews had brought this agricultural practice into association with their nomad religious traditions. In the unleavened bread they saw a sign of their ancestors' haste as they fled from Egypt (Ex 12:33-34). "Haste" always remained a characteristic of Jewish ritual at the paschal meal.*

The essential element of the ceremony, which was a nomad custom to begin with, was the immolation of a lamb. The lamb's blood was considered a protection against fluxes and maladies (Ex 12:12-22; 22:14-17; Lv 23:10-12). Perhaps at one stage celebration of such a rite happened to coincide with preservation from an Egyptian plague. For the delivered people the immolated lamb would then become the sign of its liberation, and its constitution as a free nation (Ex 12:23-29).

With the progress of the centuries the ritual of the feast was amplified. It lasted for seven days, during which all work was

*See the doctrinal theme: *eucharistic repast*, p. 306.

forbidden; and eventually absorbed the agricultural feast of unleavened bread (Dt 16:1-8; 2 K 23:21-23). However its most
distinctive character as a festival was the result of meditation by
the early prophets and of Deuteronomy. The father of the family
considered himself obliged during the course of the meal to
explain the celebrated ceremony. The addition of this catechesis
meant that participants felt really involved, and inspired to
renew within themselves the liberating rite (Ex 12:25-27; 13:7-8;
Dt 16:1-8: "It is you who have come forth from Egypt"). Then
the Old Testament insistence on the eating of the lamb rather
than its immolation or the sprinkling of the blood stressed
further the personal aspect (Dt 16:6-7; Ex 12:1-12). It was more
than a commemorative occasion. The rite of the lamb became
a symbol of personal participation, which brought about one's
own liberation.

When the prophets came to proclaim future deliverance from
the Babylonian exile they did so in terms of a new Exodus and
revived the image of the paschal lamb. And so the feast became
rooted in consciousness as that of liberation, above all liberation
from sin. Some texts, of eschatological import in this way,
such as Isaiah 10:25-27; 40:1-11; 2 M 2:7-8; Sirach 36:10-13,
may very well have been readings for the feast. In Ezechiel it
has become essentially the feast of the restoration. Expiatory
rites are multiplied (Ez 45:18-25; Lv 23:5-14; 2 Ch 30-35) with
a view to achieving the maximum of success.

When John discerns in Jesus the true lamb (Jn 13:1; 18:28),
when he has the immolation of the lambs in the temple coincide
in time with Jesus' death (Jn 19:14, 31, 42; 1 Co 5:6-8), he is
attempting to bring home to his readers the lesson that in the
sacrifice of Christ the whole paschal ritual is brought to fulfillment. This has constituted the definitive people, achieved a
veritable liberation from the power of evil, made the Christian
a pilgrim *en route* to the Promised Land (1 P 1:17) where the
Lamb, surrounded by the people he has ransomed, will reign
(Rv 5:6-13; 7:2-17; 12:11; 19:1-9).

XI. 1 Corinthians The Corinthians were accustomed to celebrate
11:23-26 the Eucharist during an agape meal. This
2nd reading gave rise too often to factionary spirit among
Holy the community. The better-off members tended
Thursday to congregate at the same tables, excluding
the poor from their good cheer (vv. 18-22).
To deal with the matter Paul is careful to remind them of the
institution by Christ (vv. 23-26), and of the close ties binding
the Eucharist to the Church, the sacramental body to the
mystical body (vv. 27-29; cf. 1 Co 10:16-17).

Luke's account of the Supper, 22:19-20 appears to be the
oldest. It is an exact reflection of Jewish liturgical practice where
the meal began with a blessing of bread, then a sharing. The
conclusion was a thanksgiving over a cup, which was called the
"cup of benediction." He makes it clear also that between the
fraction of the bread and the distribution of the cup, the meal
itself intervened ("after the repast").

Paul on the other hand, in 1 Corinthians, represents a later
discipline. The blessing of the bread is brought to the end of
the meal, side by side with the blessing of the cup. Matthew
and Mark will represent a later stage still. They juxtapose the
two blessings, but independently of any meal.

And finally, with the longer version of Luke 22:15-18, before
the rite of the Supper a paschal meal is reintroduced, with its
own blessing. Doubtless this indicates a doctrinal bias which
was anxious to stress the paschal character of the Christian
Eucharist.

a) Paul's version of the institution is fairly close to that of
Mark (Mk 14:22-25), but it already shows a Hellenistic influence and is clearly inspired by a particular liturgical usage
(perhaps that of Antioch). The repetition of the command
should be especially noted: "Do this in memory of me" (vv.
24-25). The symbolic action (do this), as a *memorial* of the
Lord, is important. A version closer to the Aramaic might

interpret Christ's command thus: "In your thanksgiving at meals, where in the ancient discipline you commemorated the marvels of God, add now a commemoration of my work." When he gives a more Hellenist turn to the commemoration, and repeats the command twice, Paul is insisting on the reality of this commemoration of Christ's death. Verse 27 leaves no doubt about his conviction that in the Church's eucharistic rite the body and blood of Christ are present.

b) On the other hand, while verse 29 too can be taken as an affirmation of belief in the real presence, its obvious purpose, above all when we remember the *body* doctrine generally of 1 Corinthians (cf. 1 Co 12:12-26), is to demonstrate how unworthy celebration means contempt for Christ's mystical body as constituted by the assembly (cf. again 1 Co 11:22, contempt for the Church of God, in this instance). Paul's general concern then is with the real meaning of the liturgical assembly. It is the symbol of the reunion of all men in the Kingdom and of the Body of Christ. Any assembly which is dispersed at different tables, so far from bearing witness as it should, becomes a countersign.

This preoccupation of his becomes more apparent when juxtaposed with the synoptic accounts of the Supper where care is taken to mention the Twelve. Paul's account is addressed to the whole assembly, telling it what it should be and what it should do in order to commemorate the Lord's Pasch. His text was the one first written. The synoptic accounts are directed to the leaders of the assembly, giving details of the actions and words that must be used, in order to ensure continuity between their Eucharist and the Supper.

Thus, contrary to the synoptics, in Paul the ministerial function of distribution is less emphasized than the actions of community in eating and drinking. Celebrating the memory of the Supper is for him clearly a community obligation.

All this is of capital importance at a time when the people of

God are coming to realize once more that eucharistic celebration is the business of everyone. Liturgical disposition then can never be altogether the province of the sacerdotal ministry. The business of the priest is to ensure that the whole assembly gives thanks to God in a manner that it finds congenial.

This being so, the concrete avocations of the assembly members, the whole texture of their lives, should find expression in their liturgy. A local community should have the power to adapt its liturgy according to local needs.

XII. John
13:1-15
Gospel
Holy
Thursday

The first verses of this passage certainly form an introduction to the full account of the Supper and the Passion. The washing of the feet was an important part of the meal ritual, and is an excellent beginning for the Paschal mystery.

a) According to one interpretation, Jesus was simply carrying out a Jewish rite of *ablution* before eating. Sometimes, on the basis of this, a whole symbolism about purification has been constructed. However, it is not at all certain that purification was the point. In fact John tells us that the incident took place "during the repast" (v. 2), and this was not the case with ablution rites. Then Christ's remark to Peter, who believed indeed that he was witnessing the inauguration of a new ablution rite (v. 9), demonstrates that the sacrifice of the cross was more cleansing than all traditional ablutions, and will in the future be the only purifying rite (v. 10; Jn 15:1-3).

b) However, in order to understand the text, the two mentions of Judas must be explained. Jesus does not exclude him from the washing rite. Yet he is "unclean," and the washing will have no effect in his case. This very detail appears to be the key to the passage. The Lord humbles himself even before the traitor-to-be. This interpretation is confirmed by the lengthy account of the preparations (vv. 4-5), and by Peter's reaction in refusing to submit himself (v. 6). When Jesus says to Peter that he will understand "afterwards," or "presently," he is not referring directly to his Passion. He is merely indicating the explanations he will give, presently, at table (vv. 12-15).

What Jesus is performing in fact is a "symbolic action," like the prophets Ezechiel and Jeremiah. He, the Lord and Master, is placing himself in the rank of the most humble *servants*. The antithesis "Lord-Servant," like that of Philippians 2:5-11, is the essential thing in the passage. The lesson is simple indeed. Jesus is giving an example of humility which the apostles must emulate. Throughout their lives they and their successors must always give concrete expression to the image of "Lord-Servant."

If this is the correct interpretation, we might inquire about John's purpose in placing the incident here in the context of the Supper. The theme of "Lord-Servant" had in fact been already treated by the synoptics. Mark and Matthew content themselves with accounts of the institution itself (Mk 14:22-25; Mt 20:25-27); but Luke adds a strange description of a dispute among the apostles about primacy in their group (Lk 22:24-27; Mk 10:42-44). Luke's narrative must indicate a rereading of the Supper account made by some primitive community. They were led to it by their own spiritual situation, in particular by the need to clarify the real meaning of ministerial functions.

The humiliation, the obedience, the spiritual sacrifice, the love of Jesus Christ are concentrated in the Eucharist.* It obliges us to make these attitudes ours. Faith should discover to us the inner meaning and shape us accordingly. Whether we be ministers or participants, we should experience sentiments of humility, obedience and mutual service. Only then will our celebration be fully valid, and the memorial be properly accomplished.

Indeed for our Holy Thursday celebration, we might well base all our reflections on this biblical theme of bread, which, through a long evolution, comes finally to symbolize this interior attitude.

*See doctrinal theme: *spiritual sacrifice*, p. 300.

There had been, in the Old Testament, an antithesis drawn between the Word of God as spiritual nourishment, and natural bread. To be nourished by one, one had to fast from the other: Exodus 24:18; 34:18; Amos 8:11. The same contrast appears in the New Testament, when Martha is preoccupied with bread and Mary with the Word (Lk 10:38-42).

A further stage is reached when the Word of God, though still contrasted with natural bread, is nevertheless symbolized by a kind of bread. The antithesis is drawn between this special bread (manna for instance, symbol of the Word) and natural bread (Dt 8:3). It is a bread come down from heaven, bearing to us the will of God. We eat it by becoming converted (Ex 16:4-15; Ps 77/78:19-30; Ws 16:20; Is 55:1-3). It differs from natural bread, which nourishes our body indeed, but does not touch us interiorly.

In most of the prophetic vocations we find this note. They are sometimes called to "eat" a book as a symbol of their ministry of the Word (Jr 15:16; Ez 2:8-3:3; Rv 10:8-11). And the angels recognize their wisdom in the "bread of angels" (Pr 9:1-5; Si 15:1-5).

So it is that Christ is nourished by a bread which is the will of the Father (Mt 4:3-4; Jn 4:31-34). He pushes the image further when he proclaims himself the bread come down from heaven, because he does the will of the Father (Jn 6:38-48). He has become so aligned with the will of the Father which is his bread, that he can claim to be that bread. And when the bread becomes his body, delivered for us in fulfillment of the Word of God, he makes actual in the Eucharist the deep Old Testament meaning of the bread of God. It is a nourishment leavened with the will of the Father which enables us to do that will.

This bread then means obedience to God's will. It can never be a simple act of eating, but must be located on the spiritual, the sacrificial, level. Like the consecrated bread in the temple, it is the emblem of interior sacrifice (Lv 24:5-9; cf. Mt 12:3-4;

Lk 12:19). So, under biblical guidance, we find the symbol of bread to be more than a symbol of nourishment. It is the sign of sacrifice, a commemoration of obedience.

XIII. Isaiah The fourth is the most important of the suffer-
52:13-53:12 ing Servant poems. It emphasizes the humil-
1st reading iation of the Servant, and finds there salvation
Good for the nations. Where it is no longer possible
Friday to discern the lineaments of a man, we see
the quite overwhelming gesture of God.

Before the mystery of this *Servant,* disfigured by humiliations yet a savior, humanity stands abashed yet responsible. It was the nations who involved Israel (the Servant) in their sin and brought about his chastisement (Dt 7:1-6; 8:20; Ez 16:25). Then suddenly chastisement is transformed into mission: the Servant, involved now in the common sin, is expiating for all (vv. 5-7; 11-12).

Israel being the primary identity of the Servant in the fourth poem, the interpretation must be collective. Nevertheless, from verse 7b onwards, the oracle envisages a personal figure, that of the prophet Jeremiah (the lamb theme is borrowed from Jr 11:19; that of silence from Jr 15:17; that of coercion from Jr 33:1; 36:5). Thus the shadowy figure of a person begins to appear, but throughout the Old Testament it continued to be shadowy. Then came the personalist interpretation of the Septuagint, which replaced the "sapling" of Isaiah 53:2 by "little child." But the personal figure did not become fully clear until the New Testament identified the Servant with Christ. A wavering and uncertainty seems evident in the Old Testament, and is reflected in the versions, as between collective and individual interpretation. It is reflected indeed in the Hebrew tradition itself. So difficult is the text of these poems, and so numerous the variants, that determination of the original text becomes well nigh impossible.

All this aside however, there is no doubt about the basic affirmation. It is by means of his sacrifice that the Servant accomplishes his redemptive mission for the "multitude" of nations.*

XIV. Hebrews Primitive Christians of Jewish origin professed
4:14-16; faith in Christ while continuing to be zealous
5:7-9 observers of the law (cf. Ac 21:20). They did
2nd reading not feel that the faith differed from Jewish
Good Friday religion to the point of requiring a change of
observance. Consequently they went on frequenting the temple (Ac 2:46; 3:1-6; 21:26) where many priests became disciples of Christ without quitting their ministry (Ac 6:7). Ideas that seem essential to us, like those of priesthood and sacrifice, were not yet clear and defined. The Eucharist was celebrated, but it is by no means certain that Jewish Christians discerned there the priestly and sacrificial implications so important at a later stage.

However, very soon a persecution of Christians by the Jews (Ac 6:11, 19) drove the former away from Jerusalem and the temple worship. This was a serious hardship for them: they seemed to be cut off from the legal priesthood and the opportunity of offering sacrifice to God.

To such expatriate "Jews" this letter is addressed. They must not really feel that they have been cut off either from the priesthood, or the opportunity of sacrifice. The true high priest is no longer the one who officiates in the Holy of Holies, but Jesus Christ who ministered on the cross once for all. The true sacrifice is no longer that of bulls or goats in the temple, but the human life offered by Jesus and the community of Christians.

a) Our passage today is concerned with the first of these

*See doctrinal theme: *redemption*, p. 264.

points. Christians no longer need the temple priesthood. Jesus is the one and only mediator.

From verse 14 onwards the author is considering the essentials of the Christian profession of faith. Christ is the "heir of all things" (He 1:2-3); he is united to the Father ("seated at his right hand"). From these basic premises, well-known to his audience, he goes on to demonstrate that Christ is priest and mediator (He 4:15-5:10).

He uses two arguments. In the first place, Christ was man, and consequently able to represent humanity perfectly (vv. 15-16). In the second, he was Son of God, and sits at the right hand of the Father. Thus, with equal adequacy, he represents the divine (He 5:1). Partaking of both natures, he is the perfect *mediator*.

He stands, in a full sense, for humanity. The human nature he assumed was nothing ideal or paradisal: it was the condition in which men live, growth and decadence, confusion and failure, routine and hope, temptation and weakness. His priesthood is not absorbed in his divinity but carries all the implications of humanity. Indeed his priesthood is exercised for our benefit through the very frailty of humanity which he transfigured. If he could bring frail human nature to that high pitch, why should not his faithful, in their turn, share the privilege?

The conclusion follows. Let us go with confidence towards the "throne of grace" (v. 16; cf. He 10:22; Est 4:11; 5:1-2), towards the king of goodness that is, who gives grace even to the guilty and is generous to the importunate.

However, that Christ be welcoming and good is not sufficient. He must be capable of reconciling humanity to God; he must exercise a priestly and sacrificial ministry that is acceptable (He 5:1). Sacrifice is the sign of communion between God and men; only one who is perfectly accredited on both sides can accomplish it. Nor can the sacrifice be perfect unless the victim too represent both worlds. The offering must be of human nature *in toto*, but under the impulse of the Spirit of God. This is what makes the priesthood and sacrifice of Christ so unique, so decisive, an act. And the faithful, in their lives and in the Eucharist, are enabled to share it (Rm 12:1; He 13:10-15; 1 P 2:5).

b) The *new high priest* fulfills practically all the required conditions for consecration as priest. If he cannot claim that of heredity like the descendants of Aaron, that is because his

priesthood is of the order of Melchisedech (vv. 5-6). The second condition he does meet: he has come from among men to represent them before God. This was true "throughout all the days of his flesh," in the imperfection and unhappiness of earthly existence, in obedience to the prayer of the suffering Servant (vv. 7-8; cf. Mt 27:46, 50; Ph 2:6-8). The ideal sacrifice described by the prophets, that which is joined with obedience (1 S 15:22-25; Am 5:21-25; Ps 39/40:7-9). has been realized.*

There is a third condition: choice by God. This is absolutely essential; the priest would not be a mediator otherwise (cf. v. 4). As the author sees it, in the case of Jesus this condition was fulfilled at the moment when the risen Christ became by God's choice the principle of salvation for all (vv. 9-10), according to the prophecy of the suffering Servant (Is 52:14). Christ's priesthood then coincides with his entry into glory (vv. 5-6). It is an eternal priesthood, which leads all that come under its influence to divine life.

XV. John   John again takes up the question he has been
18:1-19, 42 asking all through the course of his gospel:
Gospel   who is the Christ? So that his readers may
Good Friday   be able to give the proper answer, he glosses
                 over the description of Jesus' human sufferings
and stresses all indications of his divinity and glory.

He is likewise careful to stress the ecclesial significance of the Lord's death; its priestly character; its prolongation, sacra-

*See doctrinal theme: *spiritual sacrifice*, p. 300.

mentally, in water and blood; its link with the gift of the Spirit and the beginnings of the Church (represented by John and Mary). His Passion narrative has the authentic stamp of drama. The author changes the scenery for each act, places his characters on the stage, and gives each section a focus by means of a particular action and a significant declaration.

We may outline the general plan as follows:

First Act: At Gethsemane (Jn 18:1-11)
    Special theme: *defection of Judas*
    Central action: *Peter's blow with the sword* (v. 10)
    Significant declaration: *Double profession by Jesus*
        ("it is I") (v. 5 and 8)
    Three scenes: 1-2, 3-4, and 11
Interlude: Characters leave for another place (Jn 18:12-16a)
Second Act: Before Annas (Jn 18:16b-27)
    Special theme: *defection of Peter*
    Central action: *the slap* (v. 22)
    Significant declaration: *Peter's double denial* ("I am not the
        one", v. 17 and 25), *associated with, and clarifying the
        real "slap."*
    Three scenes: 16-18, 19-24, 25-27
Interlude: Characters leave for another place (Jn 18:28)
Third Act: Before Pilate (Jn 18:28-19:15)
    Special theme: *unknowingly, Pilate, the soldiers and the
        Jews proclaim the kingship of Jesus*
    Central action: *the crowning* (v. 1-3)
    Significant declarations: *Christ's declaration (v. 36) and
        Pilate's proclamation (v. 39, king of the Jews) before
        the crowning. Then another proclamation by Pilate (v.
        5, the man) and a second declaration by Christ (v. 11)
        after the crowning.*
    Three scenes: *three scenes before the crowning, where
        Pilate goes out, reenters and goes out again (v. 29, 33*

and 38), with three scenes after the crowning, where Pilate goes out, reenters and goes out again (v. 4, 8 and 13), the crowning itself serving as a dividing interlude.

Interlude: Characters leave for another place (Jn 19:16-18)

Fourth Act: At Calvary (Jn 19:19-37)

  Special theme: *crucifixion*

  Central action: *The lance-thrust* (v. 34)

  Significant declaration: *dialogue between Jesus and his mother (v. 25-27) before the lance thrust, and the texts from Scripture (v. 36-37).*

  Three scenes: *preceding the central moment (the lance thrust): 19-24, 25-27, 28-30.*

Interlude: Characters leave for another place (Jn 19:38)

Fifth Act: At the Sepulchre (Jn 19:39-42)

  Special theme: *reversal of the fourth act*

  Central action: *the anointing* (v. 39)

  Three scenes: *replica of scenes in fourth act:*

   (a) *Jesus is "carried" to the appointed "place" (v. 40-41) as he "carried" his cross.*

   (b) *he is "embalmed" and shrouded (v. 41) as he was stripped in the fourth act.*

   (c) *he is "laid" in the tomb (v. 42) as he was nailed to the cross.*

a) To the great question, "who is the Christ," we are given throughout the gospel the varying answers, that of the priests (1:19), the Samaritan woman (4:11, 29), the crowd (6:2, 26), the Jewish authorities (7:27; 8:13; 9:29).

During the Passion on two occasions Jesus asks his adversaries, "whom do you seek?" (18:4, 7) and each time meets their answer "Jesus of Nazareth" (18:5, 8) with his own "I am he." This affirmation is an allusion to Exodus 3:14 where Yahweh declares: "I am." To those then who seek only Jesus of Nazareth John is revealing the Christ's *divine personality:* "he is." To emphasize fully the divinity, he mentions the fact that the Jews fell backwards, a characteristic reaction of people who have seen God. The great question is reechoed in the one posed to Peter "Are not you among the disciples of this man?" (18:17, 25); and Pilate in his investigation is brought to the point of the decisive query "whence are you?" (19:9).

b) The deliberate stressing of the ecclesial significance of Christ's death is also striking. We have the royal investiture before Pilate (19:13-15); the priestly character of the death (reference to the seamless robe: Jn 19:23); the *sacramental* character of the water and blood that flow from Christ's side (19:34), water the sign of outpouring of the Spirit, blood the symbol of the covenant sealed in the new paschal Lamb (19:36). The phrase "he gave up his spirit" is likewise an allusion to the diffusion of the Spirit (19:30; 1:33; 20:22). The maternal function of Mary symbolizes the future role of the Church (19:26-27). Abbreviation of the description of Jesus' sufferings is meant to throw in high relief the evidences of his divinity, and the perennial character of his work in the Church.

c) Finally, at every opportunity, the *universal dimension* of the Lord's Pasch is brought forward. He who is Lord in such terms cannot be subjected to the judgment of some Jewish Sanhedrin: he has come "into the world" (Jn 18:27). When he is enthroned it is before Pilate, representative of the emperor. The sentence is written in the three languages that embrace the world of the time (Jn 19:20). Finally, at the moment when he gives up his spirit, the nations that contemplate the cross and are converted (Jn 19:37) are those foreseen by Zechariah 12:10.

B. DOCTRINE

1. The Theme of Spiritual Sacrifice

In all the civilizations of history we find sacrifice to be an essential religious rite, and the whole course of religious history has been a constant refinement and deepening of the notion. Christianity itself has not hesitated to adopt the sacrificial vocabulary (immolation, expiation, etc.), though giving it a profoundly altered significance. In one way or another the notion of sacrifice is invariably an affirmation of proper relationship with God. It will always be the most important area of existence for people to whom the religious questions are real.

Our civilization today is a profane one, altogether concerned with man and his power over nature. Atheism is the natural climate. There is little time for the religious questions, and there is less and less natural inclination to turn to God.

There is little point however for Christians being nostalgic about the past. It is possible that faith may find a better forum for authentic witness here than in sacral civilizations of the past. The biggest risk the present brings is that of devoting religious life to the service of men rather than that of God. Sacrifice has ceased to be a primary consideration. Such an anthropocentric bias, as distinct from theocentric, is indeed very serious, because it could pervert the central meaning of Christianity. If the service of men becomes the central issue, the basic thrust of the two commandments is obscured, and love for the brethren ceases to be nourished by the very life of God. The Eucharist becomes no more than a means. The apostolate itself is lowered to the level of a worldly wisdom instead of being witness to a transcendent God.

In all it is more imperative now than ever for the Christian to reflect on the theme of sacrifice, and the Holy Week liturgy can be a powerful means to that end. The matter is crucial:

on the place we allot to sacrifice will depend the quality of our lives in faith.

From sacrificial rite to spiritual sacrifice in Israel

All Israel's neighbors practiced sacrificial rites, the lives of individuals and community being patterned accordingly. The bible bears witness to the universality of the custom: all history from the earliest origins is seen in terms of the sacrifices offered.

They were indeed very diverse. For us however the forms sacrifice took are not important: we wish to identify the precise religious thrust of which they were an expression. Why immolate victims to the gods? Why destroy the first fruits of one's toil? Why sacred banquets, where the only portions of victims that might be lawfully eaten were those not reserved for the gods?

Man in his search for happiness becomes aware that he is destined for a sacral world, that in fact keeps evading him. He tries to win the benevolence of the gods or to appease their wrath. If he is to achieve happiness he must share the stability and security of the godly domain. Liturgies show him the way Sacrifice becomes the basic rite. It is the best way of ingratiating himself, of gaining a share of divine energy, if he makes a ritual expression of his dependence. If he renounces a share of his possessions, places it in the hands of the gods by sacrificing it *(sacra facere* — to make sacred), withdraws it from any possible human use by destruction or otherwise, he is acknowledging that his destiny is linked to the godly world.

When, in Israel, the regime of faith began and there was general recognition of the unique, transcendent God, sacrificial ritual gradually underwent a transformation. In the pagan view the rite was of itself valid; given the required conditions it should be efficacious, and thus of course did not involve sentiments of the heart. Things were to be different in Israel. Prophets came to point out that sacrifice without dispositions of the heart and interiorization was a vain and hypocritical gesture. Ritual might be satisfied, but God was not. Yahweh is not pleased with the purely formal sacrifice; it must express an interior sentiment of obedience and repentance, that extends to the whole texture of life.

Such reflections were destined one day to issue in the remarkable Servant of Yahweh synthesis. According to Isaiah 53 the expected Servant would offer his own life as a sacrifice of expiation. Interiority reached its maximum of intensity in this idea — the total oblation of a person for the sake of the "multitude." From now on the classic notion of sacrifice begins to lose place, and when Jesus of Nazareth comes it will only be necessary to use the language of Isaiah 53 to make his Passion comprehensible.

The spiritual sacrifice of Christ

With Jesus comes the decisive turning. The whole development in Israel had been towards a realization that the sacrificial rite is intimately associated with inner dispositions. Yahweh is not moved by purely external procedures that do not engage the heart. When Jesus comes, the one who is perfectly cooperative with the plan of the Father, sacrifice according to the ancient model is no longer required. There would be little point in his sacrificing portion of what he had: he was about to sacrifice *himself*, to consecrate himself in truth. The living victim did not require the substitution of another victim. In total obedience to the will of the Father, the incarnate Jesus carried out absolutely the divine plan for humankind. From all eternity all men are summoned to share the divine life.

Placed at a moment in time, we can see the turning point in the history of sacrifice when Jesus begins his journey to Jerusalem to die there. He carries out with his followers the ancestral rite of the Jewish Pasch, a sacrificial rite of communion. Doing so, on the eve of his own death on the cross, he transforms the rite in essence; and the time-honored immolation of the paschal lamb yields to the change. From now on there will be only one valid sacrifice, that accomplished by the priest Jesus. The new rite will be one of communion in that sacrifice: the only priesthood will be that of Jesus, according to the definitive covenant, for the benefit of all mankind.

His sacrifice, abrogating all previous sacrificial rites, is that of the man-God. A man makes a total self-renunciation, in order that the absorption of mankind as a whole into the Family of God may be accomplished. This is not destruction of being, but construction of salvation. He who dies on the cross merits resurrection, and everlasting life for soul and body. It is at the point where he asserts that he observes the will of the Father that Jesus manifests his divinity: "Before Abraham was, I am" (Jn 8:58).

The spiritual sacrifice of the Church

From now on the Church knows only one sacrifice, the commemoration of the Supper, the sacramental reenactment of the cross. Which is to say that the Church's own sacrifice must be in terms of, and in radical dependence on, the sacrifice of her founder.

By baptism the Christian enters the Church and is enabled to "serve the living God" (He 9:14). Saint Paul is explicit with the Romans: "I beseech you then, brothers, by the mercy of God, to offer your persons as a living sacrifice, holy, pleasing to God. That is the spiritual worship you must render (Rm 12:1). Saint Peter is even more so: "You yourselves, like living stones, must build the spiritual house, as a holy priesthood, offering spiritual sacrifices that are, in Jesus Christ, pleasing to God" (1 P 2:5). Baptism opens the way to the "royal priesthood" (1 P 2:9). Following Christ, the only priest of the only sacrifice, in him and by him, it becomes possible for every one who by baptism becomes a member of his Body to follow the same path of obedience and love. We are enabled to sacrifice ourselves, to be consecrated, to be living victims, holy and pleasing to God.

All this emphasis on spiritual sacrifice does not mean advocacy of an interior cult, where ritual practice is to be no more than secondary. On the contrary it is an in-depth interpretation of sacrifice which leads to a proper rhythm in living and ritual. The Eucharist is the ritual and sacrificial expression of a whole Christian community, but it is required that this expression flow over into the routine of daily life. The sacrifice is always the same because it must be rooted in that area of the person where all his being is concentrated. Before the great eucharistic prayer begins the priest proclaims: "Let us give thanks to the Lord our God." And then, immediately: "It is right and just, it is our duty and our salvation, to give you thanks, Father, *always and everywhere*" (Roman canon).

Proclamation of the gospel, the spiritual cult par excellence

In preaching the gospel to the Gentiles, Saint Paul is very keenly aware of rendering to God a spiritual worship (cf. Rm 1:9). To the Romans he describes in emphatic terms the grace from God he has received, of being "a minister of Christ among the Gentiles, a priest of the gospel of God, so that they may be acceptable as an offering, made holy by the Holy Spirit" (Rm 15:16).

This is precisely what is required from the missionary whose work is the proclamation of the gospel to pagans. He must go to the limit in rendering spiritual worship to God. The unique character of the sacrifice offered by our High-Priest is that it is an act of love. This is the link with the Father, and it makes Jesus the Savior of humanity: he died because he loved all men. So it is with the Christian too. The spiritual worship to which he is initiated by baptism draws from one source only, Christ's love for the Father and for all men, which he shares with the members of his Body. When the missionary leaves his home country for a strange one, he is creating a set of conditions which will demand the exercise of universal love. These are the terms of the spiritual worship he must render to God. But if he does this, he bears witness to the resurrection of Christ. He proclaims the gospel to the nations: he asks them, too, to be an "agreeable offering to God, made holy by the Holy Spirit."

In Saint Peter we find the very same attitude. Having reminded the recipients of his first letter that Christians are "a holy priesthood, who should offer spiritual sacrifices, pleasing, by Jesus Christ, to God," he goes on to draw the immediate conclusion. "Always behave honorably among pagans so that they can see your good works for themselves and, when the day of reckoning comes, give thanks to God for the things that now make them condemn you as criminals" (1 P 2:12). It is a less cultic formula than that of Paul, but the core of doctrine is one and the same.

Eucharistic sacrifice, the source of spiritual cult

In the eucharistic assembly the faithful are gathered for the great sacrificial rite of the new covenant. It is a sacrament consisting of a consecration and a communion; and it re-presents Christ's great single sacrifice so that his followers may share it. All participants are summoned to "give thanks" to the Father. They join in the one and only thanksgiving that ever proved pleasing to God, the sacrifice of his Son.

The great eucharistic prayer from the preface to the Our Father has a sacrificial vocabulary. It is not a lip-service thanksgiving, or the acknowledgement of dependence on God on the occasion of a holocaust or offering of first fruits. It is the affirmation at the deepest level of sincerity, of the poor creature, for love of all men, even to the death of the cross.

So close is the link that binds the sacrifice of Christ to that of the Church, his Body, that they are one and the same. The "we" used by the minister, or ministers, in the eucharistic prayer designates Jesus Christ himself, as head of the assembly, his Body. The Mass is Christ's sacrifice, and the offerer to this day is Christ. Only by incorporation in his unique sacrifice and his unique priesthood, can the faithful, as a royal priesthood, make their sacrifice too pleasing to God.

2. The Theme of Eucharistic Repast

With the promulgation of the constitution *On the Sacred Liturgy* Vatican II brought to completion a project which had been more than fifty years under way. The purpose was to restore to its proper place the eucharistic celebration. Such reforms as have taken place since the Council demonstrate that *aggiornamento* at a deep level was necessary. Not every problem has been solved, but at least the real problems have been posed.

The Mass, in the case of many Christians, fails to be effective. Apostolic groups do not for a moment question its importance, but they do not really understand it. The very best Christians, to whom "life" matters more than "rite," see little point in religious practice of itself. They consider the witness given by the exercise of charity more important. Your good Christian today tends to experience encounter with Jesus Christ not in the eucharistic celebration but among his brothers, particularly the poor.

All this is due to failure to appreciate the close relationship the Mass ought to bear to the concrete realities of daily life. So very often the homily seems to belong to an abstract world, and the very texts from scripture seem hardly understandable and without reference to real living. Even the well conducted celebration does not escape such criticisms.

Because of its exceptional prominence in the liturgical year and the actual formulas it contains, the Mass of Holy Thursday offers a good opportunity for examination of the relevance of the Eucharist to the texture of Christian daily life. The inquiry is worthwhile. On our understanding of the eucharistic mystery will depend in great part proper balance in our apostolic lives.

The eucharistic repast in Israel

The meal has a religious dimension in all "traditional" civilizations, and the sacred banquet is a feature of most religions.

Sharing the same table and eating in common creates sacred bonds among the participants which are somehow associated with the numinous. When an immolated victim constitutes the food shared, the meal is often viewed as an infallible means of securing divine favor. In the pagan religions however there was as yet no question of sealing a covenant by means of the sacred meal, or communing with the divine. The object was simply recognition of actual relations of dependence.

When the regime of faith began in Israel this primitive view of the meal was undermined, even though the temptation to revert to it as a more reassuring thing remained acute. Why the change? The covenant of Yahweh with the chosen people was in the historic order in the fullest sense of the term, not in the cosmic order. On Sinai the Totally-Other God made a covenant with a people that he selected, absolutely freely and gratuitously. As a consequence Israel became irrevocably engaged to the unforeseeable pilgrimage of faith. He took them from Egyptian slavery to lead them to the Promised Land, but they had to undergo the desert trial. The concepts of Exodus, covenant and faith are indissolubly linked.

And so, in Israel, the idea of the sacred meal takes on a new significance. It is associated with the Covenant, because it is a commemoration of the wonders that Yahweh accomplished for his people. But on the other hand the communion with Yahweh that it means is entirely his free choice. Any attempt to claim a share of divine energy disappears. The annual paschal meal, in particular, recalled the Exodus, that greatest of liberating events. In the commemoration of past marvels at this meal, the hope of salvation became more actual. It followed the rite of immolation of the lamb. The sprinkled blood of the lamb reminded every one of the original Egyptian Pasch (when the exterminating angel "spared" the first-born of the Jewish people), and also of the Sinai Covenant itself.

Observance of the meal went through the same evolution as other religious observances in Israel. Prophets opposed any overly materialist conceptions as against religion of the heart. This led to emphasis on "celebration" in the meal, and on the "sacrifice of praise." The material aspect receded into the background.

The supper and the sacrifice of the cross

On the eve of his own death, for love, on the cross, Jesus partook of the traditional paschal meal with his disciples. He presided, and the memorial aspect of the meal, the "anamnesis," took on a whole new meaning.

Hitherto it was the Exodus, and the covenant associated with it, that was contemplated, as the major event in salvation history. But at the Supper something altogether new was on the horizon. The new, definitive, covenant was to be sealed the following day in the blood of the man-God. The Sinai covenant recedes, and in the cross of Jesus human salvation will be acquired once for all.

Thus from now on the event commemorated at the paschal meal will not be the Exodus, but the cross. The true Pasch, for Israel, and for all humanity, has at last been accomplished. Jesus' own words "Do this in commemoration of me" (in commemoration that is, of my death and resurrection) are merely a ratification of what the paschal meal at which he presided became. The bread shared, and the cup of benediction derived their "sacramental" value from their absolute connection with the "body to be delivered" (Lk 22:19) and the "blood of the alliance, which is to be shed for many in remission of sins" (Mt 26:28).

The Supper brought the Jewish Pasch to fulfillment. Messianic hope achieved its object: Jesus, the mediator of the definitive covenant, in his person established communion between perfect response to the divine initiative that was found in the God and humanity. The communion is possible because of the man-God. His spiritual sacrifice, his obedience unto death on the cross for love of God and all mankind, gives the paschal meal its real meaning: God and man are brought together. With the Supper begins, in a very real sense, the sacramental economy. The sacrifice of the cross means that all who share the Supper are linked with God.

Because of all this, at the Supper eschatological tension reaches its highest pitch of intensity. "I have longed to eat this pasch with you before I suffer, because, I tell you, I shall not eat it again until it is fulfilled in the Kingdom of God" (Lk 22:15b-16). And again: "I tell you solemnly, I shall not drink any more wine until the day I drink the new wine in the Kingdom of God" (Mk 14:25).

The Eucharist, the central mystery of the Church

The word "Eucharist" has come to designate, in Christian usage, the paschal meal of Jesus and his disciples. When the gathered faithful commemorate the Lord's death, they become involved, by virtue of their communion, in the only thanksgiving that has ever been pleasing to God. The Eucharist is more than a mere commemoration of a past event; it is a participation in the eternal sacrifice of the one and only High-Priest.

When we celebrate it, we are not only celebrating the greatest marvel of all history, God's initiative in bestowing on humanity his own Son. We are sharing the salvific act of the God-*man* as active *partners:* in the living link of communion we are making ours what Jesus did.

Thus our assembly is always under the sign of charity, of limitless service to one another. The washing of the feet, as recounted by John in connection with the institution, is a clear indication of the close link between the repast and the spiritual sacrifice, consummated in love. Universal brotherhood should be the first result of our Eucharist. For proper participation it is not sufficient to be "well-disposed" for reception of the sacrament; the community aspect is absolutely essential to eucharistic theology.

Furthermore, the brotherhood must obviously be translated

into act in our daily lives. What is described in the rite as "already accomplished" must be accomplished in "life." Nothing is more essential than this to the whole ecclesial concept: a continuity between "rite" and "life." While it is true that without lasting ritual initiation there can be no true life in Christ, it is also true that ritual without concrete application of the law of universal love is hollow. The law extends to all levels of human experience.

Eucharist and mission

In the eucharistic celebration Christians are assembled in a given place. The summons for this assembly however is of its essence universal. All such groupings are symbols of the gathering of all humanity in brotherhood, round about the First-Born of the new creation. Thus there can never be apartness or exclusivism: whenever Christians are gathered for the Eucharist the communion they express is without reserve. They recognize their link with all members of the Body of Christ, as he offers the one and only thanksgiving throughout the world. But they also proclaim their openness to absent brothers, to all those throughout the world who have not yet encountered the Good News. This is the dimension of the cross, and no "anamnesis" of the death of Christ could possibly evade its implications.

The thanksgiving expressed in the rite must overflow into the whole tenor of our lives. We should exhibit as our fundamental attitude the obedience unto death to God's will, which characterized Jesus. We should try to make our own, as the source of all our actions, his fidelity in love. We shall then be true witnesses of him, before God and men: our eucharistic lives, and our apostolic lives, will be aligned. Just as the Eucharist essentially implies universal openness, ecclesial mission implies a binding of everything and everyone to God. When he shares the Eucharist the Christian is shaped for the apostolic task of evangelization and witness, whereby he renders glory to God in Jesus Christ.

The eucharistic assembly and the sign of charity

Hitherto theological thought has been greatly concentrated on objective sacramentality, which is altogether dependent on the action of Christ. "It is Christ who baptizes, Christ who offers the Eucharist." There was little real attempt to develop a theology of the eucharistic assembly itself. Vatican II redressed the balance by extending the notion of sacramentality to the relations that ought to subsist, within the framework of the Institution, between members of the Body themselves. The doctrine of collegiality for instance can only be explained in terms of the law of charity on which the Church is based. In actual fact it envisages a brotherly relationship among bishops that is altogether original.

This is the relationship that should be manifested in the eucharistic celebration. It concerns the bishops, but should also concern priests and all the faithful. Every assembly of the faithful, eucharistic or ecclesial, must have the dimension of catholicity. The Church summons to the assembly particular persons in a particular place; but straightway the gathering takes on a being of its own. The very manner of gathering is a sign of catholicity. The eucharistic assembly for instance, where the bishop presides, is a sort of model for all such groupings. We have great diversity represented, a host of different responses to the summons of salvation. But somehow all are gathered into one, a unity that is not destructive of diversity.

Purely administrative criteria must never, under any circumstances, be the decisive factor in churchly matters. Indeed, in our time, the whole ecclesiastical institution should be at the service of mission. Consequently we should all be concerned to bring the dimension of catholicity into sharp focus in our eucharistic assemblies.

3. The Theme of the Paschal Lamb

The Passion according to John (gospel of Good Friday) brings home to us the lesson that Jesus underwent the death of the cross as a victor. On the surface the actors in the drama are the Jews who condemned Jesus, and Pilate who endorsed their condemnation. They seem to direct the episode; but in reality it is Jesus who directs. All others are but the backcloth against which the great drama of human salvation is enacted.

He is not content to give us the course of the drama: the theological lesson is always in the foreground. From beginning to end the salvific implications of all that happens are in mind, and the resurrection is already with us. How much is simple witness clarified by the lucidity of faith. It was only subsequently that the disciples really understood what they had seen with their eyes.

We are invited to view the Passion likewise with the eyes of faith. It is not principally a matter of exciting our pity in contemplation of the sufferings, in every domain, of Jesus. If that were so many another man's experience would deserve equal attention from us. However awful the physical sufferings he endured, the Passion of Jesus can never be considered exclusivel· in this light. The important thing is the overwhelming love that led him to the cross, a love so limitless that man's sin and rejection were swept away by it. Each one of us should try to gain some idea of the dimensions of human salvation by measuring it against the price that was paid. So, on this day of Good Friday, confronted by the cross of Jesus, we try to plumb the depths of the great mystery of faith.

The Jewish Pasch and the blood of the lamb

The Pasch was the greatest event in the history of Israel's deliverance. Altogether gratuitously Yahweh had snatched his chosen people from the slavery of Egypt, and led them through the desert to the Promised Land. By the Sinai covenant, sealed in the desert, they were summoned to undertake the difficult road of faith.

Every act of Yahweh in subsequent Jewish history was seen in reference to the first Pasch. He is always faithful; but his liberating acts are foiled of purpose by the recurring infidelity of the people. One day his Messiah will come. Through absolute fidelity to the covenant he will obliterate all obstacles to the liberating process. He will enable the chosen people to pass from the dominion and slavery of sin to a promised land, where there will be no more sin, or suffering, or death.

The annual festival commemorated, indeed reiterated, the liberating events of exodus and covenant. In the immolation of the lamb was reproduced the original sacrifice, that safeguarded Jewish homes from the exterminating angel who smote the Egyptian first-born. The blood of the lamb recalled the blood that sealed the Sinai covenant, and established a lasting link between Yahweh and his people.

About the time of King Josias this ancient family rite became the principal temple festival. And in the postexilic period it was the feast which, above all others, attracted Jews from everywhere to the Holy City. Naturally it was heavily colored by messianism; commemoration of the past was always related to hope for future liberation. During the time of Jesus it was often the occasion of nationalist demonstrations. The Roman authorities were careful about maintaining order, and it was customary for the procurator to reside in Jerusalem during this time of year.

For the Jews, as indeed for all peoples, there was something sacred about blood. It was identified with life, and belonged to God. Its cultic use served particularly to establish contact between man and the divine. But in Israel of course blood did not have the automatic efficacy of pagan rites. Prophets denounced bloody sacrifices that did not include sacrifice of the heart.

The blood of the true paschal lamb

A great many Jews expected that the manifestation of the Messiah would be a striking event. The paschal festival seemed the ideal moment for some gesture that would herald the final liberation of the chosen people.

And so the great messianic gesture did indeed occur at the festival, but in a totally unforeseen fashion. At the very moment when the lambs were being immolated in the Temple, outside the city on a cross Jesus of Nazareth died, rejected like the Servant of Yahweh, led like a lamb to the slaughter. The coincidence in time is emphasized by the gospel of John. We have on the one hand the people in the Temple, reenacting the bloody rite of deliverance, and hoping for a new Exodus more wonderful than the first. On the other, a crucified man, condemned by the people, is performing the great redemptive and expiatory gesture which delivers humanity. The veritable Exodus is a going forth from death to life on the part of this Person, the conqueror. God is receiving from a man, his Son, the true response of love: the Kingdom has come.

Very naturally the New Testament authors reproduce the attitude of the primitive community, which saw in the crucified Jesus the paschal lamb, freely shedding his blood for the salvation of the world. The new Covenant is sealed in this blood. The perfect sacrifice is offered, in perfect obedience, and Jesus becomes the First-Born of a delivered humanity. The keystone of the arch is laid in place for God's salvific plan. Once for all, by one death, victory is won; and the author of the Apocalypse, in his prophetic vision, will see the Risen Lord not alone as a slaughtered lamb but as a victorious warrior.

Once the real lamb has been immolated, the ancient paschal rite ceases to have meaning. A perfect sacrifice is everlasting and cannot be repeated. Of the old ceremony now only the meal remains, and that in a profoundly altered way. It becomes the commemoration of the cross, and gives participants a share in the Pasch of Christ.

The Church of those ransomed by the Lamb's blood

The theme of the Lamb was crucial in baptismal catechesis (cf. Peter's first epistle). This rite made the neophyte a sharer in Christ's Pasch. Rescued from the world of sin, the faithful become the new "royal priesthood," the real "consecrated nation," who offer God their spiritual sacrifice of a life permeated by universal love. They follow the First-Born along the liberating road from death to life, and they bring in their train all humanity and all creation.

For Saint Paul the Lamb's blood has redemptive and expiatory value. It justifies, makes holy, ransoms. It brings remission of sins, and it opens the way to the Father. It reestablishes unity between Jews and gentiles, and makes the Church a people "purchased" by God.

The previous concept of eschatological hope becomes altogether changed. Jewish man lived in hope of terrestrial, paradisal happiness, which would come at the end of history. When the Messiah came, the terrestrial, mortal state would yield to the immortal, and there would be an end to the uncertainties of time. Christ did not liberate humanity and creation at all from the concrete historical condition, only from the hellish dominion of sin (cf. Jn 17:15: "I do not ask to take them out of the world, but to guard them from Evil"). Liberation in such terms made men think of the terrestrial condition as the normal one. Death itself acquires a meaning in the great pilgrimage of humanity and creation. It is here below that the "priestly people" must exercise their mission of cooperating in the salvation of humanity. Entry to the Kingdom does not detach a man from earthly responsibilities: on the contrary it leads him to undertake them in justice and in truth.

The blood of the Lamb as missionary sign

Not infrequently we hear Christians criticized by non-Christians because of their peculiar views of human liberation. The Christian concept of happiness, it is alleged, is really alienating and withdraws people from their secular responsibilities.

It must be admitted that a good many Christians do give this impression and the image they project of Christianity is distorted. The whole life of Christ, and his death on the cross, were really meant to demonstrate to men the essential nature of the earthly challenge. Christians who condemn the secular are in fact displaying an attitude that is outmoded, a Jewish one, or indeed in some instances an ancient pagan one.

For pagan man earthly existence was somehow illusory, something that lacked substance. The only path to reality, to salvation, was to share in the sacral world, the world of primordial Time and Space. Jewish man on the other hand recognized the importance of the historical event, because Yahweh had intervened in history. Yet he remained essentially oriented towards another world. Jesus of Nazareth however, who made entry to the Kingdom possible by his death, in fact restored earthly existence to its proper importance.

Thus, for the Christian, the victorious passage from death to life which is achieved by a limitless charity is in a very real sense a promotion of humanity, and of all creation. The child of the Kingdom does not avert his gaze from earthly responsibilities. On the contrary he measures them with great lucidity, and with a delicate perception of relative importance. It is in this world that the Kingdom must be built. There must be continuity between the period of construction here below, and definitive accomplishment in the world beyond. Any discontinuity must be attributed to sin.

Modern man accepts the secular world and secular responsibilities; but for the most part he tries to close his eyes to the inroads everywhere of death. The Christian is more realistic. He feels anguish, as all men do, before death; but he knows that it is only by the sacrifice of the cross that death is given a meaning at last.

Communion in the blood of the Lamb

The Good Friday liturgy does not constitute a eucharistic celebration, and recent reforms have introduced a communion service into the vigil Mass only. During a time when the Eucharist was celebrated on Sundays only, it was understandable that other days, even Good Friday, should be restricted to the liturgy of the Word. However, nowadays, when Mass is celebrated every day, that Good Friday should be the single exception is rather paradoxical. Is not the Eucharist the very best means for Christians of communing in the blood of the true Paschal Lamb? In this moment we find the veritable priestly people. And does not Saint Paul say that in sharing the body and blood of Jesus Christ, we are proclaiming the death of the Lord?

However that is, it is important that in the present form of the Good Friday service the adoration of the cross be not allowed to obscure the essentials of the liturgy. These are the communion of the vigil and today's liturgy of the Word, which is particularly rich. Centered as the latter is on the major event of salvation history, it gives Christian life its whole meaning. Whether it is participation in the eucharistic rite, or the exercise of our faith in the tenor of daily life, our business is to become more and more conformed to the death of Christ. Thus we can look forward ultimately to communing with the Risen Lord.

THE EASTER VIGIL AND EASTER

A. THE WORD

**I. Genesis
1:1-2:2
1st reading
*Vigil*** The priestly editor who is responsible for the first chapter of Genesis is the heir of a long history and of a vocabulary forged from salvation-events in that history. He is giving us not merely a history of creation; it is creation seen in the light of other salvific interventions by God.

a) It is a *victory* over chaos *(tohubohu),* just as the return from exile was (Is 35; 40:1-8; 43:16-20). A victory over darkness, endorsed by subsequent manifestations of God's glory (Is 60:1-2; 49:9; 50:1-10; Jn 1:5). A triumphant wrestling with the sea, like the victorious passage of the Red Sea (Ps 103/104: 5-9; 105/106:9; Ha 3:8-15; Is 51:9-10; Rv 20:1-13). A separation of night from day, foreshadowing the definitive victory over night (Rv 21:25). This is the primordial event of salvation history. The author sees no distinction between the orders of creation and redemption: there is one great divine plan of salvation, which is being realized.

b) We should note also the *universalist* bias of the account. One of the most important religious insights in the history of Israel was the discovery of God as creator of heaven and earth. Yahweh could no longer be looked upon as the deity of one small people; he was the God who directed the universe (Is 45:12-13; 40:27-28). We see the universalist tendency in the author's anxiety to extend to the whole universe the cultic characteristics of the Jerusalem temple. Like the temple the world has its firmament (Ps 150:1; Ez 1:22-26) over which God has his throne like the one at Sion (Ps 65/66:1). "Luminaries," a term regularly applied to the sanctuary lamps, appear throughout all creation (v. 14; Ez 35:8:14; 25:6; 27:20; 39:37; Nb 4:9-16). But they are provisional; one day the definitive temple will be lit by the glory of Yahweh (Rv 21:23). Even the blessings bestowed by God on creation (vv. 22-23) resemble those of the temple (Ps 132/133:3; 127/128:4-5; 23/24:5). Finally, at the center of this cosmic temple we find the "image" of God, man (vv. 26-29; Ps 8:5-6), destined to achieve perfection in the image of the Father, Christ (Col 1:15-17).

c) The style of the whole piece, designed as it is as a defense of the week and of *sabbath* rest, is cultic. During the author's lifetime the distinguishing mark of the chosen people was the sabbath. But sabbath rest was not to be observed now for social reasons only (as in more ancient sources); the chosen people had been given the privilege of imitating God, by freeing themselves from toil at least one day during the week.

It would be wrong to read into this passage a Jewish theory about the origins of man and the universe. Jewish faith in a creator-God has nothing to do with metaphysics or cosmogony. The whole purpose is to teach men that they are living *hic et nunc* in dependence on God. All the language about image, blessing, imitation in sabbath rest, the whole cultic presentation, is meant to inculcate this principle of dependence on God's will.

II. Genesis 22:1-18
2nd reading
Vigil

For commentary on this reading, see p. 64.

III. Exodus 14:15-15:1
3rd reading
Vigil

Here we have a description of the final episodes in the passage of the Red Sea. The piece should be interpreted according to its characteristic style. An epic style for the description of events concerning its origins is natural for any people (Ps 77/78; 104/105; 105/106; 113/114;

Ws 10:18; 11:14). The text is actually a fusion of several distinct traditions. Either the hand of Moses *(priestly tradition)*, or God and the wind *(Yahwist)*, or God's angel *(Elohist)*, accomplished the prodigy of dividing the waters. All traditions though were at one in seeing the event as a providential and spectacular intervention by God, which destroyed the horsemen and chariots of the enemy and led the people to freedom.

There was no question of personal experience of the events on the part of the compilers of the traditions. Their outlook is above all religious; they wish to show that the origins of the Jewish people are to be traced to a *divine initiative*. All the details mentioned, from the angel of Yahweh to the staff of Moses, from the column of fire to the patriarch's prayer, are expressly designed to emphasize the priority of God's action in the whole matter. In fact of course such action need not be expressed in terms of marvels, like holding the waters vertically suspended in the air. God acts on the whole within the framework of natural laws. There are indeed places along the Red Sea littoral where an arid wind could conceivably render a shallow stretch of water fordable. On this particular issue the priestly tradition (only the priestly be it noted) renders no great service either to God or the reader by its emphasis. The tendency of all peoples to resort to epic terms to recount their origins is perhaps the explanation. When added to that we have a people like the Jews who regard themselves as chosen by God, it is to be expected that God's actions in their regard will have an epic quality.

From the very origins of the paschal vigil, indeed of Judaism itself, the Canticle of Moses (Ex 15:2-18) was associated with this reading. It is a thanksgiving for God's interventions in the Exodus, during the desert sojourn, and even at the building of the temple (vv. 15-17). It might be described as the national anthem of a people whose nationhood begins with a liberation by God.

IV. Isaiah
54:1-11
4th reading
Vigil

We have here two distinct poems in honor of Jerusalem (vv. 1-3 and 4-10). Second-Isaiah is again drawing attention to the restoration of the historic city. He does so with a keen poetical sense but with less doctrinal profundity than First-Isaiah.

a) The first poem celebrates the *fruitfulness of the new Jerusalem*. The city had been barren during the exile because her children had deserted her. Now, like the patriarchs' wives long ago, she is becoming fruitful once again. She spreads herself and takes possession of the nations' land (v. 3) so that all her children may be nourished there. We are very far here from the universalism of First-Isaiah, the spiritual Jerusalem, city of all believers (Is 2:1-4; 4:2-5). For Second-Isaiah Jerusalem's relations with the nations are of the vengeful and exclusive kind. Any suggestion of real universalism is obliterated by the hope for a physical restoration of the city.

b) The second piece, with Jerusalem in mind, takes up the theme of *espousal* with God. In three strophes, each terminated by the formula "says your God," the letters of repudiation sent to the adulterous spouse by the prophets of old (Ho 1; 11:1-6; Jr 3:1-5; Ez 16) are revoked. She again receives her title of "bride of youth."

The second strophe in particular celebrates the everlasting love of God. Not even sin can arrest it, because it becomes transformed into pity and mercy, and justifies the sinner.

The new covenant is the theme of the third strophe. It is indefectible because the love of God is irrevocable. Here Second-Isaiah is developing a profound doctrinal insight. The new Jerusalem will be sustained, not by its justice, but thanks to the unchangeable love of God. The new covenant indeed is based on God's promise to convert humanity, and by his grace, make men just and free (Ga 4:21-31).

Fortunately then the author's thinking on the new covenant is more forward than his views about the new Jerusalem. We can apply his covenant-doctrine to the Church. Bearing witness means depending upon a justice that comes from God, not ourselves. It means that we recognize as due to God's love a salvation, towards the achievement of which we make no personal pretensions. It means sealing in the fidelity of the Son towards the Father the covenant celebrated in the Eucharist.

V. Isaiah 55:1-11   Here we have four short verse oracles which
  5th reading   form the conclusion to Second-Isaiah's Book
  Vigil   of Consolation (4th century). They epitomize
the core of the prophet's teaching, above all
his resolute defense of God's unicity and transcendence.

a) The first piece takes up the traditional theme of the *messianic repast* of the poor (Is 25:6), but introduces a motif from sapiental literature (cf. Pr 9:3-6; Si 24:19-22) which gives it a profoundly new bias. In future men will live, not by bread only, but by God's Word and his *knowledge*. The messianic banquet will be one of wisdom.

We must remember that the community in which Second-Isaiah lived was one of the *poor*, on whom the exile had a considerable effect. Once they had placed their hope in the frail salvation that might come by human means; but they finally placed their trust in God (Is 40:31; 41:10, 14, 17; 16:12-13). Of such quality would be the faith of those destined for assembly in the future kingdom. We are dealing here with a class tried by financial poverty whose hope nevertheless has no tincture of vengefulness. The poor will have to depend on the knowledge which comes from utter trust rather than on the good things of the messianic feast.

b) The second piece is also a rereading of oracles by First-Isaiah. He had still sought the Messiah-Savior of the people in the descendant of David (Is 7; 11:1-9). But the poor, who have become unenthusiastic about royalty, give a democratic emphasis to the theme and extend to all the people the promises originally reserved to David (v. 3b; cf. 2 S 7:1). Likewise the Servant of Yahweh, originally perhaps a royal concept, becomes here the whole people. His mission to the nations (v. 4) is seen in this light, his role as witness and as a sign in trial.

The covenant whereby the people acquires these royal prerogatives is an everlasting one. It will no longer be precarious, as in the case of David, because it is based altogether on God's will, needing no human guarantees.

c) Throughout his writing Second-Isaiah has proclaimed Yahweh's *omnipotence* and *transcendence* (Is 40:27-31; 49:14-16). The two themes are central in our poems today. The thoughts of God (in this instance, his desire to pardon) are altogether different from those of men (first poem; cf. Is 40:21-24; 43:8-12; 50:1-3) and his power is more efficacious than that of false gods and idols (second poem; cf. Is 40:12-26).

In the preceding chapters he had been concerned with demonstrating how the events of history, whether favorable or unfavorable, far from being the whims of false gods or forces outside Yahweh's control are in fact controlled by God himself for the good of his people. Throughout vicissitudes that sometimes bring disturbance and unrest God is always present, calmly working out his plan. Even where the plan or the advancement of humanity (vv. 8-9) appears to be foiled it is nevertheless being accomplished. When man's sin seems too great to be pardonable, God reveals a thought which transcends human notions of justice and renders possible the conversion of the worst of sinners.

In his resolute defense of monotheism (Is 41:8-14, 17-20) he is affirming implicitly a singleness of design in history. God being unique, there is no other force involved with him in the control of history. Every stage is willed by him; everything leads toward the eschatological future: his plan (symbolized here by the "Word," vv. 10-11) cannot be countered. Thus, belief in a unique and transcendent God is the very cornerstone of faith.

Today's Christian has little difficulty in affirming God's transcendence, but it is important to determine whether his affirmation is based on the revelation of Isaiah and Jesus or on Western theology. Isaiah does not say that God's divinity is measured by the diminution of man's stature, focusing everything as it were on the world which transcends man. On the contrary, for him, God's transcendence is principally manifest when he stretches man to his fullest stature. Jesus understood this when he asserted that the one who sent him was the Father (Jn 14:9). The father was in him; there was in him some greater force, but he *was* that force.

VI. Baruch
3:9-15, 32; 4:4
6th reading
Vigil

This is an extract from a long sapiental poem (Ba 3:9-4:4), which was composed in the second century B.C., doubtless with the idea of encouraging piety among Jews of the Diaspora. In specific terms, there is manifest anxiety to rekindle taste for obedience to the Law. The plan is simple. Jews isolated in a pagan milieu wonder how they can know God (v. 15). The answer is given that the wisdom of God is apparent in nature (vv. 32-36), and was communicated to Israel (v. 37) by means of the Law (4:1). Consequently to obey the law means to search the wisdom of God.

The sentiments expressed suggest some reflection about the relation of Jewish faith, and of Christian faith, to philosophic systems. Centuries before Christ the Jews contemplated nature, and tried to penetrate to the secret that lay behind. Their answer was the "Word" (Logos), the thought of God, which maintained the universe in equilibrium and gave it some intelligibility. To some extent the author of the poem shares this philosophic view: nature seems to him so well ordered that it ought to lead to God. He parts with it though in his insistence that God manifests himself gratuitously (vv. 37-38). Man's philosophic quest is transformed into a study of divine history and divine manifestation. The only possible way to penetrate the meaning of things is the encounter with a God who reveals himself. Reveals himself, that is, not alone in the sense of explaining the meaning of nature and order (which is a purely rational investigation), but as a God with a will that challenges the will of man, a God who promulgates a law (Ba 4:1). In that sense God is too transcendent to be satisfied with answering our questions. He localizes the encounter on a different plane; he is the freedom which challenges the freedom of man.

The wisdom therefore which controls the universe is something other than Greek philosophy. For one thing, it renders history harmonious; in the second place it deals in terms of freedom and will rather than intellect.

VII. Romans 6:3-11
Epistle Vigil

Throughout the whole letter to the Romans Paul is contrasting the justice that men, whether Jews or Gentiles, try to procure for themselves, and that bestowed by God which requires faith. Baptism is the means towards this divine justification; it is the point of encounter between God's justice and man's faith.

a) The essential theme of today's passage is *death with Christ*. It is biblical doctrine that God is life and his plan a plan of life. To the Jew physical death was an accident to be attributed to sin (Gn 3:3, 19; Ez 18:23, 32; 33:11; Si 25:24; Ws 1:13;

2:23-24). It is with this perspective that Paul associates natural death with the spiritual death of sin. The link should be properly understood. Paul is not saying that physical death is as it were an exterior punishment determined by God for human sin. The teaching is that man by shutting himself in sin, depending that is on his own resources only to realize his destiny, becomes shut in also inevitably in death. Only God's initiative, and openness to God on man's own part, can succeed in liberating him. In this sense sin and death are associated.

Now Christ was the first person to experience death, not in sin, not with the determination, that is, to depend on his own resources. On the contrary he showed an absolute fidelity and loyalty to his Father, confident that he would be saved by him. In this way his death destroyed the link that had been between death and sin. It became a force that liberated from sin, because it was the death of someone who showed himself emancipated from death and capable of resurrection, simply because of his dependence on the Father. Death is now no longer an obstacle to God's plan for diffusing life: it is the very means whereby God communicates his life to man.

b) *Baptism*, Paul tells us, unites us to the death of Christ. It does so in the sense that it leads us to depend on the Father rather than ourselves, that it is the rite whereby we affirm our purpose of realizing our human destiny through communion with God (vv. 3-6). It is like dying with Christ (v. 4) because we make his attitudes ours, and depend absolutely like him on the Father's salvific initiative. We remain of course, like all men, liable to physical death; but thanks to our baptism we can encounter it as God encountered it, in absolute openness. We can overcome the spiritual death of sin, because sin means refusing to recognize God's portion in the realization of human destiny. From another angle still, the death-experience is our best road to the Father because it means total stripping of ourselves. The one thing we do know about God since Jesus Christ is that life for him means giving oneself, to the very point of dying. If we would live with the life of God, we must have that complete openness of self to others, to the point of dying. Baptism makes this possible for us.

c) There is a further point. As well as dying to sin in baptism, we are enabled to share in God's plan of life. For all that we are doomed to death, we live with a *new life*,* which is God's gift (vv. 4-5). As we live it we come to look on death as something already experienced. He who is dead is emancipated from sin (v. 7; cf. Col 3:3; Rm 6:10-11). The baptized person has undergone the essentials of death, the spiritual death of sin; and thanks to God's intervention he has emerged.

The idea of a future restoration had evolved in the Old Testament, together with that of a preliminary resurrection for the just, those deemed worthy of sharing the restoration. It was natural to conclude that the living could pray and expiate for the sins of the dead, so that they might share this privilege (2 M).

Apostolic catechesis had the same perspective, but added a proclamation that in Jesus Christ the resurrection of the just had begun. From the moment that the Lord was established as judge of the living and the dead, the restoration of the holy people was embarked upon. Nevertheless the letters to the Thessalonians and the Corinthians are totally concerned with the future resurrection when we shall be "with" the Lord, sharing his glory and incorruptibility.

The letter to the Romans goes further still. Paul insists that Christ's resurrection is not an isolated thing, the pledge of our future resurrection, but something that engages us here and now. We are already dead "with him" (v. 3), already buried "with him" (v. 4): we live already "with him" as new life (v. 5). This word "with" is repeated five times in the few verses, in order to emphasize the truth that baptism involves the Christian in the great process leading to resurrection and restora-

*See doctrinal theme: *newness,* p. 339.

tion of the just. Natural death cannot possibly arrest a process that sends divine life coursing through our being. The intensity of this transformation in us will depend on the extent of our imitation of Christ in service, in self-emptying, in love that leads to death.

VIII. Matthew **28:1-10** *Gospel* *1st cycle* *Vigil*	All four evangelists give us an account of the resurrection, and all place it at dawn on the first day of the week, which is actually Sunday (Jn 20:1, 26; 21:1; Rv 1:10). The new creation, like the first, begins on the first day of the week.

The style followed in the description is altogether apocalyptic. The whole impression given is that it is impossible to recount this phenomenon according to the criteria of history in human language. Accordingly the author has recourse to a genre that transcends the ordinary, and conveys in his own way the mysterious reality of the resurrection.

Unlike the other evangelists, Matthew's account is reminiscent of the context of the great apocalyptic *theophanies* of the Old Testament. We have earthquake, an angel coming down from heaven (Luke and Mark mention a "man" only), the terror of the guards, who become as dead people, the whiteness of the messenger (angel of God: Gn 22:11-13; death; Ex 3:1-6; 20:18-21; awesome environment: Ha 3:3-15; Ps 28/29:3-9; 76/77: 17-19). His use of all these cliches of theophany is designed to stress the fact that the resurrection is no mere survival or spiritual immortality; but, like the other great salvific acts, a direct intervention by Yahweh.

The angel's message is essentially a reminder that the resurrection had taken place "just as Jesus had said." After his ascent to Jerusalem Jesus had foretold not alone his death, but his resurrection "on the third day" (Mt 20:17-19).

Matthew localizes the apparitions in Galilee, whereas for Luke they are in Judaea. Doubtless we have here the traditions of two different communities who did not attempt any synchronization.

The gospels display great anxiety about details in recounting the resuscitation of the daughter of Jairus, or that of Lazarus. That they are silent where the resurrection of Jesus is concerned is extremely significant. None of them describes the actual occurance because it is more than an historical event. There was no witness; it transcended the laws and methodology of history. Yet it is precisely because of this that the gospels command credence. People anxious to perpetrate a forgery would have been prolific in detail. What their silence demonstrates is their genuineness.

IX. Mark   Between this account, which is parallel to
    16:1-8   Matthew (Mt 28:1-7), and Matthew's there
    Gospel   are only differences of nuance. Mark gives
    2nd cycle   evidence of more detachment. He says nothing
    Vigil   of the guards at the tomb, or of the signs
of the "day of Yahweh" which concerned
Matthew. However he adds Salome to the list of women at the tomb and he gives special mention to Peter. Peter becomes the first witness of faith in the resurrection; he is destined to have primacy in the Church and to confirm the faith of the brethren.

Despite any divergence in the accounts of the evangelists, their witness to the resurrection is unanimous in these points:
    — the women's visit to the tomb on the first day of the week,
    — the discovery of the empty tomb,
    — the women's awareness of their "mission" where the apostles are concerned.

All this seems to suggest an apologetic concern. Confronted by Jewish incredulity, Christians had to formulate their reasons for *belief in the resurrection*. It could not be the product of fantasy on the apostles' part, because it was revealed, incidentally only, to some women whose only purpose was the care of a corpse. The women had no vision of the Lord; they could only testify to the empty tomb.

Faith in the resurrection could never be based on merely human testimony: the formula "he is risen" (v. 6) was not pronounced originally by human lips, but by those of a mysterious being. In Mark the silence of the women (v. 8) is emphatic, all the more so in that Matthew and Luke allow the women to speak (Mt 28:8; Lk 24:8-11; cf. Jn 20:18). It is as if in this sacred matter no human utterance was valid. The truth is that for Matthew and Luke the resurrection is the dawning of a new world. For Mark (who wrote perhaps during a time of persecution) it is on the other hand the beginning of silence and secrecy in the Church.

X. Luke 24:1-12   All the evangelists drew on a common source
Gospel   for their accounts of the resurrection, but
3rd cycle   each contributes a particular detail or doc-
Vigil   trinal nuance. They are all unanimous in
describing the three stages of events on the first Easter: the visit of the women (v. 1), their discovery of the empty tomb (vv. 2-3), their awareness of a mission to the apostles concerning their experience (v. 9). We shall confine ourselves to the specifically Lucan elements: the message of the angel (vv. 6-7) and Peter's arrival at the tomb (v. 12).

a) Luke deliberately ascribes to the "two men" who appeared to the women the type of discourse that Jesus will later give his apostles to convince them of his resurrection (Lk 24:25-27, 44-47), and that they themselves will reproduce in catchesis (Ac 2:23-41; 3:12-4:12). This really reinforces the primitive catechesis. So far from being a construct of the apostles, it represents a tradition already fixed. The message of the angels and of Christ himself is anterior to any proclamation of the faith. The two "men" indeed authenticate the tradition (cf. Dt 19:15). In all the Lucan texts (Lk 9:30; 24:4; Ac 1:10) their role is this.

b) The mention of Peter's *arrival at the empty tomb* (v. 12) is doubtless a later addition to Luke, but the impact of the verse is not for that reason weakened. Repeated in the case of the woman, and of Peter, this amounts to being a proof, negative but necessary, of the resurrection. To be aware of the Risen Lord, one must "see," not with the eyes of man (Jn 20:14, 29). The full vision of faith fills up what is wanting.*

Peter and the holy women illustrate, according to their fashion, the demands of missionary witness. This witness will only be really worth while, when we have previously plumbed the limits of all human means of knowledge and salvation. Many a time we see that an apparently Christian viewpoint meets with quite violent rejection; and the reason may be failure on the Christian's part to see the limits of his own vision, failure to accept the message entrusted to him in obedience and fidelity.

In the Eucharist persons who are aware of their own limits are exposed to the Word. They are then enabled to rejoice in the presence of the Risen Lord, and to bear witness to his message in the texture of daily life.

XI. Acts 10:34a, 37-43
1st reading
Easter

This is an extract from Peter's discourse to Cornelius of Caesarea and his household, when preparing them for conversion and baptism. The missionary discourses of the Acts may be classified according to the addresses: Jews (Ac 2:14-36; 3:12-26; 4:9-12; 5:29-32; 10:34-43; 13:16-42) or Gentiles (Ac 14:15-17; 17:22-31; cf. Th 1:9-10).

*The Risen Lord demands a similar purification in requiring Peter to progress from ordinary love (*philein*) to that of agape (Jn 21: 15-17).

The six discourses to the Jews resemble one another very much; and Luke's hand as editor seems very evident, even if the use of earlier documents is admitted. Exegetes have still to determine how much material is Lucan, and how much traceable to his sources.

We may regard the introductions in each case (here vv. 34-35) as Lucan. Likewise the resume of the public life (vv. 36-38) which is a particular feature of this discourse. It corresponds to the plan of Luke's gospel.

The descriptions of the passion however and the resurrection (vv. 39-40) are derived from a "summary" of the passion that must have circulated amongst primitive communities (cf. Mk 8:31; 9:31; 10:33). Luke would have embellished them with an argument probably borrowed from primitive preaching. It made the Jews, or at least the Jews of Jerusalem, responsible for Christ's death. The accusation however is rather more sharp in the other discourses.

a) A notable feature of these passion and resurrection summaries is the mention of the *third day*. It was extremely common in primitive catechesis and is still in our Creed. In fact it is an allusion to Hosea 1:2 (where the verb "he will raise up" is the same in Greek as that used for the resurrection). The Talmud applied this oracle of Hosea to the final resurrection of the body. The three days were regarded as the interval necessary for raising up all the dead of Israel and allowing them to possess Jerusalem. Accordingly Christ's resurrection is the first of many others (cf. Mt 27:52-53): the great resurrection of the just which heralds the definitive restoration of the people has begun (Ez 37: Dn 12:1-3; 2 M 7:9).

b) The resurrection of Jesus is presented not as his own accomplishment ("Jesus has arisen") but as the work of God ("God has raised him up"). Here Luke is making his own a phrase from the general resurrection vocabulary, the resurrection awaited by Israel. He wants to convey that the *resurrection of the dead,* foreseen by the prophets as a preliminary to the last days, has begun with the resurrection of Christ. Thus the restoration of the new people is not now an object of hope: the vision of faith proclaims it a present reality.

c) Apparently verses 41-42, about witness, are also due to Saint Luke. However he is back again in the context of the Jewish final resurrection when he says that Christ is "constituted judge of the living and the dead". He means that Jesus is the central figure in the *eschatological judgment* which will divide the wicked from the just, and enable the latter to share the resurrection and the restoration of the Kingdom. Jesus is first among those arisen because he is destined to be the leader of the new people.

And so, the issue is clarified. Primitive Christian belief in the resurrection of Jesus is colored yet by Jewish ideas about the resurrection of the flesh, and the restoration of the people in the last days. According to these beliefs, the great resurrection is initiated by that of the Lord, and the restoration of the people has begun with the establishment of Christ as judge of the living and the dead (Ac 1:6).

XII. Colossians
3:1-4
2nd reading
Easter
This passage is at once a conclusion and an introduction. It brings to an end Paul's discussion about Christian liberty, which is under challenge from the alienating forces of paganism and heresy (Col 2:16-3:4). Paul shows that the Christian who has died with Christ is beyond the reach of human efforts at salvation (v. 3). Simultaneously, he begins the paraenetic portion of his letter by showing how life with Christ (vv. 1-2) entails a totally new behavior in the world.

If Christian life had its source here below, in this world, that is to say, it would be automatically frozen in a thousand and one prescripts of "religion." But coming from above as it does, from the region where Christ is now, this *life* is "bestowed" on the Christian, by resurrection as it were. Because of this, because it always goes on being a gift from above, there is no need to use human techniques of salvation for its maintenance.

But there can be no compromise. Believing that this life is a gift of God means breaking with a world which is always concerned to be its own source of life, by the use of fallible and sinful means. For the Christian however, who like Christ is dead to the world in *baptism,* the break has been already made.

Man seeks the absolute. His own experience will sometimes let him touch it fleetingly; the confidence and security he yearns for can come only from the absolute. Religious history demonstrates this. Always it has been a matter of looking for techniques and methods to make life absolute; the pagan "elements of the world," the Jewish law.

The Christian not only seeks the absolute: he believes the absolute, the spirit of Jesus Christ, is present in his personal life. His existence does not depend upon some vague absolute, that he must devise means himself of touching; he depends upon a person who never ceases to give him life.

It is then the lesson of faith that we do not live of ourselves. Christ is our life. When we say 'yes' to him, the life we live is ours indeed; but we live each moment of it as something that a Person has bestowed on us. That is what living the risen life means, knowing that the life in us always comes from "on high." If we seek autonomy, that would mean basing ourselves "here below"; it would mean acceptance of death.

XIII. John 20:1-9 By strict chronology this account, called that
      Gospel   of the "empty tomb," should be read before
      Easter   the account of the apparitions. However this
                  is a very late tradition, markedly distinct from

the synoptic witness. To begin with, Magdalen's motive for visiting the tomb is not mentioned (v. 1). When she sees that the stone has been taken away she thinks it possible the corpse has been removed, doubtless by the officials (Jn 20:13). She hastens to tell the apostles, hoping they will be able to recover the body.

Since there is question of disappearance only, the apostles believe her and come themselves to verify the matter (vv. 2-5: differing from Lk 24:11 and Mk 16:11). The tomb is empty, but the cerements shrouding the body of Christ are on the ground (vv. 5-8). This precludes the hypothesis or removal. So the apostles "begin to believe" (v. 8, a reading preferable to "he believed"). The body could not have been transported to another tomb. Could Jesus be arisen? The answer to this question was to be found in scripture (above all Ho 6:2; Ps 16/17:10); but at this moment the apostles did not have the key (v. 9).

a) What we are getting then in the account is the *pilgrimage* of the apostles towards faith in the resurrection. They first think of the possibility of removal. Then, realizing that this does not meet the case (the presence of the cerements) they "begin to believe." Nevertheless their pilgrimage will not be complete without the aid of the scriptures. In other words what is required from them is not mere verbal witness to something that happened, but the witness of faith, which must necessarily be based on the scriptures. The resurrection of Christ cannot be considered apart from the concrete, and totally unexpected, fashion in which it was an accomplishment of his messianic vocation. Indeed it is the fulfillment of the scriptures (v. 9) in Christ that constitutes the essential object of Christian faith. The apparitions of the Risen Lord must always be combined with reflection on the messianic hope that was realized in the earthly sojourn of Jesus.

It is for this reason the scriptural argument assumes such

importance in the missionary discourses of the apostles. Their new insight in this domain made them realize that in Jesus Christ, always, mysteriously at work, each man is called to share the divine sonship and to cooperate in building up the messianic Kingdom.

b) It is not *Peter's mission* to move too hastily (v. 4). He lets more ardent disciples outstrip him. Yet he and his successors have the responsibility. He is the first to enter the tomb, to satisfy himself about the frailty of everything over which the shadow of death has fallen, even the cerements that touched the body of Christ. He is the first to believe.

For faith to be born, it was necessary to undergo the trial of the empty tomb. Peter had to lose all artificial assurance by experiencing in his turn emptiness. The whole Church in the same way must have the courage to enter the modern world, which is the "tomb of God." On the other side of emptiness lies faith.

| **XIV.** Luke 24:13-35 *Gospel Easter evening* | Here we have an account of the second palpable appearance of the Risen Lord. It took place with the disciples at Emmaus on the evening of the Pasch. |

a) Luke's apparition narrative has three tableaux: the appearance to the women (24:1-2), to the disciples at Emmaus (24:13-35), and to the Twelve (24:36-49). The three represent three groups who were intimate with Christ, and whom we find throughout Luke's gospel (Ac 1:14: apostles, women and brethren of Christ; Lk 8:1-2: apostles, women). Luke draws on the common tradition for the account of the women and the apostles, but has a special source which he is the only one to use for the disciples at Emmaus. Unlike the other evangelists,

he is concerned to give considerable prominence to these
"disciples" (Lk 10:1-20). It is possible that they constituted a
fringe group, distinct from the community of the Twelve, who
were later to be the nucleus of the Gentile community at
Jerusalem that was occasionally in conflict with the "Hebrews"
(Ac 6:1-6). In stressing the fact that Christ appeared to the
disciples too, Luke seems anxious to go beyond the "Hebrew"
witness to the resurrection. However, if he is using a special
source, he does not hesitate to color the account fairly freely
with primitive *Christian experience*. The disciples' remarks (vv.
19-20) are a resume of primitive catechesis (Ac 2:22-23;
10:38-39). The Lord's commentary on scripture (vv. 26-27) is
the doctrine of accomplishment from primitive tradition (Ac
2:23-36; 3:18, 27; 8:26-40; 1 Co 15:3-5). The rite in which the
disciples recognize the Lord is the breaking of bread, the fraternal repast of the primitive communities (Ac 2:42, 46; 20:7,
11). Finally, the account concludes with a profession of faith
(v. 34) which is that of primitive Christians (1 Co 15:3-5;
Rm 6:4-9; Ac 10:41).

Thus what we have in the Emmaus account is the projection
on the apparition itself of the life of the primitive community.
The purpose is not, as in the case of the other apparition
accounts, apologetic. It is to show that the veritable encounter
with Christ takes place in the Word, the breaking of the bread,
and the profession of faith, all basic components of the Christian
assemblies.

b) There is a direct relation between Luke's composition of
place, and his vocabulary, and the predictions of the Passion,
especially Luke 18:31-34. The disciples did not comprehend at
that time the meaning of scripture, still less the meaning of
Jesus' words. But now there is a change. The prophecies and
the person of Jesus become clear. The disciples themselves are
ready to "go up to Jerusalem" (v. 33) and bear witness to their
faith. To understand scripture and act in that understanding,
faith in the Risen Lord is necessary.

There is a certain doctrinal cresendo about these Paschal gospels. The empty tomb is the first experience and it is insufficient to arouse faith. It proves nothing, and the persons who witness to it are of secondary importance.

The true proof of the resurrection is the apparition: it is an event in the spiritual and mystical order, which only a believer can appreciate. Indeed it is significant that Jesus frequently appears in a palpable way, but that does not necessarily create faith. He can be seen by the unbeliever. The appearance only achieves its true purpose at the moment when the risen Jesus is no longer sensibly seen, but becomes the object of faith. We have this development in the case of the disciples at Emmaus, and it is likewise with other apparitions.

The essential apparitions to the apostles should be carefully distinguished from those to the disciples and the women. The persons in the latter instance are secondary. We have much more detail (precisions about time and place, names of people, etc.) than in the case of the apostles. For the apostles there is a stylized format: very little description, very little detail about place and circumstance, just the dogmatic principle about faith in the Risen Lord and the mission of the Church in the world. It seems likely that these have been already established as condensations of the dogmatic and paschal experience during the fifty days that followed the Passion events. They are less anecdotal than the Emmaus account for instance; but they are notably more doctrinal.

B. DOCTRINE

The Theme of Newness

Those who are born Christian, accustomed as they are to hearing the name, fail as a rule to realize the newness that faith in Jesus Christ, as lived by the Church, means. To describe the salvation awaited, or already accomplished, both Old and New Testaments are always using this term. But surely, newness must be something to which one never grows accustomed.

The formularies we read on this day of the Pasch suggest reflection about the new life initiated by baptism. We hear about new birth, new life, a new world. What does this newness mean, where does it lead?

Sometimes Christians, very often the best of Christians, are nowadays taken aback to find among non-Christians, or even atheists, moral attitudes of which they, as Christians, thought they had the monopoly. Faith of course is something that ought to overflow into the concrete circumstances of living. Consequently pastors above all have to translate their theological insights into moral criteria. This exposes one to the risk of devaluing the faith, of blurring the essential quality that distinguishes Christian moral life. If conversion to Jesus Christ is merely an evangelical ideal, are we not leaving something out? The newness indicated by this sort of conversion, even if it be to an evangelical ideal, is something within the reach of human resources, or at least it seems to be.

Where then is the newness of the Christian attitude, if it be not a moral attitude? What do we mean when we talk of newness that bears witness to the salvation acquired once for all in the man-God? That the Christian have an answer to such questions as this seems absolutely essential.

The Jewish version of newness

In all traditional religions newness is an essential note of salvation. When the religion is cosmic in character newness is seen in terms of constant rebirth, a ceaseless restoration, through contact with the sacral, of terrestrial things. Of themselves these would be subject to decline, would age, and involve man too in their downfall. It is natural too in such circumstances that everything new in the world takes on a sacral character, the first-born, the return of spring, etc. Custom on the other hand makes stale, secularises: duration means growing old.

In Jewish religion this notion of newness is radically altered. The myth of eternal return and cyclic regeneration is dethroned in favor of salvific intervention by Yahweh in history. The event, Yahweh's intervention, brings newness. The very constitution of the people is always presented as a veritable birthgiving.

Yet terrestrial things continued to seem subject to erosion and decay, and this was thought to be the result of sin. Man does not inhabit the sort of earth God prepared for him at creation. By sin he was cast out of paradise, and plunged into a world of suffering, age and death. God's salvific intervention in favor of his people would normally bring about a transformation in human existence. That there was no such transformation was due to Israel's infidelity.

The gaze of the prophets was fixed on the future. Israel might be unfaithful, but Yahweh was faithful. One day salvation would come, and all would be rendered new. Sin frustrated the first creation; the first exodus was greeted by the people's infidelity, the first covenant by their hardened hearts. On the day of Yahweh, thanks to the fidelity of the expected Messiah, there would be a new heaven and a new earth. The marvels of the exodus from Egypt would be eclipsed by the prodigies of the new exodus. Yahweh "would do a new deed . . . make a road in the wilderness, paths in the wilds" (Is 43:19). The old covenant would be supplanted by a new; Yahweh would give man a new heart and a new spirit; the law would be its source.

Jesus Christ the new man

Jesus presented himself as the expected Messiah. His person inaugurated the eschatological era of the Spirit. The prophets were not deceived; he brought with him the new exodus, the new covenant, the new creation. He brought the law to fulfillment by renewing it. A new commandment, that of universal love without limit, was to be central.

Yet how very surprising this renewal was. He recalled the messianic image of the Son of Man. But where were the characteristics found in Daniel? Jesus partook totally of the human condition, and everyone knew whence he came. What of the new heaven and the new earth of Jewish hope? No such thing had come about. He said himself, during his public life, that he would be baptized in death. Not even the one without sin, then, escapes death. And it is on the cross, in deliberate acceptance of death, that the Messiah accomplishes human salvation. If death is conquered, it is not annihilated.

The whole concept of newness has to be restructured in Jesus of Nazareth. The kingdom he inaugurates is rightly called the Family of God. He himself is the Son, and his fidelity as man to the Father's antecedent initiative makes him rightly the first-born of the Kingdom. In him it becomes possible for every man to be an adoptive son of the Father, and to be a real partner in the work of building the Family of God. In this basic fashion he changed the concept of newness: man's hope is fulfilled beyond his wildest dreams.

There is no question of reversal in terms of man's terrestrial existence. Suffering and death are not obliterated; but their meaning in the great project of advancement for man and creation is clarified. If we confront it in obedience, in love for God and for all men, death becomes the road to resurrection.

That is what, in God's plan, fidelity to our creaturely condition means.

So, when we say that Christ is the new man, the new Adam, we should be very sure of our terms. What we mean by new man is true man, man the way God from all eternity determined him to be, faithful to his human condition. The difference between the old and the new man has nothing to do with his ontological and existential state. The difference is that between sin and grace. The old man nourishes the illusion that he can accomplish his destiny through his own resources: he is sinful man seeking to divinize himself by escaping somehow or another his terrestrial state. The new man on the contrary is perfectly aligned with God's plan, because only God can raise him to the "filial" state. He realizes that fidelity to his human condition consists for him in obedience unto death. He knows that his "yes" as child of God must be based on a creatural "yes".

Only Christ of course, because he was the man-God, could bring the human vocation to perfection. All others could move towards that ideal, and try to realize their destiny by "awaiting" God's salvific intervention. No one however, unless it is the Virgin Mary, accomplished this successfully. Men in fact opted for sin, the old man's solution.

The Church, the New Jerusalem

All that we have just said of Jesus applies to the Church also, his Body. The real new Jerusalem did in fact fulfill Jewish hope, but her visage was not the one anticipated. She is of course altogether a work of grace, the fruit of the Father's antecedent initiative. But it was only in the case of Jesus Christ, the cornerstone of the new edifice, that God's initiative met with a perfect response. In him all men are called to share in building the true Jerusalem. The building is an earthly task, which goes forward in the certainty of final accomplishment on the other side.

Everything then is new for the Christian, but with the newness of Christ. In baptism he is reborn according to the Spirit, becomes an adoptive son and an active member of the new Jerusalem. Without ceasing to be a creature he is really divinized, and can now cooperate in building the Kingdom and hastening its accomplishment. The new birth is more than a fulfillment of previous hope. Putting on the new man means shedding the old, being purged of the old leaven. "For anyone who is in Christ there is a new creation. The old creation has gone and now the new one is here" (2 Co 5:17).

Because they are reborn in the Spirit by baptism, the members of the Body can gradually restore in themselves the Creator's image (cf. Col 3:8-10). They will no longer seek human destiny by evading the human condition. It is here and now, in the concrete practice of universal charity, that the new Jerusalem is being built. If they imitate Christ in obedience for love even to the death of the cross, they will be restoring man to his true human destiny, participation in the divine life.

This task of renewal extends moreover to all creation. Fidelity of man to the condition of creature, who is made in the image and likeness of God, involves the whole universe in the great transformation from death to life. This is what will bring a new heaven and a new earth.

Proclaiming the Good News to the World

The Good News is news of access to the Father, possible now in Jesus Christ by entry to the Church. Preachers of the gospel, when they summon men to be born in the Spirit, are asking them to abandon the fallacious means of evading the creaturely condition, to shed the old man and put on the new, Jesus Christ. The invitation is addressed to every man. He can enter the narrow, poverty-stricken, creaturely way of obedience, and play an active role in the realization of God's plan for all creation. That is conversion to Jesus Christ, and it will require always that he muster all his energies for the genuine advancement of humankind. There is indeed a close connection between the building of the Kingdom here below and the enterprise of civilization. It is because of sin that civilization itself continues to be inchoate and distorted.

This task, at once divine and human, to which all are called in Jesus Christ, is one of unity on a universal scale, and reconciliation on a cosmic scale. It has been set in motion by Jesus of Nazareth, the new man *par excellence*. In the flesh, Saint Paul says, he reconciled Jews and Gentiles. And Saint John in similar fashion speaks of the gathering together of the dispersed children of God. In the furtherance of this task, the places throughout the world where the mystery of the Church has already taken root play a capital role. Man's ultimate responsibilities, and his hopes, must always be matters of concern there.

Because of his increasing mastery over nature, modern man is much less inclined to resort to evasive tactics *vis-a-vis* the terrestrial state, where so many essential tasks confront him. Indeed he is liable to charge the Christian (and very generally all religious) with such evasion. Furthermore there is point in his charge, because many Christians do not have a lucid understanding of the real meaning of newness in Christianity. When they do have, they become the most obviously humane, the best exponents of real acceptance of the terrestrial state. The modern man who comes to know them, who hears the call of faith, will realize that it was he who was attempting to divinize himself, to escape the creaturely state.

The Eucharist, a gradual insight into new realities

No one can shed the old man and don the new unless he is vitally linked with Christ. Only he was Son by right, only he was capable of obedience unto death for love of all men. Baptism is but the first step in a process of initiation which should change a man's life radically, and touch the very depths of his being. To be united with Christ one must in a very real sense "put him on." Such a process can only be accomplished in the always renewed initiation of the Eucharist.

But we must beware of thinking that there can be anything automatic about a Christian rite. The doctrine of *ex opere operato* does not dispense a Christian from putting into practice, in daily life, what he receives in the liturgical celebration. The rite will only produce fruits when it spreads into his life. Nor does the doctrine relieve the Church of a very great responsibility: that of making the eucharistic celebration the heart of a great ecclesial act of evangelization, valid for the times. In this sense there is need for continuous liturgical reform that will keep the Word and the homily constantly to the fore. The Word gives insight into salvation history; but the proclamation of it takes place in time and space, and must be actual. It must lead Christians to read correctly the "signs" of God's Today. Then they will understand the newness of which they must be witnesses before all men.

TABLE OF READINGS